The
Past *as*
Present

The Past *as* Present

in the Drama of August Wilson

Harry J. Elam, Jr.

The University of Michigan Press
Ann Arbor

For my grandparents and for the ancestors

First paperback edition 2006
Copyright © by the University of Michigan 2004, 2006
All rights reserved
Published in the United States of America by
The University of Michigan Press
Manufactured in the United States of America
⊗ Printed on acid-free paper

2009   2008   2007   2006   6   5   4   3

*A CIP catalog record for this book is available
from the British Library.*

Library of Congress Cataloging-in-Publication Data

Elam, Harry Justin.
    The past as present in the drama of August Wilson / Harry J. Elam, Jr.
        p.   cm.
    Includes bibliographical references and index.
    ISBN 0-472-11368-2 (alk. paper)
        1. Wilson, August—Criticism and interpretation.   2. Historical drama,
American—History and criticism.   3. Literature and history—United
States.   4. African Americans in literature.   I. Title.
    PS3573.I45677 Z65   2004
    812'.54—dc22   2003015075

ISBN 0-472-03163-5 (pbk. : alk. paper)
ISBN 978-0-472-03163-4 (pbk. : alk. paper)

Acknowledgments

I must start by thanking Leonade D. Jones, who was there at the inception of this project. Let me also express my heartfelt appreciation to August Wilson himself, for giving of his time and his materials. I will never forget sitting with him for over three hours between the matinee and evening shows of *King Hedley II* at the Mark Taper Forum in Los Angeles on September 9, 2000. I am also very appreciative of all the support provided by his assistant, Dena Levitin.

This book has been quite a process in coming. Along the way I spent time at the Stanford Humanities Center, and I thank the Center and its staff, most particularly my good friend Susan Sebbard, for all of its resources and support. I also thank my small cohort of colleagues at the Center with whom I met often and discussed issues of race and representation, Vilashini Cooppan, Susan Gillman, Ariela Gross, and Richard Roberts. I thank the members of my graduate and undergraduate August Wilson Seminar at Stanford, in the spring of 1998, for their incredible energy and insight into his work. These students, particularly Margaret Booker and Venus Opal Reese, had a profound impact on my work.

Several friends and colleagues have also contributed to this project. My good friend Imani Abalos helped me with reference questions and commented on matters of style. Ebony E.A. Coletu provided key philosophical insights. When I called, Alice Rayner and Janelle Reinelt were always there with superb advice on negotiating critical problems. Jim Grammar, who grew up in Pittsburgh, talked with me and sent me materials on the Pittsburgh of August Wilson. Kathleen Graham shared articles from Minneapolis newspapers on August Wilson. Michal Kobialka wisely referred me to the work of critic Giorgio Agamben. Celine Parrenas-Shimizu provided me with readings on race and psychoanalytic theory. Sandra Richards helped me think through questions of the Yoruban influence present in Wilson's work. Jenny Spencer gave me an excellent critical reading of the manuscript as a whole that greatly aided my shaping of its final version.

My assistant for two years, Nicole Fleetwood, was an incredible asset in so many ways, from negotiating contracts for the production images in the book, to working on the Wilson bibliography. Seraphina Uludong very ably finished the work on the photographs. Lisa Thompson also did extremely valuable work on the bibliography, and then Shawn Kairschner carefully completed the final stages. Ron Davies and Arden Thomas were extraordinary in proofing and preparing the manuscript for the press.

I thank my family, my mother and father, Barbara Elam and Harry J. Elam, Sr., my brother Keith and sisters Patricia Elam and Jocelyn Perron, my aunts Harriet Elam-Thomas and Thelma O'Brien for all their love and support.

I thank my editor at the University of Michigan Press, LeAnn Fields, for her wise counsel and guidance along the way and for her commitment to publishing critical work in the fields of theater and drama that has enabled our discipline to grow.

Finally, and most importantly, I thank Michele Elam, without whose efforts and loving support this book would not be what it is now. She read draft after draft, made excellent suggestions for revisions, deftly talked me through problems, and sent me critical articles and references to look up in the library. Her incisive readings informed and challenged me. She helped me tighten my argument and focus my writing. She inspired me, sustained me, and believed in me in such a way that I felt her presence as I wrote every page.

Contents

The Overture
"To Disembark"

A series of wooden crates sits in the corner of a room. They emit barely audible sounds—Billie Holiday's "Strange Fruit" and "Travelling Light." A black man who bears a striking resemblance to Abraham Lincoln is shot by an assassin who shouts, "Thus, to Tyrants!"[1] A gay, black doctoral student and his 189-year-old grandfather travel back in time to slavery and the insurrection of Nat Turner; their vehicle is a bed that lands, *Wizard of Oz* style, on the evil "Massa Mo'tel," whose feet dangle from underneath it. Emerging from a watery grave, the ghost of a murdered baby haunts her mother's postemancipation home. Imagining himself the archangel Gabriel, a World War II veteran with a metal plate in his head performs a strange, possessed dance, and through it opens up the gates of Heaven for his deceased brother to enter.

These divergent images, produced in the 1980s and 1990s by African American artists, trouble the interconnections between the African American past and the present. The final reference comes from the Pulitzer Prize–winning play *Fences*[1] by August Wilson, the author who is the focus of this study. I set Wilson's work in relation to these other images in order to reinforce my contention that the creation of his twentieth-century cycle of plays does not happen in a vacuum, but within a confluence of artistic creation that includes visual, literary, and dramatic texts. The first representation cited is part of an installation included in conceptual artist Glen Ligon's exhibit at the Hirshhorn Museum in Washington, D.C., from November 1993 to February 1994 entitled "To Disembark." The crates, which vary slightly in size and design, approximate the proportions of the box in which the slave Henry "Box" Brown traveled from Richmond, Virginia, to freedom in Philadelphia in 1849. The title "To Disembark" connotes the transitional process of unloading at the end of the voyage, the impersonal disburdening of black Africans, like cargo from the hull of slave ships. In another section of the gallery hang lithographs that imitate nineteenth-century wanted posters for escaped slaves in which all the descriptions of the runaway slaves concern Ligon himself. Entitling this exhibition that visually foregrounds the impact of slavery on the contemporary African American subject "To Disembark," Ligon implies that African Americans are still in the process of disembarking, still discharging historic baggage, always and already on the physical and psychological journey toward liberated self-definition.

The texts from which the other images come also negotiate issues of disembarkation as they foreground the impact of the African American past on the present. Playwright Suzan-Lori Park's imaginative work, *The America Play* (1990–93), which contemplates the profound effects that the myth and legacy of Lincoln's freeing the slaves continue to have on the African Americans, is the source of the second image. Irreverently questioning the lack of a gay presence in the history of slavery, Robert O'Hara's play *Insurrection: Holding History* (1999) is the source of the third. The fourth comes from Toni Morrison's now classic novel *Beloved* (1987). Set in the period of emancipation, Morrison's novel wakes the dead in order to provoke the processes of African American living. The last occurs during the climax of *Fences*, a play that explores and, with this final invocation of ritual, transcends the tensions of black family life in Pittsburgh, 1957.

I begin my examination of August Wilson's twentieth-century history cycle with this reference to *Fences* and to other African American works of the 1980s and 1990s in order to situate Wilson's historical cycle within a larger sociohistoric context. Throughout this volume, my allusions and references will not be limited to the African American dramatic canon but will draw from other genres of black cultural expression as well. Wilson's dramaturgy, like the cultural productions of all those mentioned above, depends on the circulation of images and conditions conducive to such historical explorations. In the 1980s and 1990s, as scholars and artists came increasingly to understand race as a social, political, and historical construction, they correspondingly came to consider how the political and cultural constructions of history helped to constitute the meanings of race.[2] And yet, concern for the politics of history and historiography is not particularly new within African American culture. The inability to suppress, control, manipulate, and right histories of race has repeatedly affected the social and cultural dynamics of African American life. W. E. B. Du Bois in his 1935 treatise *Black Reconstruction in America* took issue with the representation of race within American history at that time, arguing that "the story of Reconstruction from the point of view of the Negro is yet to be written. When it is written, one may read its tragedy and get its truth."[3] David Blight notes that the final chapter in Du Bois's work, "The Propaganda of History," served as "an indictment of American historiography and a probing statement of the meaning of race in American historical memory. . . . the stakes in *Black Reconstruction* were the struggle over the nature of history itself."[4] Correspondingly, these artistic imaginings of history in the 1980s and 1990s, let me suggest, are part of a continuing battle over "the nature of history."

The emergence of this artistic return-to-the-past movement testifies to a present desire to reckon with unfinished business. Yet these artistic engagements do not simply offer a compensatory history for that which has been lost or omitted within the American historic lexicon. Rather, in keeping with the historical materialism expressed by Walter Benjamin in his "Theses on the Philosophy of History," they "brush history against the grain" not only to fill in gaps in historic knowledge but to expose history's relativism, as they explore how history means in the present.[5] In one of nine etchings with chin collé that mimic the frontispieces by white abolitionists of nineteenth-century slave narratives included in "To Disembark," Ligon writes, "The Narrative of the Life and Uncommon Sufferings of Glen Ligon, a colored man, who at a tender age discovered his affection for the bodies of other men, and has endured scorn and tribulations ever since."[6] The etching's style and words write Ligon's personal history into the slave past. Yet the etching also points to Ligon's own negotiations of identity in the present, how he is figured within a history, ghosted by the past. Critical to his and other interpretations of history, including that of Wilson, is an understanding that history is formulated in the now. According to James Baldwin, "If history were past, history wouldn't matter. History is the present. . . . You and I are history. We carry our history. We act our history."[7] With their fantastical, mystical, spiritual imaginings of the past, these artists see history not as static fact, but as malleable perceptions open to interpretation, as a place to envision the past as it ought to have been in order to understand the present and to achieve a future they desire.

Sparked in part by the sociopolitical circumstance of the times, this African American literary and theatrical archaeology in the 1980s and

1990s evidences an approach to the interaction between art, politics, and community more perhaps nuanced than that expressed in the Black Arts movement of the 1960s and 1970s. As Philip Bryan Harper notes, that movement "was characterized by a drive for nationalistic unity among people of African descent."[8] This mandate led in many cases to relational artistic practices that explicitly linked black advancement to the destruction of white hegemony, that sought to combat the "white thing," as Mike Sell calls it,[9] in terms of both form and content. The Black Arts orientation was decidedly presentist, critiquing Western aesthetics, challenging white privilege in order to effect immediate change. The movement preached a functional aesthetic that envisioned art as a powerful tool in the struggle for black liberation. Yet, writing in the early 1990s, after the black urgencies of the previous decades had largely dissipated, critics such as Harper and David Lionel Smith have pointed to the constraints that such an aesthetic imposed on black artists.[10] Rebelling against past, prescriptive paradigms that posited the fight against racism and white oppression at the center of all black artistic creation, playwright Suzan-Lori Parks writes:

> There are many ways of defining Blackness and there are many ways of presenting Blackness onstage. The Klan does not have to be outside the door for black people to have lives worthy of dramatic literature. . . . And what happens when we choose a concern other than race to focus on? What kind of drama do we get? Let's do the math: BLACK PEOPLE + x = NEW DRAMATIC CONFLICT (NEW TERRITORY).[11]

The "new dramatic territory" that she imagines does not mean an art evacuated of social efficacy. Rather than an obliteration of the politics of race, Parks calls for a freedom to explore new visions of what constitutes black art and the liberty to discover how, within this art, the complex social dynamics and political impulses of black life find expression. Glen Ligon expresses a similar sentiment: "The work of artists of color is often reduced to being simply about race and nothing else as if our gender, sexual, class, and other identities didn't complicate any discussions of race as subject matter, or as if race was our natural subject matter."[12] Ligon speaks to the stereotypical expectations placed on black artists from external sources, while Parks discusses the agency of black artists themselves to create beyond the constraints of conventional racial politics. For both, as for Wilson, turning back toward history offers a place to construct "new dramatic territory," to disembark; to explore race and yet to operate seemingly removed from the immediacies of current racial contexts.

Significantly, the fire of the Black Arts movement of the 1960s—even as critics and artists assault its failures, its missed opportunities as well as applaud its successes—still haunts today's black artists. The movement calls out to Wilson and others to achieve its romanticized ideals of real social commitment, material social change, and a functional black unity. Its conjunction of arts and politics raises certain critical questions for artistic practice that challenge African American artists even now: How can we claim a racial unity, celebrate "black power," and cry out that "black is beautiful" without enforcing essentialism? How can we assert our collective blackness while allowing for intraracial differences? How can we marshal or recapture that sense of urgency that we found in black politics of the 1960s? Paradoxically, with such contemporary questions, historical analysis becomes increasingly important, and artists have turned to that past for answers. They seek to reevaluate that past in order to understand the present better. In such an effort, history serves not simply as the site of nostalgia and longing, nor only as progress or as rational, logical process. Rather, this return to the past in the present represents what Giorgio Agamben terms "a critical demolition of the ideas of process, development, and progress."[13] The result, then, is a new experience of history, a new contestatory and contingent engagement with the past that puts into question the historical categorization of race as it interrogates the meanings of blackness. For Parks, Ligon, O'Hara, Morrison, and Wilson, revisionist historicism has enabled complex renegotiations of blackness and new delineations of community.

Wilson's self-imposed project, to write a play for each decade of the twentieth century, both links him to and separates him from the other aforementioned history projects. With two Pulitzer Prizes, two Tony Awards and numerous other accolades, August Wilson stands out as one of the preeminent playwrights in contemporary American theater. He has changed the face of American theater, and his emergence has enabled other black writers to follow. As director Marion McClinton states, "A lot of black writers had doors opened to them basically because August Wilson knocked them out. . . . American theatre now looks toward African-Americans as viable members."[14] The viability of

Africans in America, their place within the American dream, is central to Wilson's theatrical project. His singular commitment to exploring the experiences of African Americans over time has enabled him to delve into the particular, but also see the process of historic evolution. With this cycle he has shaped a history that is at once personal and collective, figurative and real. John Lahr writes that "his plays are not textbooks; they paint the big picture indirectly from the little incidents of life."[15] The plays explore African American history through Wilson's own memories, "his story." Ethics and aesthetics conjoin as the personal dynamics of his characters' lives have profound political consequences. He terms his project "a 400 year old autobiography, which is the black experience."[16] In this African American "autobiography," history both shackles his African American characters and empowers them. They must discover how both to embrace the past and to let it go. Because of Wilson's investment in "the souls of black folk" (as W. E. B. Du Bois would say), there is not simply a matter of unfinished business with the past but a hunger for redress and regeneration in the present. As regenerative models of healing, his cycle integrates the political, the historical, and the spiritual in ways that push the realms of conventional realism and evoke a spirit that is both timeless and timely.

Wilson's own movement in writing these plays in his cycle has been far from linear, moving back and forward through time and negotiating the past's impact on the present.[17] In fact, he did not originally set out to write a cycle, but in the process of writing discovered that this was exactly what he was doing.

> Somewhere along the way it dawned on me that I was writing one play for each decade. Once I became conscious of that, I realized I was trying to focus on what I felt were the important issues confronting Black Americans for that decade, so ultimately they could stand as a record of Black experience over the past hundred years presented in the form of dramatic literature.[18]

Although not written in chronological order, Wilson has to date completed plays on the 1900s, *Gem of the Ocean*, 1910s, *Joe Turner's Come and Gone* (1988), 1920s, *Ma Rainey's Black Bottom* (1984), 1930s, *The Piano Lesson* (1990), 1940s, *Seven Guitars* (1996), 1950s, *Fences* (1987), 1960s, *Two Trains Running* (1992), 1970s, *Jitney* (2000), and 1980s, *King Hedley II* (2001). His play of the century's first decade, *Gem of the*

Ocean, premiered at the Goodman Theater in Chicago in April 2003 and moved from there to the Mark Taper Forum in Los Angeles in July 2003.

With each work, Wilson re-creates and reevaluates the choices that blacks have made in the past by refracting them through the lens of the present. In his most recent plays, he has decided not only to unearth the continuities and disjunctures of African American experience in time, but also to mine the relationship between his own texts. Wilson's *King Hedley II* explicitly revisits characters seen close to forty years earlier in *Seven Guitars.* In his final two plays of the cycle, *Gem of the Ocean* and a newer play to be set in 1999, Wilson intends to "build an umbrella under which the rest of the plays can sit. My relating the '00s to the '90s play should provide a bridge. The subject matter of these two plays is going to be very similar and connected thematically, meaning that the other eight will be part and parcel to these two. You should be able to see how they all fit inside these last two plays."[19] *Gem of the Ocean,* set in 1904, focuses on Aunt Ester, a character as old as the black presence in America, and the action that transpires when Citizen Barlow arrives at her house, seeking sanctuary from spiritual turmoil. While Wilson previously discusses Aunt Ester in *Two Trains Running* and *King Hedley II, Gem of the Ocean* marks the first appearance of this figure he now believes is "the most significant person of the cycle. The characters after all, are her children."[20] In this play that marks the ultimate inception and near culmination of the cycle, Wilson has worked his way around to staging Aunt Ester.

Because Wilson repeats and revises certain ideas, concepts, phrases, and ritualized actions within the plays—such as Aunt Ester—I have organized this book around key questions and critical thematic issues that evolve through his dramaturgy. Rather than constructing the chapters around individual plays, I examine Wilson's self-reflexive intertextuality. His plays purposefully speak to each other; they develop a common agenda. Therefore, examining them in consort and dialogue with each other is crucial. By considering the intersections and continuities across the cycle, I intend this analysis not only to provide insight into the individual plays but, more significantly, to explore how the cycle as whole makes meaning and to theorize how Wilson (w)rights history.

Invoking the concept of (w)righting, I consciously riff on the meanings of *writing, righting, right,* and *rites* to frame and analyze Wilson's processes of reckoning with the African American past. (W)righting underscores the etymology and the denotations of the word *playwright*. Just as a wheel*wright* makes wheels, a play*wright* functions not simply as *writer* but as a play *maker*. Playwriting is a selective and collective act of creation. "(W)righting history" implies that Wilson, through his three-dimensional constructions of the past, his meditations on black experiences in each decade of the twentieth century, is making history. Carefully situating each play at critical junctures in African American history, Wilson explores the pain and perseverance, the determination and dignity in these black lives. In the introduction that follows, "(W)righting History: A Meditation in Four Beats," I will further develop the concept of (w)righting, as I establish a theoretical overview around the concepts of history, memory, time, and ritual that will prove critical to this study and that are fundamental to an understanding of Wilson's dramaturgy.

Wilson's (w)righting history, his project of dramaturgically documenting the African American past, raises important questions of authenticity and essentialism in representation: How can one play capture, as Wilson proposes, "the most important issues confronting black Americans for that decade"?[21] Does Wilson's (w)righting therefore limit and essentialize blackness? Unlike Ligon's "To Disembark" or O'Hara's *Insurrection,* Wilson's African American history never refers to black homosexuality, nor does Wilson, like Lynn Nottage or Kathleen Collins, depict the historic images of the black bourgeoisie.[22] He intends to take up the subject of the black middle class in his final play of the cycle that he will set in 1999. Wilson has situated all his plays to date within very particular social, cultural, sexual, and even geographic spectrums. Can the Hill District of Pittsburgh serve as the symbolic home of all black America? Discussing his April 2001 production of Wilson's *Piano Lesson* for the San Jose Repertory Theatre, director Kenny Leon proclaimed, "It's like these characters represent all the African-Americans who have ever lived."[23] Certainly Leon is not alone in such contentions, as the very nature of Wilson's historical project lends itself to such generalizations. Given our current understanding of the diversity within African American life and of race and history as constructions, however, any criticism that takes Wilson's cycle simply as representative of all African Americans is problematic. Yet I would argue that the "limits" of Wilson representation do not need to be understood as essential, or romanticized as definitive portraits of authentic black experience. Rather, the critical task with Wilson's dramaturgy is that we recognize the utility of the representation without reading it as totalizing; that we note the possibility of responding to its symbolic meaning without corresponding absolutely to it or subordinating oneself to its authority. For theater and performance are always sites of surrogacy, where the figurative becomes charged increasingly with symbolic import and where collective recognition, empathy, and sentiment can be generated in the shared experience of spectatorship.[24]

One day as I was working on this Overture, my mother, whose social and educational background are very different from that of Wilson or his characters, remarked, "August Wilson's theater makes me proud to be a black person." Not to be overly sentimental, I think her statement encapsulates complex relations of history, racial identity, and identification at play in Wilson's representation and reception. Wilson through his own style of realism, his three-dimensional portraits, his storytelling bravado, validates a history of black experience. Rather than locating blacks in positions of victimization, subordination, or objectification, Wilson places them as subjects of his drama. Given the history and politics of black representation in America, this is a significant move, as signaled by my mother's comment. She identifies with his creation. Even in her difference, it resonates. Wilson's imaginative, selective grounding of black America feels "real" and engenders racial pride. And yet my mother's remark, as well as Leon's, suggest the weight that Wilson bears in the public sphere. As the singular African American playwright, he must be responsible to all black people; he must uplift the race. Do we expect too much of him? Perhaps. Still, as evidenced by his interviews and speeches, Wilson takes on the mantle of social responsibility willingly. How Wilson, employing the vernacular, "keeps it real" historically, theatrically, and culturally is a question of critical import in this analysis of Wilson and his cycle.

Wilson writes that his "blood memory" is a guide for his creation.[25] Blood memory—the idea that there are some intrinsic experiences, some ontological knowledge that blacks remember just because they are black—also has the potential to seem essentialized. Suzan-Lori Parks, in her play In the Blood (2000), critiques the very notions of a fixed blackness. Her central character, Hester, is a black, homeless woman with a multicultural brood of children, each with a different father. Through her representation, Parks raises questions about what is in the blood and how blood is racialized. My sense is that Wilson's invocation of blood memory equally interrogates what is in the blood, functioning as a metaphor that is at once something and nothing. For memory is never a perfect mirror, and ideas of race are constantly in flux. Or as Ralph Ellison writes, "I said black is . . . an' black ain't."[26] Blood memory, in Wilson's theatrical construction, operates as a metaphor for his central idea of reimagining history and for appreciating how the African and African American past is implicated in the present. Wilson constructs blood memory on and through his dramas not as a biological essence but as a symbolic representation that dramaturgically blurs the lines between the figurative and the real.

Wilson's personal history, in fact, exemplifies the symbolic construction of blood memory operating in his cycle and testifies to the ways in which collective memory and race are the products of historical, cultural, and social construction. Wilson was born Frederick August Kittel on April 27, 1945. He was the fourth of six children. His father, Frederick Kittel, a white German baker, hardly lived with the family. His mother, Daisy Wilson, worked as a cleaning woman and later married David Bedford, a black ex-convict and former high-school football star. As is signaled by his decision to change his surname from Kittel to his mother's name, August Wilson self-identifies as black, not as mixed. In his now famous speech to the Theatre Communications Group in January 1996 Wilson states,

> Growing up in my mother's house at 1727 Bedford Ave in Pittsburgh Pa., I learned the language, the eating habits, the religious beliefs, the notions of common sense, attitudes towards sex, concepts of beauty and justice, and the responses to pleasure and pain that my mother had learned from her mother, and which you could trace back to the first African who set foot on the continent. It is this culture that stands solidly on these shores today as a testament to the resiliency of the African-American spirit.[27]

Wilson notes that he constructs memory through the learned behaviors passed on in his mother's house. The meanings of the cultural traditions he describes in his mother's house, then, are produced in the present. How they come to signify on the past comes through current understandings of self, identity, and of subjectivity. "The resiliency of the African-American spirit" is a testimony to black endurance, adaptation, and the ability to evolve. Central to Wilson's dramaturgical project is the idea that one can move forward into the future only by first going back. Wilson's cycle suggests that African Americans need to confront more integrally the African dimension of their Du Boisian double consciousness, the penultimate principle of *both/and* in African American experience.[28] They must embrace the legacy of slavery, celebrate the African retentions that remain within African American cultural practices, and acknowledge the psychological scars that still endure.

Even as it starts with the 1900s and concludes with a play set in 1997, Wilson's history cycle reveals an African American continuum that is always in process, stretching back into Africa and reaching into the future. Within West African cultures, life is similarly imagined as a circular process that does not end but is linked in a continuum with the world of the ancestors as well as that of the unborn. Sandra Richards argues that for Wilson, the United States, like Africa, "is a site of cultural becomings. . . . though the idea of democracy may be constant, its substantive meanings and referents are continually changing."[29] In the cross-cultural connections that Wilson develops, the notion of disembarking, of moving on toward liberated self-definition, is continuous. His cycle, then, does not constitute an end but a beginning. And so we disembark.

Introduction
(W)righting History:
A Meditation in Four Beats

Well, I think if you—if we disappeared off the face of the planet and some Martians or some people come here and the only thing that survived was these ten plays, they should be able to put together a cultural portrait of the people. These were their ideas and attitudes. These were the ways they dealt with this here. This was their attitude toward death. This was their attitude toward love, this was their attitude toward this. For someone working as an anthropologist to look at those plays and be able to paint a reasonable portrait of black America—that's what I hope. Not that it's necessarily historically accurate in the events and things of that sort, but the cultural portrait of the people—the ideas and attitudes, their belief system.

—August Wilson (2000)

Despite my interest in history, I have always been more concerned with culture, and while my plays have an overall historical feel, their settings are fictions, and they are peopled with invented characters whose personal histories fit within the historical context in which they live.

I have tried to extract some measure of truth from their lives as they struggle to remain whole in the face of so many things that threaten to pull them asunder. I am not a historian. I happen to think that the content of my mother's life—her myths, her superstitions, her prayers, the contents of her pantry, the smell of her kitchen, the song that escaped from her sometimes parched lips, her thoughtful repose and pregnant laughter—are all worthy of art.

—August Wilson (1995)

In the tumultuous moment that ends the first act of August Wilson's *Joe Turner's Come and Gone* (1987),[1] the traumatized, obsessed, and possessed central figure, Herald Loomis, returns to Seth's Pittsburgh boardinghouse, where he and his daughter Zonia have been staying, and enters into a world in which time stops. Past and present, history and memory, ritual and reality all collide. On entering the house, he

"What you done seen, Herald Loomis?" Joe Turner's Come and Gone, *Trinity Repertory Company, Downstairs Theater, 1989, with Lawrence James (Seth), Michael Rogers (Herald), David Kennet (Rutherford), and Ed Hall (Bynum). (Photography by Mark Morelli.)*

spies and menacingly interrupts the other residents engaged in praising God through dancing the Juba; the Juba, a dance performed by African Americans in postslavery times to praise their adopted Christian God through movements, gestures, rhythms that still hearkened back to African roots and forms of religious observances. Wilson's meticulous stage directions reinforce the African origins of these Afro-Christian rites: "The Juba is reminiscent of the ring shouts of African slaves. . . . It should be as African as possible."[2] Haunted by his own spirits, besieged by his own lack of faith in a Christian God, a divisive Loomis chastises the others, ridicules their faith, blasphemes the authority of Christianity, and then turns to exit until he is rocked back, knocked to the floor by a horrific vision that engulfs him. "What you done seen, Herald Loomis," Bynum, the root worker and conjure man, asks (*Joe Turner*, 1.4.250). Loomis, transformed into a visionary, replies, "I come to this place . . . to this water that was bigger than the whole world. And I looked out . . . and I seen these bones rise up out of the water. Rise up and walk on top of it" (1.4.250). Tellingly, Loomis reimagines the Middle Passage, a historic site of loss but also a critical location of struggle and survival for African Americans. His frightening, yet mystical, "rememory"[3] of "bones walking on top of the water" captures the dichotomy of those perilous journeys aboard slave ships that marked both death and new life, that ensured the profound disconnection from, as well as the endurance of, the spirit of Africa, that initiated the complex gestation and difficult birth of African Americans. Herald's apparition equally constitutes an individual trauma and a collective rememory of that initiating rupture for African Americans. As the scene escalates, his vision becomes a shared remembrance and an antiphonal rite of call-and-response with Bynum. Under Bynum's syncopated coaxing and anticipatory interrogation, Loomis discloses his fervent desire to join the legion of marching bones as they become flesh and walk onto the land. This revelation is not simply personal. The implications of this admission and his ensuing journey are at once individual and communal. Loomis's odyssey, his desire to stand and walk along with the bones people, symbolizes the need of African Americans to reconnect with their past and with each other, to renegotiate their perceptions of and relationships to history. Within the ritualized remembrances of this signal moment of *Joe Turner* and within the body of his twentieth-century cycle as a whole, August Wilson (w)rights history.

As expressed in Herald Loomis's and Bynum's visionary incantation of the Middle Passage, Wilson (w)rights history through performative rites that pull the action out of time or even ritualize time in order to change the power and potentialities of the now. This process of (w)righting history necessarily critiques how history is constituted and what history means. It reinterprets how history operates in relation to race and space, time and memory. The parentheses around the *w* also imply a silence and contingency; (w)righting can sometimes mean righting. Wilson seeks to "right" and remake American history by recuper-

3

ating African American narratives that have been erased, avoided, or ignored. He focuses on the daily lives of ordinary black people within particular historical circumstances. Yet, perhaps most significantly, as expressed in Loomis's and Bynum's collective conjuration, Wilson (w)rights history through such highly charged, ritualized enactments, in which his characters and their embodied actions render new and potentially incomprehensible situations meaningful and bring traditional structures to bear. Bynum's call-and-response with Loomis transmutes Loomis's seemingly crazed possession into a healing communion. Such (w)rightings symbolically transform the meanings of the past in the present. Walter Benjamin argues that "History is a subject of a structure whose site is not homogeneous, empty time but time filled with the presence of the now."[4] For Wilson, as for Benjamin, time is never empty or homogeneous, and the concept of the historical must unite with a vision of the messianic. Spiritual salvation is not antithetical to, but a necessary component of a progressive historicism and revolutionary politics. Wilson (w)rights history by invoking rites that connect the spiritual, the cultural, the social, and the political, not simply to correct the past but to interpret it in ways that powerfully impact the present. In a space and time outside of time, within the liminal dimensions of theater, Wilson (w)rights history.

Beat 1: Out of Time

> Every concept of history is invariably accompanied by a certain experience of time, which is implicit in it, conditions it, and thereby has to be elucidated. Similarly, every culture is first and foremost a particular experience of time . . . the original task of a genuine revolution, therefore is never merely to "change the world," but also—and above all—to "change time."
>
> —Giorgio Agamben

From the outset of *Joe Turner*, Herald Loomis finds himself outside of time and on a mission to resituate himself within time, place, and history. His experience of time has been shaped by his particular history of enslavement and loss, a loss of connection, a loss of history, that he desires desperately somehow to right. After seven years of forced servitude on Joe Turner's plantation, he returns to his former home to find that his wife, Martha, has left him. With daughter Zonia in tow, he sets out in search for Martha, a search that has now lasted four years as he blows through the doors of Seth's boardinghouse in Pittsburgh 1911 and into the action of *Joe Turner*. Cathy Caruth argues in *Unclaimed Experience* that "What causes trauma . . . is a shock that appears to work very much like a bodily threat but is in fact a break in the mind's experience of time."[5] Loomis's mind has endured such a break. His original trauma is the realization of being ripped out of time—a reenactment of slavery, literally stolen out of the moment by Joe Turner and his henchman. Traumatized by this condition of servitude, dislocated and alienated from the world around him, Loomis seeks a starting place, a return to time past in order to live in time present.

Like Frantz Fanon's concept of "sociogeny"[6] outlined in *White Skins/Black Masks,* Wilson's dramaturgy demonstrates that the cultural—current social conditions and past oppression—can have an impact on the psychological trauma, the social dis-ease eating at the fabric of black American lives. Cultural healing as well as cultural reclamation are critical objectives in Wilson's dramaturgical project. He wants his black figures like Loomis to achieve wellness, to be both black and whole. Paradoxically, throughout his cycle, Wilson turns to characters who are suffering, such as Loomis, or figures like Gabriel in *Fences* (1987) and Hambone in *Two Trains Running* (1992), who seem naive and deficient, to heal, symbolically, the whole community through their actions. Later, in chapter 2, "Fools and Babes," I examine how Wilson uses children and madmen, characters who are perceived as mentally disabled, to further his message through their unique proximity to the ancestral past and their special relationship with the supernatural. The spirit works on and through them. These children and madmen may appear marginal figures, but in Wilson's dramaturgy the marginal refigures the center. In an intriguing parallel, Wilson, a high school dropout, once existing on the outskirts of society, has written himself into the center of contemporary American theater. Wilson champions the subjugated, those whom society has discarded and forgotten. His fools and babes—who function as a metaphor perhaps for his vision of African Americans as a whole, a people whom "the larger society has thought less of than we thought of ourselves"[7]—bring particular insights into Wilson's refiguring of time and the presence of the past. (W)righting history through his exposition of Loomis's trauma as well as his outline for and of cultural healing in the cycle as a whole,

Wilson seeks the genuine revolution identified by Agamben and attempts to change time.[8]

Of course Wilson's revolution is within the theater and within the codes and conventions of theatricalized time. The theater, like any culture as noted by Agamben, structures a certain relation to time. Separated from the present as well as the past, we enter the theater and submit ourselves to a place in which time stops for the time period of the play. The performance we see may be set years in the past or may transpire in the world of the future, and yet it always and already happens before us in the performative now. At the same time that the world of theater is outside of time, it is placed within a very real time frame. Episodes, blackouts, divisions into acts and scenes, all delimit and focus time. Regional theaters often announce with placards in the lobby the ending time of the theatrical event. "Tonight's performance of *Joe Turner's Come and Gone* ends at 10:45." We know that when a play is successful, four hours in the theater can seem like no time at all. Yet when an actor forgets a line for a few seconds, the resultant pause for those on stage and even in the audience can seem an eternity. Bert O. States writes that "a play plucks human experience from time and offers an aesthetic completion to a process we know to be endless. The play imitates the timely in order to remove it from time, to give time a shape."[9] The play gives time shape even as it removes "the timely from time" and exults in the timelessness of the experience. The theater exposes and examines the gaps in time and understandings of time. Wilson in *Joe Turner*, as well as in the rest of his twentieth-century cycle, places the action within a particular time frame, but even as it explores a different historical period, he is interested in its impact on the now. The plasticity of the theater enables Wilson to engage historic continuities as well as ruptures and change. Rather than being driven by action or plot, Wilson's plays work toward an internal reordering of temporality on the part of his characters. As a consequence, in this age of sound bytes and short attention spans, Wilson's plays may seem languorous to the impatient or uninitiated. His reply to this criticism is to point his critics to an earlier time and to the length of Shakespeare's plays and explain that some things just take more time to work themselves out.

For Wilson there is also a particular relationship between race and time and ways in which time becomes racialized in his plays. This is not to suggest an essentialized or ontological concept of a thing called "black time." Yet and still, I want to posit that the social, cultural, and historic conditions of black life affect the way blacks have experienced time in America. To this end, the concept of "CP time," Colored People's time, is telling. Simply defined, it means that black people are always late, that they function in their own time. Yet what the phrase infers is a subversive strategy in which black people seek to possess, control, or master time. The history of enslavement meant that African Americans, as property and possessions, could not command their own time. Their time, in fact, could be sold. A slave knew that a prime factor in how much more work they would have to do was a direct function of how long it took to complete a particular task. Consequently, laziness or slowness became a method of stealing back time and represented a form of what Saidiya Hartman terms "stealing away": "Stealing away involved unlicensed movement, collective assembly and an abrogation of the terms of subjection in acts as simple as sneaking off to laugh and talk with friends or making nocturnal visits to loved ones."[10] Stealing away, seemingly a small thing, was an act of resistance that asserted self in defiance of the system that constituted the slave as property. "Through stealing away, counterclaims about justice and freedom were advanced that denied the sanctity or legitimacy of property rights in a double gesture that played on the meaning of theft."[11]

At the outset of *Ma Rainey's Black Bottom*, the title character is late, and the other characters must wait for her to begin a recording session. By implication, she is, as the white record producer Sturdyvant implies, "always late" and thus on CP time. When she arrives, however, we discover that she has been detained by a white police officer after an altercation with a white cab driver who refused to pick her up. The police officer even accompanies her to the studio until he finds someone—a white person—to vouch for her. Despite her fame within the black community, Ma Rainey is still not in control of her time. Throughout the play and the recording session, then, Ma seeks subversively to steal away and possess her time. Other efforts at possession and resistance play out in a myriad of ways in the Wilson cycle as black characters attempt to reconcile their own identities, their perceptions of self, with the ways they are positioned within and determined by time.

One of the ways in which Wilson's characters first seek to recover time lost is by spatializing it. Outside of time, lost without a history, Loomis spatializes time in order to find his "starting place in the world. Find me a world I can fit in" (*Joe Turner*, 2.3.273). And so he searches for his lost wife. Loomis can only move forward psychically by going back, by connecting to a time past and to a tangible foundation and history in order to progress in time present. His movement is analogous to that set out by Wilson to underline the processes of black regeneration and self-discovery that mark his cycle as a whole. Yet and still, the idea of spatializing time is not a particularly Wilsonian project, nor is it merely a "black thing." Since and before Hegel philosophers have considered the integral relationship between time and space. Agamben notes, "Since the human mind has the experience of time but not its representation, it necessarily pictures time by means of spatial images."[12] Following a similar line of thinking, Henri Lefebvre adds that "in nature, time is apprehended within space—in the very heart of space: the hour of the day, the season, the elevation of the sun above the horizon, the position of the moon and stars in the heavens, the cold and heat, the age of each natural being and so on. . . . Time was thus inscribed by space, and natural space was merely the lyrical and tragic script of natural time."[13]

While Wilson's spatialization of time is not unique, its trajectory backward into history is significant. The journey points toward Africa and joins, for me, with the West African concept of "Sankofa" in providing insight into the presence of the past in Wilson's work. In Twi, the term *Sankofa,* symbolized by the Sankofa bird, who as legend goes, flies forward with his head turned backward, means that one must understand the past in order to move present into the future. Moreover, within the West African worldview, the past, present, and future coexist and continually interact. Wilson's theater, as evidenced by Herald Loomis's vision of past in the present, engages such simultaneity. In Wilson's work, Africa functions as Gunilla Theander Kester suggests, "as a native soil and empirical abstraction and a metaphorical space."[14] The idea of Africa as metaphor, I believe, is critical as it enables Wilson to escape the romanticization and essentialization of Africa, but rather allows his "Africa" to be constructed, to be (w)ritten within the context of the moment. Wilson spatializes and even attempts to racialize time through a turn back toward this multidimensional image of Africa.[15]

Beat 2: History

> The past leads us if we force it to. Otherwise it contains us in its asylum
> with no gates. We make history or it makes us.
> —Marge Piercy

> I take issue with history because it doesn't serve me—it doesn't serve me
> because there isn't enough of it. In this play, I am simply asking,
> "Where is history?," because I don't see it. I don't see any history out
> there, so I've made up some.
> —Suzan-Lori Parks

As he returns to the past that is his present, Herald Loomis's vision of the Middle Passage is a site not only of contested histories of African Americans, but also of historical amnesia. Suppressed or forgotten within his psyche is the legacy of the African homeland and culture from which he has descended. Wilson writes in his introduction to the play, "From the deep and near South the sons and daughters of newly freed African slaves wander into the city. Isolated, cut off from memory, having forgotten the names of the gods and only guessing at their faces, they arrive dazed and stunned, their hearts kicking in their chest with a song worth singing (*Joe Turner,* 203). For Wilson the history of black migration in the early 1900s from the South to northern cities such as Pittsburgh and the feelings of separation and dislocation that ensued are predicated on even more fundamental and inciting incidents of rupture and loss. Here then is one of the ways that Wilson seeks to (w)right history, by reimagining the significance of the past lost in Africa, a past that he believes is retained within African American cultural practices and beliefs. But other losses of the Middle Passage can never be recovered: the particular histories of those who died onboard; those Africans who could not endure and succumbed to sickness; mothers who threw their children overboard rather than submit them to the unknown terrors ahead; brave souls who vainly fought to escape and suffered the consequences; the infirm or traumatized that just passed silently away. The fact that we can never recuperate these particular, individual histories shows that history can and does disappear. Within this history of loss and the loss of history, Wilson, like Suzan-Lori Parks, "makes some up." The silence of traditional American history, the historical amnesia around the fate of African Americans, not only before and during the

Middle Passage but after, has led to artistic interventions such as that offered by Parks.

Even more pointedly, the notion of making up history underscores the particular role that performance has played within African American history and culture. Alan Nadel argues of Wilson,

> If reality is authorized for black Americans by performance and for white America by text, Wilson's plays, as both text and performance, mediate between the site of dominant discourse and the practices of black American life. In this regard, we can view his project to create a decade-by-decade cycle of plays as an attempt to make history, that is, an attempt both to construct an event and to construct the story in which it figures.[16]

For Nadel, the making of history involves both text, "the story," and performance, the "constructing of the event" that Wilson dramaturgically negotiates. Yet the lack of "the text," the written-down form of history—"You should write it down and you should hide it under uh rock," Park's chorus in *Death of the Last Black Man* intones[17]—for African Americans has often meant that performance becomes a subversive strategy and agency that acts as a form of resistance to the omission of the black presence from history. Negro spirituals such as "Swing Low Sweet Chariot" contained coded messages about real plans for escape to the North within the figurative tale of a chariot coming to carry them to the afterlife in Heaven. Such masking or "double voicedness" enabled black performances to function on a variety of levels.[18] Even as they performed for the entertainment of the white master, slaves could ridicule or potentially undermine his control simultaneously through the mechanism of performance. Everyday survival on the plantation also necessitated the employment of certain coded performances, playing the role of deferential subservience or feigned ignorance. Thus, the history of African American performance is always already implicated in the history of African American social, cultural, and political struggles for freedom. In addition, through performance African Americans can and do make history, and these performances constitute history in themselves, historical records, or what Nadel calls a "truer form of history than white historical discourse."[19]

Correspondingly, Wilson's title *Joe Turner's Come and Gone* is appropriated from a blues song written by W. C. Handy, "the father of the blues," and reflects a particular history and reality for African

Americans. From Handy's account, black women sang this lament after their men were taken into servitude by Joe Turney, the brother of Pete Turney, the governor of Tennessee (1883–97). "He come with forty links of chain, Oh Lady! Got my man and gone." Judith Williams points out that within black folklore the character of Joe Turner took on many personifications.

> The musical chronicle of Joe Turner has a chameleon-like nature; Joe Turner has had several incarnations. In Handy's "Joe Turner Blues," he casts Joe Turner as the long-suffering victim of unrequited love. Bill Big Broonzy sings of a benevolent Joe Turner who is both the white man who provided material aid to black and white victims of a flood, and the black man who delivered that aid.[20]

The various incarnations of Joe Turner, the move to change the name of the historical figure of Joe Turney to Joe Turner, all function as rhetorical strategies within African American performance practices in which history is disseminated, adapted, and even made up. Wilson's move within *Joe Turner* is similarly inspired. His account of Herald Loomis's encounter with Joe Turner conflates myth and history, endows the fictive with the real and the real with the fictitious such that the fictitious becomes more real.

Nadel acknowledges that the history that Wilson makes in his cycle is a "figurative history," but he notes that the figurative has always played a significant role within "the claim for human rights for black Americans."[21] He reminds us that history for African Americans has constantly reified the figurative. In order to acknowledge the presence of slaves in drawing congressional boundaries while justifying the system of slavery at the same time, the Constitution at its inception proclaimed that a black person constituted only three-fifths of a human. With the growth of the slave economy as well as northern abolition efforts, the Mason-Dixon line came to demarcate the separation between an African American's status as slave or free individual.[22] At this same time, the one-drop rule determined that a person with any black blood was, in fact, black and therefore to be denied the rights of citizenship. Through these legal mandates, fictions of race structure black reality. Ariela Gross in *Double Character* examines the paradoxes in slavery and slave law "that arose from slave's double identity as human subjects and objects of property *at one in the same time.*"[23]

Understanding such dual positionality is critical to understanding how the figurative became real and consequential for blacks and structured their subjectivity.

Wilson has his characters make history through processes of oral transmission, replicating oral practices from early African cultures that continued throughout the diaspora. The African griot or oral historian engaged, as Eric Hobsbawm and Terence Ranger explain, in the process of "invented history," as oral transmission not only passed on the tribe's or community's history, but constituted an actual historical record.[24] Following in this oral tradition, in the first act of *The Piano Lesson,* Doaker, the uncle of the central combative figures, Berniece and Boy Willie Charles, functioning as New World African griot, relates the history of the piano that stands at the core of the conflict between brother and sister. Doaker invents history: his revelation of the family's travails over the ownership of the piano are an "authentic" historical record with multiple and multilayered meanings. The convention of storytelling is critical to Wilson's dramaturgy, with characters repeatedly speaking their history as they and we consider its meaning within their current circumstances. Troy Maxson, the central figure in *Fences,* through a series of backyard tales engages in an educative and historiographic project that expands the canvas of the play. In vivid and captivating detail, Troy recalls his journey into the present, his battles with his father, leaving his father's house, his early life of crime that led to manslaughter and imprisonment, his redemption through baseball and marriage to Rose. Troy's stories reach beyond the conventional temporal and spatial limits. Reexamining history, re-creating and positioning himself within the fabric of the historic narrative, Troy constructs his past in the present. This oral mode of historical transmission, communication, and performance embodies what Kenyan scholar, novelist, and director Ngugi wa Thiong'o calls *orature.* Joseph Roach defines orature as

> a range of forms, which, though they may invest themselves variously in gesture, song dance processions, storytelling, proverbs, gossip, customs, rites and rituals are nevertheless produced alongside or within mediated literacies of various kinds and degrees. In other words, orature goes beyond a schematized opposition of literacy and orality as transcendent categories; rather, it acknowledges that these modes of communication have produced one another interactively over time and that their historic operations may be usefully examined under the rubric of performance.[25]

Performance moves Wilson's words from the page to the presence of the audience continually mediating between literacy and orality. In the tension and gap between these two, Wilson (w)rights history.

History provides both background and foreground for Wilson, who sets his plays at critical moments of historic transition, significant periods of liminality for his characters and for African Americans. With *Ma Rainey's Black Bottom* (1984) the time is 1927, a moment when the popularity of African American rural blues of Ma Rainey was fading, to be replaced by the up-tempo jazzier sounds and urban dance rhythms of Bessie Smith. *Fences* begins in 1957, not long after *Brown v. Board of Education* and just before the Memphis garbage strike and the Montgomery bus boycott. He ends the play in 1965 at the cusp of the Civil Rights movement, which would galvanize the social sentiments of people, capturing the attention of a nation. Four years later, in 1969—a time of social upheaval, as black liberation strategies evolved from the integrationist and nonviolent paradigms of civil rights into the violent, radical separatism of Black Power—Wilson sets *Two Trains Running*. Wilson locates the play in a small Pittsburgh restaurant that is at once within as well as outside the urgencies of these times. The shop must be torn down as part of the process of urban renewal. Outside its confines, a funeral for the fictitious Prophet Samuel and a rally for the real slain black leader Malcolm X are held. Inside the shop, the characters confront issues of identity and black power, black capitalism and patriarchal hegemony. The play is at once timely and timeless, operating within a specific historical context and at the same time commenting on the present. Here and throughout the Wilson's cycle as a whole, the liminality of the times provides a metaphor for the characters' own dilemma and developments. The characters and Wilson's dramaturgy are at once within and outside of history.

In each work this liminality figures prominently. Characters have unfinished business, unresolved issues with their history. The piano player Toledo in *Ma Rainey* chastises the other band members and declares that the colored man is a "leftover from history."[26] As "leftovers," African Americans are liminal figures, outside the trajectory of white American history. Toledo goes on to ask, "Now what's the colored man to do with himself?" (*Ma Rainey*, 1.47). This question hovers over the cycle as a whole, as Wilson wonders about the empowered acts African Americans can take in the present or will take in the future.

Toledo's use of the masculine pronoun is not just traditional, but significant and should be noted. At the center of Wilson's dramas are "colored men" struggling for meaning, "native sons" wondering how to reclaim their place within the promise of America and an inheritance that they believe is rightly theirs. His work is decidedly malecentric, and the fourth chapter of this book analyzes Wilson's constructions of masculinity as his characters move toward self-determination. Wilson asks how black men rendered irrelevant in the postslavery economy can create meaning. He makes history with these "leftovers from history."

What Wilson develops is an alternative history—a concept of history that is not simply linear but the result of stops and starts, contested and contradictory moments, individual battles for subjectivity and identity. The struggles occur within the space and through the agency of performance. On the one hand, Wilson's focus on the transitional situates his plays within a conventional model of history as progress, yet Wilson contests and complicates this linear view of history by constructing characters who resist historic change based on their own experience. Ma Rainey refuses to play the new version of the title song arranged by the brash young trumpet player, Levee, because she fiercely believes that she knows her fans and her music. Her manager tries to convince her by telling her, "Times are changing. Levee's arrangement gives the people what they want." Ma responds, "If he got what the people want, let him take it somewhere else. I'm singing Ma Rainey's song" (*Ma Rainey*, 1.51). Because segregation and prejudice in baseball restricted his own chance to achieve, Troy in *Fences* rebuffs his son Cory's efforts to be recruited by a college football recruiter. Despite evidence to the contrary, Troy believes that whites will never let Cory succeed in sports and acts to protect him. John Timpane writes, "To allow Cory to play would acknowledge the inadequacy of his [Troy's] reading of the world. His refusal has tragic consequences for both Troy and Cory."[27] In *Two Trains Running*, Memphis, the restaurant owner, fights the forces of urban renewal that will tear down his business, insisting he receive from the city the value that his property is truly worth. Similarly, Becker and his cabbies in *Jitney* determine that they will hire a lawyer and will resist the city ordinance to move out of their jitney cab stand.

In each case resistance is based on a personal history that privileges individual experience. These particularized resistances reinforce the notion that the past indeed has weight and that at times change is hard to accept. Yet this does not contradict the Wilsonian philosophy that one must go back in order to move forward, that the past will "lead us if we force it to." Wilson asks what if we think of a history that is not teleological in that it presumes some future moment in which we can reflect on and understand the past, or deterministic in that it leads inexorably to a next preordained moment? What if history is not simply a master narrative in which the great events are plotted? Then perhaps the particularity of individual lives, the peculiar and idiosyncratic, can be represented. Within such representations lies the possibility of change and a chance for individual agency.[28]

Beat 3: Memory

> You rememory me?
> Yes. I remember you.
> You never forget me?
> Your face is mine.
> > —Toni Morrison, *Beloved*

> Black Man with Watermelon: Miss me
> Black Woman with Fried Drumstick: Miss me.
> Black Man with Watermelon: Re-member me.
> Black Woman with Fried Drumstick: Re-member me. Call on me
> sometime. Call on me sometime. Hear? Hear?
> > —Suzan-Lori Parks, *Death of the Last Black Man in the
> > Whole Entire World*

> Herald Loomis: I done forgot how to touch.
> > —August Wilson, *Joe Turner's Come and Gone*

"They tell me Joe Turner's Come and Gone," Bynum sings, and Loomis trembles and quakes with pain at each verse. "Stop singing that song!" he commands. Loomis wants to forget, but Bynum forces him to remember back to his enslavement as a way of confronting that history; as a means of going back in order to move forward; as a step toward letting go in order to recover his song. Here memory functions as an active agent, interpreting the past and illuminating present action. Walter Benjamin writes, "To articulate the past historically does not mean to recognize it 'the way it really was.' . . . It means to seize hold of a memory as it flashes up at a moment of danger."²⁹ Urgent situations within the present dictate the course of remembrance, and the power of memory is strong and painful as it meets with history and time. Memory as a palimpsest becomes a way that figurative and literal history merge in the individual. Repeatedly in his dramaturgy, Wilson conflates real memory with figural memory and real and figural history. At the end of the first act of *Two Trains Running,* Memphis recalls the impact of his mother's death and its contribution to his present determination to fight for what he justly deserves: "I'm ready to walk through fire. I don't bother nobody. The last person I bothered is dead. My mama died in '54. I said then I wasn't going for no more draws."³⁰ The last line "I ain't going for no more draws" emerges from Wilson's own memory of an off-duty city bus driver who got into a minor traffic accident with another man and exploded with rage. "The one guy jumped out of his car, slammed his hand on the hood, and said, 'I ain't going for no more draws.' He was banging on his car and screaming, 'I ain't going for no more draws' and he lost it." From this memory, Wilson constructed a figural history for this man: "So I figured that everything in his life was a tie, tie, tie. He said, 'Look I don't mind losin'. I wanna win, but I don't mind losin'. But I ain't going for no more draws."³¹ Wilson borrows this memory for Memphis, who refuses to accept less than the price he has established for his property. Eddie's Restaurant, frequented by Wilson in his youth, becomes the prototype for Memphis's establishment in *Two Trains Running.* Lutz's Butcher Shop and West's Funeral Home in *Two Trains Running* were real locations in Pittsburgh. Due to the growth of West's as the largest black funeral home, black people would joke, "Keep messing with me and West will dress you and God will bless you."³²

Thus, Wilson's cycle is a site for reworking his own memories that have both personal and political consequence in the present. Conversations heard in the barbershop and on the street corner in the Hill district of Pittsburgh are repeated and revised within the plays. Says Wilson, "I guess standing on a street corner in Pittsburgh for fifteen years, you just absorb those kind of things."³³ His own friends growing up, Earl and Jesse, are now remembered as the offstage friends of Cory in *Fences.* Its revelations of father-son conflict, as in *Jitney,* are places for Wilson to rework his own memories of his stepfather David Bedford and his biological father, August Kittel. And in his one man show entitled, *How I*

"They ain't gonna give you no twenty-five thousand dollars for this building. It ain't worth that." Two Trains Running, *Center Stage Theatre, 1994, with Damien Leake (West) and Anthony Chisholm (Memphis). (Photograph by Richard Anderson.)*

Learned What I Learned, first staged in May 2003 at the Seattle Repertory Theatre, Wilson performs his own history, a history that is at once figurative and real. As he recalls stories, people, and memories from his past, in effect, he situates himself as a character within his African American cycle. On the one hand there are direct links between his life and the plays: he tells a story of time spent in jail and the lawyer he called Steve Bartaromo. Joseph Bartaromo is the lawyer that the character Memphis hires in *Two Trains Running.* Even more significantly, within this performance, Wilson understands his own life in terms of the pageant of African American history, describing, for example, his experience of jail as particular to him but also representative of the conditions black men faced in America during the 1960s.

For Wilson, history is a function of his personal memory. Perhaps this is why, as Sandra Shannon notes, he eschews historical research:

> Wilson's ten-play chronicle challenges the authority of history. Preferring dramatic conflicts that evolve fundamentally from his own memory, he consciously avoids historical research and turns instead to the blues for inspiration for mood, place, time, subject and dialogue for each play. The blues evoke an atmosphere conducive to remembering.[34]

As will be discussed at length in the next chapter, "The Music is the Message," the blues in Wilson's plays become a space of collective cultural memory, an element in both form and content, a conduit for connecting past to present. In Chapter One, I analyze how music, particularly the blues, figures in his historical project, informing both the form and the content of his plays. In Wilson's dramaturgy the recuperation, the recognition, the reaffirmation of song is critical to reintegrating African Americans with their African past, with their spiritual and cultural roots. Through the blues and through narrative, memories are passed on or borrowed by one character from another. Yet, significantly, memories also traverse between real life and the world of the play, and thus memory in Wilson is tropological rather than simply historical.

Throughout the cycle, the revelations of memories both personal and collective function symbolically and materially to inform the characters' struggle to be black and whole. In *Piano Lesson*, Berniece's memory of her mother's suffering over the piano conditions her own interactions with it. "Mama Ola polished this piano with her tears for seventeen years. For seventeen years she rubbed on it till her hands bled. Then she rubbed the blood in . . . mixed it up with the rest of the blood on it" (1.2.52). Her remembrance of the matrilineal care and lineage of the piano sharply contrasts with Boy Willie's memories and with the strong patriarchal history of the piano's conquest and eventual delivery into Berniece's possession by the men in the Charles family. Her memories shape who she is as a woman, but her inability to fully confront these memories constrains her and prevents her from truly moving on.

Chapter 3, "The Women Question," looks at Wilson's depiction of women and examines how they operate within the conditions and constraints of Wilson's male-focused dramaturgy as well as within the historical restraints of patriarchy. My approach is not simply to note Wilson's limitations, but to consider how the subjectivity of African American women is critical to his project of historical recovery. Only through the collective communion of men and women can Wilson's characters achieve levels of liberatory self-definition and collective healing. The movement of *Piano Lesson* is both backward and forward in time, in internal and external space and memory, as Berniece finds herself through "re-membering" her ancestral legacy. Berniece comes to historical consciousness through memory that links her with her ancestors. This memory, in the words of Jeanette Malkin, is "not individual and ephemeral" but "collective, material and historically potent."[35]

My invocation of "re-membering" signifies on theories circulating within contemporary African American cultural production and criticism. Through re-membering, one addresses unfinished business of the past within the circumstances of the now. Re-membering is nonlinear and disrupts chronology as it sutures individual and collective wounds. This notion draws on Toni Morrison's invocation of "rememory," expressed in her Pulitzer Prize–winning historical novel *Beloved* (1987) in which the horrors of the past find enactment and confrontation in the present. At the end of the novel Paul D. suggests that you must embrace the past to let go of it. He tells Sethe, "We got more yesterday than anybody. We need some kind of tomorrow."[36] More specifically, however, I am appropriating this concept from *Death of the Last Black Man in the Whole Entire World* (1989–1992), in which playwright Suzan-Lori Parks speaks of re-membering as an act that reunites or re-members the collective black body, that joins past to present and that overcomes loss by recuperating and actively maintaining a living African American history in the present. Memories, both personal and collective, for African Americans serve to problematize concepts of historical truth and at the same time to uncover or, as David Palumbo-Liu phrases it, to "un-forget," that which had been previously covered up in historical accounts.[37] Memory in Wilson allows for strategic forgetting and at the same time enables the "un-forgetting" to which Palumbo-Liu refers.

History and collective memory intersect in the words and images of the poetic un-forgettings that introduce the published versions of the earliest three plays, *Ma Rainey, Fences,* and *Joe Turner.* On a fundamental level, these moments establish a starting place, the specific historical time frame that each play looks back on. Yet, on another level, they reveal how cultural and social memory open up alternative histories. Wilson announces in his introduction to *Ma Rainey*, "It is early March in Chicago, 1927" and that "Chicago in 1927 is a rough city, a bruising city." He also writes that the "negro" music called "the blues" defies definition but "is music that breathes and touches. That connects" (9). The music then contests the hardness of the city and the limits placed on black lives. Thus, prior to the action of the play, Wilson establishes that re-membering the blues provides an alternative understanding of black cultural survival.

The introduction to *Fences* also concerns questions of cultural survival. Introducing the published version of *Fences*, Wilson muses: "Near the turn of the century, the destitute of Europe sprang on the city with tenacious claws and honest and solid dreams. The city devoured them." In contrast, he posits that "the descendants of African slaves were offered no such welcome or participation."[38] Wilson's account powerfully contradicts the American grand historical narrative of opportunity for all. Written in the mid-1980s at the height of the Reagan-Bush era, Wilson's historical memory moment sharply contests the Republican romantic rhetoric of "morning in America" that hearkened back to the 1950s as an exemplary time of American family values and prosperity. Wilson foregrounds the disillusionment and strife that African Americans faced in their "New World." With the introduction to *Joe Turner,* Wilson underlines further the psychological scars of displacement that blacks encountered as they underwent the Great Migration north.

> Foreigners in a strange land, they carry as part and parcel of their baggage a long line of separation and disbursement which informs their sensibilities and marks their conduct as they search for ways to reconnect, to reassemble, to give clear and luminous meaning to the song which is both a wail and a whelp of joy. (203)

Wilson reinterprets the northern movement of blacks and (w)rights African American history by positing African Americans not as "migrants" to the North but as "foreigners in a strange land." Implicitly he sets the South as an ancestral homeland for African Americans. This moment and the other impressionistic moments of introduction imagine alternative cultural histories. They flash insurgence and disrupt the traditional historical memory as they suggest ways in which the plays that follow will interrogate issues of black social, psychological, and cultural survival.

Wilson, in perhaps an ironic bit of repetition and revision, calls each of these introductions to the published plays "The Play." Yet, they are not the play but precede the actual text we know as the play. In fact, outside of setting the date and time, they do not provide the director and designers with practical information upon which to structure their concepts for the play. Rather these interludes "play" with the concept of play and with the (w)righting of history as they create mood, texture, feeling, affect that inform the work. They comment on the collective social memories that are always at play and that act upon how African Americans perceive themselves and are perceived. Amritjit Singh, Joseph T. Skerrett, Robert Egan and Arjun Appaduria, remind us "Not only do we create and maintain the memories we need to survive and prevail, but those collective memories both shape and contain us."[39] Wilson's introductory narratives of play speak to the profound ways in which historically African Americans construct and are constructed and constrained within memory. These issues then play out within the play texts that follow.

These introductory moments constitute what Pierre Nora terms *lieux de mémoire,* or sites of memory. Within *lieux de mémoire,* history and memory intersect in "moments of history torn away from the moment of history." Nora explains that *lieux de mémoire* are "created by a play of memory and history, an interaction of two factors that results in their reciprocal overdetermination." Consequently these sites are "material, symbolic and functional."[40] Nora argues that the need for *lieux de mémoire* surfaces in a time marked by historic discontinuity and the instability of meaning. For African Americans, whose social reality is conditioned by performance and for whom cultural expressivity has always been central, the "synchronic remains of the present" in sites of history and memory can prove critical.[41] Geneviève Fabre and Robert O'Meally argue that the concept of *lieux de mémoire* can significantly inform reconsiderations in African American studies by facilitating reinterpretations of "poems, slave narratives, autobiographies and oral testimonies as crucial parts of the historical record. These varied repositories of individual memories, taken together create a collective communal memory."[42] Wilson moments of "play" are similarly wrapped in "a heap of signifying," a communal conjunction of history and memory.[43] These introductions as *lieux de mémoire* redefine what of the past is memorable even as they affirm the value of cultural memory.

Within the play texts themselves Wilson constructs *lieux de mémoire* that provide interplay between the personal and collective, and thus creates alternative sites of historical signification and cultural meaning. In *Seven Guitars,* at the top of act 1, scene 5, the characters gather around in the backyard to hear the radio broadcast of the second heavyweight title fight between black champion Joe Louis and the white former champion Billy Conn. According to the historical record, Louis proves victorious knocking out Conn in the eighth round. The mere record of the victory, however, does not account for the profound power that the cultural memory of the Brown Bomber, the son of an Alabama sharecropper, had within the African American community. His victories were experienced vicariously and collectively. They became symbolic triumphs over oppression. Thus, the characters in *Seven Guitars* share the victory communally as they contemplate their own personal struggles against white hegemony. They celebrate the Brown Bomber's win with another form of *lieux de mémoire,* a dance known as the "Jump Back." The fact that a dance serves as *lieux de mémoire* is telling because the dance functions as a performance within a performance, and performance and memory are inextricably linked, as Joseph Roach tells us: "Performance, in other words, stands in for an elusive entity that it is not but that it must vainly aspire to embody and replace. Hence flourish the abiding yet vexed affinities between performance and memory, out of which blossom the most florid nostalgias for authenticity and origin."[44] This moment of dance recalls with nostalgia a time in the forties when swing dancing and the Jump Back were the vogue. The actors must embody this memory, learned through the rehearsal process in order to convey it authentically before the audience. In Morrison's *Beloved,* the character Sixto, a defiant first-generation slave who is eventually burned, shot, and killed for inciting insurrection, dances with the hope that his child will inherit the memory. Morrison writes, "Sixto went among the trees at night. For dancing, he said, to keep his bloodlines open, he said."[45] The idea here, then, is that the performance contains a "blood memory" that can be passed on.[46] His dancing ensures the genealogical transmission of culture. Similarly, Wilson constantly considers aspects of blood memory and cultural transmission in performance. In each play, dances, songs, narratives, and oral testimonies function as performances within the performance, as *lieux de mémoire* that are invested with political, symbolic significance. They join the personal and the collective as they comment on processes of remembering.

Beat 4: Ritual

> Ritual action involves an inextricable interaction with its immediate world, often drawing it into the very activity of the rite in multiple ways. Exactly how this is done, how often and with what stylistic features will depend on the cultural and social situation with its traditions, conventions and innovations.
>
> —Catherine Bell, *Ritual*

In the final, powerfully ritualized moment of *Joe Turner,* Loomis's lost wife appears, and Loomis hands Zonia to her, but this connection with her, this act of return, is not enough for Loomis. He pulls a knife, initially to strike Bynum, who he feels has betrayed him. Instead Loomis cuts his own chest in a ritual act of syncretism that joins Christian and African rites; he bleeds for himself. "I don't need no one to bleed for me," Loomis intones as he covers his face in purifying blood. The act symbolically frees him, and with a newfound sense of self and of his song, he exclaims to Bynum, "I'm standing!" His standing links him in a new way with his past, and he walks out of the boardinghouse into his future. Metonymically, Loomis's actions here, as in other ritualized junctures in Wilson's cycle, return us to originating moments of rupture within African American history—particularly the Middle Passage and slavery. Such scenes work to refigure the forgetting, the amnesia, the losses of history and the history of loss; they are signal moments in which Wilson ritualizes time, memory, and history.

Wilson's rituals function as both endings and beginnings that unite past and present in a particularly African American cosmology. Thus, Loomis's performance of self-mutilation resonates with both African and Euro-Christian rites of blood sacrifice, and in its unique syncretism and in its social and symbolic meanings represents an act that is decidedly African American. Within such ritual practices, historical patterns are "reproduced but also reinterpreted or transformed."[47] They operate as "symbolic mediations"[48] linking the characters as well as the audience to an African and African American continuum of struggle and survival. Context is critical to ritual, as Catherine Bell stresses, and Wilson creates circumstances conducive to ritual action that is also—as Loomis's bloodletting—a practical response. Functioning as a "signifying practice,"[49] Loomis's individual rite of purification and other moments of ritual in Wilson's cycle convey a communal good on those who bear witness—the gathered community as a whole benefits. Wilson's rituals reaffirm collective faith even as they advocate self-definition and self-determination. As signifying practices,[50] these rituals operate in ways that are both situational and strategic: they seek to restructure the given reality; they construct meaning and mediate the dynamics of power; they bring the African past and African American present into relation. Given the import of the ritual and symbolism for Wilson's (w)righting, my examination of Wilson's cycle culminates in the fifth chapter, "Ogun in Pittsburgh: Resurrecting the Spirit," with a discussion of the intimate link between very practical matters of social change and ritual, African spirituality, and the symbolic. For Wilson, ritual and the symbolic become "a central arena for cultural mediation, the means by which various combinations of structure and history, past and present, meanings and needs, are brought together."[51]

As chapter 5 explores, Wilson's characters' embodiment of spirit and spirituality proves crucial to his dramaturgy and its processes of cultural healing and regeneration. Bell notes that central to understanding of ritual as cultural practice is

> the primacy of the body moving within a specially constructed space, simultaneously defining (imposing) and experiencing (receiving) the values ordering the environment. For example the body movements of ritually knowledgeable agents actually define the special qualities of the environment, yet the agents understand themselves as reacting or responding to this environment.[52]

Herald Loomis's self-scarification is a moment of embodied ritual that simultaneously defines and engages the values ordering that environment, communicating even as it constructs the meaning of the event. He sees himself as reacting to the forces around him but is in fact also shaping these circumstances. His embodied rite produces a complex interaction with systems of power, history, and knowledge. His practice links him to powerful spiritual forces beyond himself but also locates the force

of God, of spirit, within. Loomis becomes a "qualified" agent of authority bestowing a hopeful benediction on the African American future but,
as Bell suggests, does not understand the mutually constitutive tension
between the self and external conditions. As I will explore further in
chapter 5, embodiment is critical to Wilson's rites and their enactment
by the actors as well as the characters. Loomis's blood ritual is a highly
charged, highly theatricalized moment experienced not only by the gathered community on stage, but by the community of spectators.

Through ritualized re-membering, then, Wilson's form becomes
what Terry Eagleton terms the internal, cultural logic of content; it
refigures breaks both personal and collective in time, space, and identity, to restructure reality.[53] His rituals stop processes of conventional
theatrical realism with their liminality and metatheatricality; they happen within the realistic template of the play and yet transcend conventional theatrical realism. More and more insistently, Wilson's dramaturgical style within the cycle—moving from *Ma Rainey* in 1984 to
Gem of the Ocean in 2003—has evolved to a place where the symbolic
becomes the methodology for conjoining the past and the present, the
self and the surrounding sociopolitical environment. The trajectory of
Wilson's work is toward an eschatological apocalypse that affirms a
new future through the revelations of the past's impact on the present.
Embodied ritualized acts in his plays offer practical sites for personal
and social transformation.

Perhaps a spiritual solution to social ills seems removed from the
material conditions and social realities that plague African Americans.
Perhaps one of the reasons for Wilson's success with white audiences is
that his proposed racial radicalisms do not overtly threaten whites but
hide behind the distance of history and the safety of spirituality. Perhaps Wilson's powerful call for a new black theater movement at the
Theatre Communications Group National Convention in 1996 caught
white theater practitioners and funders off guard because his virulent
call for black theater activism was no longer couched—as are his dramas—in mysticism or separated by time. The speech garnered both support and criticism from a variety of factions and led to a televised
debate with nemesis Robert Brustein in January 1997. Spurred on by the
vociferous responses to this speech, to the debate, to the demands that
he live his convictions, Wilson helped to organize a National Black Theatre Summit at Dartmouth College in March 1997. Wilson, reborn as

playwright in his midthirties, now finds himself in his fifties reconstituted as an activist leader. And in the sixth and final chapter of this book, "The Rhetoric of Resistance in Way of Conclusion," I consider how Wilson's artistic practice relates to his social performance. I read closely Wilson's TCG speech in relation to his practical theater work. I examine the cycle's marking of both an ending and a beginning for history, always a process and in process, contested and constructed in the present. Despite the cross-cultural appeal of his dramaturgy, Wilson sees his own roots within the Black Power movement of the 1960s and identifies himself with black cultural nationalism of that time and the processes of black revolutionary theater.

Thus, the intersections of his own identity politics, his spoken words and written dramaturgy, with their moments of ritualistic jubilee, create their own intriguing ruptures, complexities, and discontinuities that demand interrogation.

As Wilson (w)rights history, he recovers an earlier concept of revolution and revolutionary processes. Hannah Arendt points out that the word *revolution* was "originally an astronomical term. . . . In its scientific usage it . . . indicates a recurring cyclical movement. In the seventeenth century it was used for a movement revolving back to some pre-established point."[54] Following this line, I propose that we see Wilson's process as re-evolutionary, returning us to the past, to the cycle of time, to the recurring movements and moments within African American history. He repeats and revises these re-evolutionary moments in order to open up the possibility for a new beginning—a beginning that is possible only after we confront the past, negotiating its meanings and its presence.

Chapter 1
The Music Is the Message

The page is finite. Once you put the words down on paper you've fossilized your thought. Bugs in amber, nigger. But music is life itself. Music is time. Played live, played at seventy-eight rpms, thirty-three and a third, backwards, looped whatever. There's no need for translation.
—Paul Beatty, *The White Boy Shuffle*

Gathered around the kitchen table in the first act of *The Piano Lesson*, Boy Willie, his friend Lymon, and his uncles Doaker and Wining Boy passionately sing a work song they all learned while kept in servitude, at different times, on Parchman Prison Farm.

O Lord Berta Berta, O lord gal oh-ah
O Lord Berta Berta O Lord gal well.
(1.39)

They accent their a cappella harmonies by clinking glasses against bottles, clapping their hands and stomping their feet as they perform "with great fervor and style." It is a moment of embodied performance within a performance, within and yet beyond the limitations of theatrical time, at once inside and outside the action of the play. The lyrics tell of unrequited love, "Berta in Meridan . . . I'm on old Parchman." The scene symbolizes the personal hardship and collective social memory of unfulfilled dreams and compensatory separations that blacks suffered under forced enslavement. Yet, even as the song expresses the pain of these men, it also proclaims their will to survive. The cultural response of this blues song enables them to endure the hardship of the labor camp. They sing now as survivors, recalling that past, but removed from Parchman's particular inhumanities. Their a cappella ode is thus

(The men begin to play) Seven Guitars, *Goodman Theatre, 1995, with Jerome Preston Bates (Floyd), Albert Hall (Hedley), Ruben Santiago-Hudson (Canewell), and Tommy Hollis (Red). (Photograph by Goodman Theatre.)*

time bound and yet transcendent, triumphant and yet tragic. It is a communal, dichotomous moment that contains "both a wail and a whelp of joy."

This "Parchman" musical interlude in *Piano Lesson* exemplifies the incisive functionality and multidimensionality of music within Wilson's (w)righting of history. I quote here at length Robert O'Meally's insightful analysis of Ellison's Invisible Man's discovery of the blues and black vernacular history because of how it can also apply to Wilson's dramaturgical project:

> What he [the Invisible Man] must face is that yes, although blues music is not the only history of the United States, it is a vital one. Perhaps it is the most vital one. It's Ellison, remember, who in essay after essay has

insisted that the blues may come closest to expressing Americans' sense of their comic/tragic predicament in a country full of blues. If the sidewalk blues music seems too incidental or vague, then it is still true that like the cultural signs of the boys on the subway—with their ceremonies suggesting a death as well as a hope to prevail even in the face of death; with their sly humor suggesting that they are mockingly insightful as well as poised for action—the recording must be read with extreme care. In a sense it *is* the true history of the times, one of America's most dramatic forms of incipient action.[1]

O'Meally's argument that the vernacular operates in Ellison as a "true history" repeats Alan Nadel's statement on performance and history in African American culture, quoted in the introduction. *Piano Lesson*'s performed Parchman song echoes back to the real, notorious Parchman work farm, where black men endured indignities, monotony, and grueling work with the help of song. Within the immediacy of performance, the men's passionate singing summons specific memories for each of the characters involved, revisits African American cultural history, and usually generates enthusiastic responses from the audience. "Music is time," Paul Beatty intones in the epigraph to this chapter. Like time, music is always moving, able to conflate past, present, and future. Music has its own time, meter, rhythms, but the narrative of music in time also connects to concepts of memory and allows us to imagine and remember times. Equally important, such musical interludes as "Ol' Berta" disrupt and transcend theatrical time, as the song occurs in the performative now. The music in Wilson is always historical, set within a specific historical moment. And yet in its performance, music such as this Parchman song can transcend history through emotional dimensionality. The work song performance acts as a *lieu de mémoire* that joins history and memory, mediating historical discontinuities and practically enabling survival.

Throughout the work of August Wilson, music, most particularly the blues, functions as both metaphor and metonym, as vehicles for cultural transmission and re-membrance. Musical instruments, blues songs, recurring lyrical tropes represent, embody, and express the "souls of black folks." Wilson depicts black people in liminal space, displaced and disconnected from their history, separated from their individual identity and in search of spiritual resurrection and socio-political reconnection. Wilson suffuses their search with musical imagery: his alienated and dislocated black characters must rediscover their "song." This song, as Wilson writes in the introduction to *Joe Turner's Come and Gone*, "is both a wail and a whelp of joy" (203). It evokes pleasure and pain, struggle and survival, the complexities and contradictions inherent in African American experience. In Wilson's dramaturgy, then, the recuperation of, the recognition of, the reaffirmation of this song is critical to reintegrating African Americans with their African past, with their spiritual and cultural roots.

As Wilson draws on black music, he seeks to capture in theatrical form music's expressive force, and in this process, he links himself to other black writers past and present. In "Music as Metaphor," Margaret Wilkerson writes, "Black music born out of the need for an expressive as well as a coded private language, is as implicitly political as the lives of these writers [new black women playwrights] depict. And writers from Langston Hughes to Alice Walker, from Richard Wright to Lorraine Hansberry to Ntozake Shange, have attempted to emulate the efficiency and evocative qualities of that form."[2] Just as black music operates as "coded private language," Wilson's plays speak to a particular constituency through specific cultural references and language. At the same time, like music that finds listeners across racial and ethnic borders, Wilson's works contain meanings and messages that are accessible to a wider audience. Wilson captures the poetry and music found in the rhythms of black speech in his dialogue. In so doing he counters pejorative claims that black English is a subordinate, inarticulate form rather than, in James Baldwin's words, "this passion, this skill . . . this incredible music."[3] Wilson validates the vernacular, a vernacular that is inherently musical. Given Wilson's engagement with the musicality of black speech, we must understand that meaning in performance is not simply located in the connotations and contexts of the dialogue but also in the sounds, the inflections, the accent of the lines. Wilson invites the audience to participate aurally in the proceedings, to hear, as Kimberly Benston argues, "the poet *as* musician." For the community of audience and performers there is "the intimacy of shared presence rather than the distance of re-presentation."[4]

Yet and still the trope of black musicality is often too generalized, too overused, too overdetermined to the point it has become essentialized, limiting black people to the stereotypical claims that "we all got rhythm," the expectation that we can all sing and dance. Repeatedly,

Wilson incorporates live musical performances that flirt with the historic stereotype of the black performer as amusing song-and-dance minstrel. At the same time, he subverts the stereotype by exploring the pain, as well as the pleasure within the performance. Early in *Seven Guitars,* as Floyd Barton strums his guitar, Red Carter pulls out drumsticks and keeps a beat on the chairs and table around him. Canewell joins in on his harmonica. Desiring to participate, the mysterious West Indian character, Hedley, grabs a board, bangs in a nail, and ties on a string, creating a one-string instrument that he plucks. Their improvisation pleases the audiences and breaks the rhythm of the action. Wilson's dramaturgy encourages such interventions. Hedley and the rest of the men in this musical moment from *Seven Guitars* make music out of nothing. They engage the physical burdens and limitations of life through cultural expression and improvisation, through music, through song. Wilson plays on the notion of cultural ownership, that the "song" belongs particularly to blacks. And yet as evidenced by the carved piano in *Piano Lesson,* a European instrument that the African American Charles family adopts and appropriates and makes its own, or the one-string that Hedley creates in *Seven Guitars,* African American culture has always involved adaptation, appropriation, and hybridity. Consequently, questions of authenticity, purity, and ownership are particularly complex and at times contradictory. Culture is always in process, always multidirectional, always about positioning. Culture is not simply a static set of shared beliefs and customs inherited by people of the same ethnicity; rather, it operates as what Baz Kershaw calls a "signifying system," "signs via which groups, organizations and communities recognise and communicate with each other."[5] Hence particular care must be taken when analyzing the signification of the trope of black musicality in Wilsonian criticism for fear of essentializing Wilson's practice and depreciating the complexities of the musical interchange.

Paul Carter Harrison and other critics have argued that Wilson's musical aesthetic aligns him with the activist poets and playwrights of the Black Arts movement of the 1960s and 1970s, who proclaimed that African American musical traditions best exemplified a "black aesthetic,"[6] a black way of creating. These writers sought to replicate the identifiable black musical aesthetic in other artistic forms. The Black Arts movement carved out a decidedly political agenda for art and firmly believed that ethics and aesthetics should not be separated. Harrison proclaims that Wilson's work is the fruition of the Black Arts movement's vision and agenda, congruent with the position of key critic and advocate for the movement Larry Neal:

> Wilson's work faithfully corresponds with Neal's demand for black self-authentication. . . . Stylistically, Wilson's plays are compatible with Neal's call for the self-determination of artistic purpose that is located in an oral tradition codified by the aesthetics of black church oratory and folk blues performances.[7]

Harrison points out the ways that Wilson's work embodies black music traditions found not only in black folk blues and music performances, but in church orature as well as the practices and language of everyday life. This articulation is affirmed by Wilson himself: "I stand myself and my art squarely on the self-defining ground of the slave quarters, and find the ground to be hallowed and made fertile by the blood and bones of the men and women who can be described as warriors on the cultural battlefield that affirmed their self-worth."[8]

Yet, even as Wilson's own design for, and the critical response to, his theater root him in a particularly black cultural tradition, his work traverses such cultural borders. Neal and black aesthetic activists in the 1960s proclaimed that an idealized black community was to be the sole source, audience, and critic for black theater. Wilson, on the other hand, produces plays in predominantly white theaters and receives positive reception from white critics and audiences. Wilson's work, like black music, is multidirectional, marked by race, culture, and historic context, yet able to negotiate barriers of skin, nationality, and language. Once located solely in the black rural South and evidence of a specifically black musical aesthetic, the blues now depend economically on white listenership, feature white artists, and are patronized by white spectators. Rap music, which emerged from black urban environs, now boasts a large fan base of suburban white teens, and its most successful current practitioner, Eminem, is white.

In the concluding chapter of this book, I will discuss the dynamics of such cross-cultural appreciation, appropriation, commodification, and commercialization in relation to Wilson's own critical commentary as well as to his own art. Here I want to explore Wilson's musicality by noting that it works as a contextualized cultural practice constructing meanings in the present even as it resurrects the past. In Wilson's dramaturgy "song" as a key signifier of black difference is constructed through specific processes and within particular contexts of black life. Wilson stylistically infuses his plays with musicality and pushes against the limits of conventional realism. He himself functions as a bluesman, "improvising on a theme" or themes. Accordingly, his scripts for the performer and director, his dramatic texts and performances for the scholar and critic, must be recognized for their blues voice, their particular rhythms and musical inflection and for what Houston Baker in his theorizing on the blues terms an "invitation to inventive play."[9]

Language of the Blues

Wilson describes the blues as one of his principal creative influences. He discovered the blues in 1965 while listening to an old recording of Bessie Smith's "Nobody in Town Can Bake a Sweet Jellyroll Like Mine." This recording transformed his life and his cultural ideology. The blues not only became a guiding force in his writing but also a foundation for African American expressive culture and for what he believes is a distinctly African American way of "being."

> I saw the blues as a cultural response of a nonliterate people whose history and culture were rooted in the oral tradition. The response to a world that was not of their making, in which the idea of themselves as a people of eminent worth that believed their recent history was continually assaulted. . . . In such an environment, the blues was a flag bearer of self-definition. . . . It was a spiritual conduit that gave spontaneous expression to the spirit that was locked in combat and devising new strategies for engaging life and enlarging itself.[10]

According to Wilson the cultural, social, political, and spiritual all interact within the blues. Forged in and from the economics of slavery as a method of ameliorating its pains and dehumanization, the blues are purposefully duplicitous, containing a matrix of meanings. In *Ma Rainey's Black Bottom*, Ma reminds her band leader and guitar player, Cutler, "The blues always been here" (2.68). Houston A. Baker, Jr., similarly calls the blues "an economically determined and uniquely black 'already-said.'"[11] The blues for Wilson offer a methodology for negotiating the difficult spaces of African American existence and achieving African American survival, operating with the unique combination of the tragic and the comic, of poetry and ritual that Ralph Ellison saw in the blues.[12]

In each of the plays, Wilson's characters engage in vernacular games—the dozens and signifyin'—that are extensions of the blues or variations on a blues theme. Wilson sets his works in sites that enable such communal engagement, verbal jousting, and oral transmission of culture. He places the band's interaction in *Ma Rainey* in the band room downstairs from the recording studio. The band room represents what Houston A. Baker terms, a "blues matrix,"[13] which Baker envisions as a "point of ceaseless input and output, a web of intersecting, crisscrossing impulses always in productive transit."[14] For Baker, the prototypical site of the blues matrix is a railroad crossing, "the juncture of multidirectionality," a place "betwixt and between."[15] Situated at the blues matrix, the blues singer transcends spatial and socio-historical limitations. The band room as blues matrix is a site of power and potential. It is a space of unfinished business, where the band must rehearse its songs and await the arrival of Ma Rainey. It is a metaphorical space where the band members enact rituals and tales of survival that replicate the patterns of black experiences in America.

Similarly, Seth's boardinghouse in *Joe Turner's Come and Gone*, Memphis's restaurant in *Two Trains Running*, and Becker's jitney cab station in *Jitney* are liminal spaces, blues matrices, "betwixt and between." The boardinghouse serves as a way station for African Americans during the great migration from the South to find work. Seth remarks that "word get out they need men to work in the mill and put in these roads . . . and niggers drop everything and head North looking for freedom" (*Joe Turner*, 209). The characters come to Seth's boardinghouse in search of a new life, a new sense of self. Or, as Wilson notes, "they search for ways to reconnect, to reassemble, to give clear and luminous meaning to the song" (*Joe Turner*, 203). Memphis's restaurant also functions as a way station for its regular customers. As the play opens, the restaurant is threatened by the impeding reality that it soon will be torn down with the advent of urban renewal. Thus its liminality is confirmed. The restaurant exists between its past glory and its uncertain future. Memphis laments, "At one time you couldn't get a seat in here. Had the jukebox working and everything. Time somebody get up somebody sit down before they could get out the door" (*Two Trains Running*, 1.1.9–10). Similarly, in *Jitney*, Becker's cab stand is scheduled for demolition by urban renewal. While Memphis determines a way to sell his restaurant for the best price, Becker and his drivers decide to stay and fight for their space. In each case, the stage environment as blues matrix represents a site of inventive resistance. The liminality of the spaces makes them locations of great creative and destructive potential. They are sites in which Wilson employs the "productive transit" of the blues.

In Wilson's "bluesology," the plays are driven by character and the lyrical music of the dialogue rather than plot or action. Wilson, who was a poet before he became a playwright, celebrates the poetic power in the speech of poor and uneducated people. His characters voice their history in the verbal equivalent of musical solos. Troy Maxson, an illiterate garbageman in *Fences,* fashions himself through bold expressive tales. Like the ancient city of Troy, he is an epic force, impregnable and larger than life. Allan Wallach points out that "the play swells to match his oversized dimensions."[16] During one storytelling riff, Troy describes a wrestling match he had with Death. Later, he relates how the Devil came to his house offering furniture on credit. Rose, his wife, interjects a practical perspective that contradicts the veracity of Troy's tales: "Troy lying. We got that furniture from Mr. Glickman" (*Fences,* 1.1.117). Yet the truth of the stories is not as significant as the power of the African and African American oral traditions that Wilson celebrates and asserts through Troy's performance.

Wilson's attention to the rhythms, logic, and linguistic structure of black speech enables his plays to celebrate the poetry within everyday life even as they assert black difference and the power of the vernacular. His youth spent hanging out in Pittsburgh's Hill District observing the conversations of older men, the regulars who congregated at the neighborhood cigar store, becomes a source for the patterns of black speech he seeks to capture. Wilson shows the ultimate reverence for the "ways blacks talk." Wilson works to be true to the musical sounds of black speech: "I found out that the musicality is built into the language. It's built in the way in which black folks talk. . . . And it's a language that I grew up with."[17] Linguists John and Russell Rickford in *Spoken Soul* credit Wilson with an ability "to re-create and evoke the beauty, poetry and wisdom of everyday black speech" as he "deploys a battery of the [black] grammatical vernacular features including completive *done* ("they *done* trumped") and habitual *be* ("he *be* making out")."[18] Yet, even as Wilson records authentic black dialect and attends to historic detail, he employs patterns of language and rhythm that are particular to his dramaturgy. Phrases such as "I ain't studying you," he repeats from play to play. Thus, a Wilson play requires actors who have the acumen for Wilson-speak and his specific formalism. Just as actors like Rebecca Pigeon and William Macy have been highly successful in translating the staccato rhythms of David Mamet on stage, actors such as Charles Dutton and L. Scott Caldwell have effectively interpreted Wilson.[19] Paradoxically, mastering the formal structure of Wilson's dialogue enables its musicality and produces the illusion of a free and spontaneous discourse.

One of Wilson's central methods for achieving musicality is repetition with revision, found in blues and jazz music, but also often connected in contemporary critical discourse to the formal language of Suzan-Lori Parks in such early works as *Death of the Last Black Man in the Whole Entire World* and *The America Play*.[20] The process of repetition and revision in jazz refigures the idea of forward progress as the music follows a more circuitous pattern. Sounds are repeated but do not repeat. When I directed Wilson's *Fences* at TheatreWorks in Palo Alto, California, in March 2000, I became aware of one brief but telling repetition and revision through Tony Haney's powerful performance as Troy. Frustrated by Cory's lying to him about working at the A&P, Troy complains to his friend Bono and son Lyons,

> That boy ain't working down there. He lying to me. *Telling* me he got his job back . . . *telling* me he working weekends . . . *telling* me he working after school . . . Mr. Stawicki *tell* me he ain't working down there at all! . . . When it get to the point where he wanna disobey me . . . then it's time for him to move on. Bono'll *tell* you that.
>
> (Fences, 1.4.146; emphasis added)

The repetition and sound of duosyllabic "telling" contrast aurally in performance with the singular "tell." Accordingly, for Troy, Cory's "telling" of lies contradicts the facts that Mr. Stawicki or Bono "tell." Wilson's repetition and revision of tell and telling suggest the power of indirection that scholars such as Geneva Smitherman and Henry Louis Gates, Jr., have pointed out is critical to black vernacular communication and is fundamental to Wilson's dramaturgy.[21]

The interpolation of live performances also becomes another form of cultural transmission, another way in which Wilson re-presents blues tropes and traditions. In *Piano Lesson,* not long after he has joined Boy Willie, Lymon, and Doaker in the singing of the Parchman song, Wining Boy wanders over to the piano and plays a blues song about travel and rambling.

I am a rambling gambling man
I gambled in many towns
I rambled this wide world over
I rambled this world around.
(1.2.47)

The concept of travel is critical to the blues and its legacy. Born in the postslavery period of black migratory energy, the blues celebrated movement. The desire to transcend the immediate difficulty of social circumstances, the restlessness experienced by many, translated into a music that, in its sounds, its lyrical fluidity, embodied a spirit of resilience and contestatory progress. The blues affinity for movement is a trope that Wilson repeats and revises in his cycle (and that I will take up again in relation to Wilson's women in chapter 5). Central to the blues idea of travel are trains and the railroad. Houston A. Baker, Jr., explains, "This possibility came from the locomotive's thrust, its promise of unrestrained mobility and unlimited freedom. The blues musician at the crossing, as I have already suggested, became an expert at reproducing or translating these locomotive energies."[22] Railroad crossings also signified the displacement of sharecroppers with the onslaught of trains and new industry and thus the need to migrate north to find employment and a better life. As a bluesman improvising on a theme, Wilson returns repeatedly to the trope of the railroad. He foregrounds it in the title to his play of the 1960s, *Two Trains Running,* which indicates the divergent directions one's life path can take. Act 2 of *Piano Lesson* opens with Doaker, the railroad man, singing a song about the trains: "Gonna leave Jackson Mississippi and go to Memphis" (2.1.55). Doaker sings of the unbridled, free transit enabled by the train. For black former slaves, victims of constraints and restrictions, his song suggests that the railroad can bring a new experience of life and liberty. Present in these railroad blues is the possibility of change, of action, and of new potentiality. The song represents a historical record as well as the personal memory of Doaker's experience as railroad man.

Mikhail Bakhtin offers that "language does not merely represent: it is itself an object of representation. Novelistic discourse is always self-critical."[23] Translating this to the drama of Wilson, the songs in the plays not only constitute historic blues and archives of black culture, they work to define and transport the culture of the blues.[24] Wilson is particularly referential in this process, echoing the history of the blues, the songs that he listens to as he writes.

Wilson listens to blues music specific to the period for each play he writes; the music provides him with clues to the lives of the people but also with a texture for the work. With *King Hedley II*, his play of the 1980s, however, he shifted and instead listened principally to jazz as he composed.[25] Asked if *King Hedley II* was therefore a jazz play, Wilson cautioned, "It's a blues play. No, you see because the music—the blues is basic, bottom music. Jazz comes out of the blues, gospel comes out of the blues. It's all blues."[26] His comment underscores the centrality of blues in his artistic production and in his social vision of black experience. Wilson's plays operate with what Ralph Ellison terms a "blues impulse," that is, "an impulse to keep the painful details and episodes of a brutal experience alive in one's aching consciousness, to finger its jagged grain, and to transcend it, not by the consolation of philosophy but by squeezing from it a near tragic, near comic lyricism."[27] Wilson's characters confront and finger that jagged grain. They seek that tragicomic "song" which enables them to persevere.

In order to further provoke the near tragic, near comic lyricism, Wilson in *Ma Rainey's Black Bottom* composes his blues musician characters—like Levee the young, fiery trumpet player, who blares and blasts with rage and desperation—to correspond with the instruments that they play. According to Wilson, "With the trumpet you have to force yourself out through the horn. Half-consciously I tried to make Levee's voice a trumpet. . . . Levee is a brassy voice."[28] Correspondingly, Slow Drag, the bass player, maintains the bass line in the play. He is a slow and deliberate voice, who reinforces the action around him. Cutler, the bandleader and guitar player, strikes a practical note. He is not one to improvise but has the power to embellish a theme, as when he tells the involved story of Reverend Gates, a black preacher humiliated by white racism. Toledo, the piano player, is the only member of the group who can read. He is a philosopher who engages in monologues and storytelling riffs that are analogous to virtuoso, improvised piano solos.

Understood as musical instruments within a "blues impulse" and "invitation to play" and the liberating formalism of Wilsonian style, the characters vamp, solo, and improvise. The instruments also sound antiphonally as in the blues: Levee's blare clashes with Ma's blues voice and with the notes of Toledo's piano. Functioning as sound, as blues, as music, as antiphonal harmonies, the play's climactic moments, Levee's firing by Ma and his killing of Toledo, embrace and exude the ambiguity and complexities of the jagged blues edge that Ellison describes. They are moments that, as Albert Murray says, acknowledge and confront "the fundamental facts of life, without illusion, facts that are sometimes as incomprehensibly absurd as they are ugly."[29]

In the performance of *Jitney*, the characters' voices and actions, composed by Wilson in concert with his director Marion McClinton, become a musical jam session that provides both antiphonal critique and collective communion. Ben Brantley, in his review for the *New York Times*, called the play an "urban symphony."[30] Within the world of Becker's cab station, Wilson constructs the individual cab drivers and their particular histories and idiosyncrasies. The stories unfold, of Youngblood's desire to buy a house, of Fielding's drinking problems, of Turnbo's overwhelming desire to involve himself in everybody else's business. And yet, at the same time the play and its action also join the characters together in an ensemble that culminates in their solemn communion following Becker's funeral. The director McClinton explains: "Hearing *Jitney* is like listening to the Modern Jazz Quartet. Each of the characters has his or her solo, but they have got to be there as backup for the others."[31] The concept of sidemen and jazz soloist in *Jitney* is one that McClinton, the cast, and Wilson developed through the rehearsal process. According to Barry Shabaka Henley, who originated the role of Doub at the Second State Off-Broadway, the play's musicality is something that the actors must be prepared for: "You come in with your own instrument every night and you've got to be ready to jump in and play as hard as you can. You get juiced up and feed off each other's riffs."[32] The riffs and antiphonal melodies are spaces within which the conflict of the play explodes and the characters clash in call-and-response with each other. Youngblood reacts to Turnbo's insidious implications and unwanted involvement in his love life. Most centrally, Becker and his son Booster strike opposite chords, finding little place for agreement or active harmony. The image of a jazz ensemble not only connotes individual artistry and solo virtuosity, it also compels an awareness of the players' need to function together and find spaces of unity. They need to hear, appreciate, and support each other's rhythms. The music must resolve. The final scene of the play, the funeral for Becker, constitutes such a moment when the rhythms and music come together, the characters harmonize. There is collective understanding of the need to work, "to play," together for the benefit of all.

If *Jitney* is a jazz jam session, then *King Hedley II* embodies the feeling of a jazz opera in which the characters' arias reveal their loves and losses in ways that reconstitute the past in the present. These jazzy monologues are particularly gendered. While the women speak of love and maternity, the men discuss issues of honor, duty, and pride. Ruby, King's mother, remembers her career as a singer and how she fended off the advances of her employer bandleader, Walter Kelly. Tonya, King's wife, details why she has determined not to bring another baby into the world. King, the title character, explains how he took the life of the man who scarred his face. Elmore, King's mother's erstwhile lover, discloses how he came to murder King's real father Leroy. These operatic confessions, long monologues even for Wilson, operate on a mythic level, larger than life, filled with grand motives of rage, deception, and revenge. Yet they also function in a very real space of human frailty and within the tragic continuum of black-on-black violence. In suspended time, as singular performances that are at once inside and outside the forward action of the play, the men, Elmore and King, acknowledge pain, passion, pathos, all present in one moment of life-altering violence. Elmore explains:

> Leroy started to get out the [barber] chair. He was coming straight at me when I fired the gun. Gator [the barber] said, "Damn Elmore. Damn." The bullet hit him right smack in the middle of the forehead. That was the first bullet. I couldn't stop firing. Blood went everywhere. A piece of skull bounced off the mirror and landed about ten feet away. I found myself wondering what that was. I didn't find out till later. . . . I didn't say anything, I just walked out. Got outside and said, "Now what? That's over. Now what?" The bottom had fallen out of everything.[33]

Elmore's description is extremely graphic. He paints a vivid picture of the event for himself and for the gathered community. In the Seattle, Los Angeles, and Washington, D.C., productions, the actor Charles

Brown accented the gunshots by mimicking the gesture of pulling a trigger. The movement, the jolt of his hand with each retort from the pistol, reinforced the effect. Much as a John Coltrane jazz piece progresses through a "variety of recollections and disruptions of harmonic schemes,"[34] Elmore's monologue revisits that past through a series of signal moments, social frames, previous encounters with Leroy, and telling incidents of self-reflection. These individual, not necessarily sequential, memories climax in the critical barbershop bloodshed, the murder of Leroy. The process, then, does not simply reconfigure memory but reworks its meaning in the present.

Cultural Literacy and the Music

The fact that there is meaning in the musicality of dialogue as well as the words suggests a way in which Wilson's dramaturgy critiques and comments on concepts of literacy. Music constitutes for Wilson a key modality of cultural literacy. For African Americans, historically prevented from learning to read and write, other forms of cultural literacy necessarily emerged. Wilson, in his cycle, repeatedly riffs on modes of literacy and their relation to the transmission of African American culture. As he posits different forms of literacy, it reveals them not as antithetical, not as hierarchical, but as culturally and socially marked and constructed sites of difference. Wilson's men are often illiterate in the traditional sense and compensate by other means. In *Ma Rainey,* although all the men can play music, only Toledo can read the list of songs they are to record that day. Still, all the men know their instruments, can improvise and can play the verbal dozens. Floyd in *Seven Guitars* cannot read the letter of agreement that he receives from the president of Savoy Records, and yet he sends love letters crafted by a surrogate in Chicago back to Vera in Pittsburgh. Despite not being able to read, Troy in *Fences* revolts against the unwritten restrictions placed on black garbagemen and becomes the first black garbage truck driver—without a driver's license. Later, Troy uses his illiteracy as a defense when Rose asks why he signed papers that confine his brother Gabriel to a mental institution. Lacking the power to read and write, Wilson's figures must develop other forms of social and cultural literacy in order to survive. Most prominently, they learn the blues skill of improvisation on a theme.

Musical improvisation, ability to play the blues, is critical as an alternative mode of literacy, as Wilson demonstrates most profoundly in a small scene from *Piano Lesson* between Boy Willie and his niece Maretha at the piano. Boy Willie asks Maretha to play something for him, and she plays "something any beginner first learns" (1.1.21). Boy Willie quickly replaces her at the piano and plays a rousing boogie-woogie. Memorably enacted by Charles Dutton in the Broadway production, the boogie-woogie, accompanied by Dutton's freeform dance as he played, elicited laughs, rhythmic clapping to the beat, and a round of applause from the audience. "See what I'm doing? That's what you call the boogie-woogie. See now . . . you can get up and dance to that. That's how good it sound" (1.1.21). Boy Willie's performance functions as signifying revision of Maretha's naive technical playing. The self-taught musician Boy Willie brings "soul" to his piano playing. His unconstrained, improvisational performance contrasts with Maretha's need to rely on reading music. He tells her, "You don't need no paper. Go on. Do just like that there" (1.1.21). Maretha's reluctance to improvise on the piano without the sheet music symbolizes her removal from the creative heritage and oral traditions of black expressive culture and her sheltered tutelage by her mother Berniece. Wilson (w)rights history here by showing that improvisational skill in music is not ontological, not essentially black but a product of cultural experience and practices that inform social reality. The ability to read music potentially constrains Maretha. How the various forms of literacy and competency interact, then, is at issue.

In Wilson, written texts and the ability to read are not simply oppositional to orality and blues improvisation; rather, he demonstrates the ways in which they are relational and can coproduce meaning. Written texts such as legal documents often function as tools of white hegemony that black survival skills must confront or even circumvent. Ma Rainey must sign the release papers that give Sturdyvant and Irvin control over her voice on record. Her delay in signing is an exercise of resistance to the power of the written document. Floyd in *Seven Guitars* needs and can't find a piece of paper from the workhouse in order to receive his payment for time served. "She told me if I didn't have the paper I can't get my money. I told her all that wasn't gonna change nothing. The government still owed me thirty cents a day for my time in the workhouse" (1.4.33). King, the title character of *King Hedley II*, believes that he should be able to redeem his roll of pictures from Sears after he has produced the receipt.

Historically, legal and other written documents controlled black freedom; white sheets of paper were powerful texts that governed black mobility. For former slaves "having papers" signified that you were free. These papers functioned performatively, since by possessing them, blacks could enact freedom. Despite the presence of the live black body, these papers declared black liberated subjectivity and equally referenced the presence of unmarked white hegemony behind the document. The written text not only held promise and possibility but also contained the power to deceive, to reinforce the import of the figurative. Accordingly, Ma Rainey's oppositional performance of delay in signing the release forms operates as an alternative text that must be read, another example of orature. Wilson, the poet turned playwright, the ninth-grade dropout, constantly signifies on the relation between the written and the oral. His introductions to the plays, phrased in imagistic prose, are directed at an audience of readers and are not to be performed. On the other hand, only in performance can an audience appreciate the power of Ma's singing or the vibrancy of Boy Willie's boogie-woogie. Wilson puts the literary in conversation with the performative, aware of the diverse functions and audiences for the performance text and the written text.

The Blues Musician

It follows, given the import that Wilson allots to the music, that he privileges the blues musician and posits the blues musician as a potentially powerful site of black resistive agency.

> Blues is the best literature we have. If you look at the singers, they actually follow a long line all the way back to Africa, and various other parts of the world. They are carriers of the culture, carriers of ideas. . . . Except in American society they were not valued, except among the black folks who understood. I've always thought of them as sacred because of the sacred tasks they took upon themselves—to disseminate the information and carry these cultural values of the people.[35]

Locating the blues as literature underscores the points made earlier on Wilson's reorientation of literacy. For Wilson, blues musicians can convey the value of this alternative literacy; they have a spiritual and cultural power. Ma Rainey is such a blues musician who recognizes that the blues can become both a self-accentuating song and a declaration of the collective, cultural memory of African Americans. Ma believes that singing the blues is not simply therapy but rather an engagement with a complex and enabling force. "You don't sing to feel better. . . . You sing 'cause it's a way of understanding life" (*Ma Rainey*, 2.67). Similarly, in his essay, "Blues People," Ralph Ellison argues that the blues can transcend "conditions created within the Negro community by the denial of social justice."[36] Ma, as blues singer, situates herself inventively and uses the resources she has at her disposal to control and mediate the world around her. She asserts the power of blues singer to overcome material limitations.

Too often, however, Wilson's musicians do not realize the power they possess. Lyons in *Fences*, Jeremy in *Joe Turner's Come and Gone*, Wining Boy in *The Piano Lesson*, Floyd in *Seven Guitars* all represent blues musicians who to varying degrees have not recognized the spiritual force of the blues song and the cultural responsibility inherent in their musical ability. As a result, they are exploited for their music and fall victim to those who wish to control their spirit and song. The band members in *Ma Rainey*, similarly, do not realize the spiritual and political potential of their music, their blues voice. Toledo, the piano player, chastises his fellow band members by saying, "You lucky they [white people] let you be an entertainer. They ain't got to accept your way of entertaining. You lucky and don't even know it" (*Ma Rainey*, 2.77). Unfortunately, Toledo's words do not activate an increased social awareness in the brash young trumpeter, Levee, or in the other band members.

In sharp contrast to Ma Rainey, Levee, the play's pivotal character, is perhaps the prime example in Wilson's dramaturgy of a blues musician who fails to understand his relationship to the music, and never realizes his blues song. Levee, the youngest member of Ma Rainey's band, presents himself with a boldness that the others lack. His self-importance is both stubborn naïveté and camouflage. Levee desires to fit in with the band, to be accepted, to achieve within a world that devalues African American spirit and accomplishment. Significantly, Levee represents the forces of modernity in conflict with tradition; as Paul Carter Harrison writes, Levee's very name signifies "possible kinship with the new music soundings of jazz being created along the Mis-

"I ain't started the blues way of singing. The blues always been there."
Ma Rainey's Black Bottom, *Studio Theatre, 1986, with Bill Harris (Cutler) and Alfredine P. Brown (Ma Rainey). (Photograph by Joan Marcus.)*

sissippi levees of New Orleans during the period."[37] Levee rejects and ridicules the "jug band" songs of Ma Rainey. He desires to play music that makes people move and that he can "lay down in the people's lap." Yet Levee does not recognize that his new urban blues sound and jazz beats are deeply indebted to earlier African and African American sounds and sociocultural traditions. One of the most significant and repeated messages in Wilson's (w)righting is that modernity cannot erase but must embrace tradition, that the past constantly and continually affects the present.

Tragically individualistic, Levee speaks of personal ownership and individual achievement. He wants to play "his" music, write "his" songs, and form "his" band. He is unable to heed Toledo's warning to embrace communality and to think collectively: "It ain't just me, fool! It's everybody! What you think . . . I'm gonna solve the colored man's problems by myself? I said, we. You understand that? We. That's every living colored man in the world got to do his share" (*Ma Rainey*, 1.33). Levee does not think in terms of "we," but instead isolates and alienates himself from the other band members and systems of African American communal empowerment. Rejecting communality, Levee believes that he is on a mission to sing his song. Yet he does not understand the technologies of capitalism and white racism that constrict him and prevent such self-actualization. Levee disavows African American community and allows his music, his song to be commodified and controlled by the white record producer, giving Sturdyvant his songs and expecting that Sturdyvant will help him to form his own band.

In *Ma Rainey*, as in Wilson's subsequent works, the dominant culture seeks to suppress, to control, and to commodify the black blues song. Unlike any of the other plays in his cycle to date, *Ma Rainey* opens with two white characters, Ma Rainey's manager Irvin and Sturdyvant, the recording studio owner and a producer of "race records," on the stage. Together Irvin and Sturdyvant strategize on how to capture Ma Rainey's blues voice in the recording session. Sturdyvant reminds Irvin, "I just want to get her in here . . . record the songs on that list . . . and get her out. Just like clock work, huh?" (*Ma Rainey*, 1.12). Wilson juxtaposes Irvin and Sturdyvant's plan to commercialize Ma Rainey's blues song with Ma's own resolve to protect the integrity of her music. Ma testifies to Wilson's contention that the blues are a uniquely black voice that whites desire, but cannot understand: "White folks don't understand about the blues. They hear it come out, but they don't know how it got there" (*Ma Rainey*, 2.67). Throughout his historical cycle of plays, Wilson replays this theme, as whites repeatedly attempt to seize or possess black music, the black blues song. Wilson maintains, "The music [blues] is ours [African Americans], since it contains our soul, so to speak—it contains all our ideas and responses to the world. We need it to help us claim the African-ness and we would be a stronger people for it. It's presently in the hands of someone else who sits over it as custodian, without even allowing us its source."[38] Again I read this as a strategic claim, for cultural ownership is decidedly problematic. Wilson's assertion of cultural authority and ownership reworks the relation of cultural power and hegemony and affirms the social significance of black culture by constructing whites as always-desiring subjects. Early in *The Piano Lesson,* when the protagonist, Boy Willie, inquires about potential buyers for the family's heirloom, a carved piano, his uncle Doaker tells him that there is a white man going around trying to buy up black people's musical instruments. Even more significantly, the ghost of the recently deceased white southern landowner, Sutter, materializes in the Pittsburgh home of Doaker and Boy Willie's sister, Berniece, in an effort to reclaim the family's piano, the symbol of their African American struggle and survival. In *Joe Turner* Jeremy, a young boarder, reveals how a white man exploited him for his music in a guitar contest. Through the invisible presence and symbolic activities of offstage white characters, Wilson suggests that the dominant culture has continually sought to subjugate African American humanity and suppress the power and ability of African Americans to sing their song.

This musical metaphor has considerable contemporary significance. It reflects on the ways black cultural expression has been commercialized and exploited in today's mediatized culture. The raw, hard edge and social critique of black urban rap music, for example, has been commodified and softened to sell everything from soft drinks to hamburgers. Ma Rainey's obstinacy in the face of white hegemony parallels Wilson's own struggle against co-optation as a black artist and his desire to maintain his creative integrity and autonomy. Wilson's fierce resolve not to allow the film version of *Fences* to go forward without a black director evidences his determination to protect his agency as a black artist.[39]

In *Seven Guitars,* Wilson repeats and revises both the image of a mis-guided blues musician from *Ma Rainey* and the trope of white exploita-tion of the black song. Just as Levee mistakenly trusts the white record producer, Sturdyvant, Floyd Barton puts his faith in white producer and agent Mr. T. L. Hall. Floyd "Schoolboy" Barton dreams of returning to Chicago to record another hit record. According to Floyd, "Mr. T. L. Hall showed me a record he got from the record company. Say, 'Be there on June tenth to make some more records.' "[40] Yet, as noted ear-lier, Floyd is illiterate and cannot read his contract or any other com-munication from Hall. Although his hit record plays on the radio, Floyd receives no residuals. As his sideman, Canewell, points out, Floyd has "no hit-record money." Late in the second act Red Carter, the band's drummer, reveals that Hall has been arrested for "selling fake insur-ance. Say he sold over fifty thousand dollars worth" (*Seven Guitars,* 81). Clearly, Hall is not a man to be trusted. Like Levee, Floyd banks his future on someone who only intends to use him. Although Levee is only a band member, Floyd is the leader of his band. Levee dreams of success and longs to record his own music. Floyd, in contrast, already has a song playing on the radio. Still, both are seduced and blinded by the enticements of white-controlled commodity capitalism. The power they assign to the music is commercial, not communal or political, and they can envision only financial transcendence. Floyd's myopic, self-centered desire for fame and fortune in Chicago results in his betrayal of the power of the blues and values of community. With his capitulation to the forces of commodification symbolized by the pawning of his guitar, the instrument of his cultural potency, Floyd's demise is inevitable.

Mistakenly, Levee believes that his interactions with Sturdyvant build upon lessons he learned from his father on how to "deal with the white man." At the end of *Ma Rainey's* first act, Levee tells of his father's act of retribution against the white men who gang-raped his wife, Levee's mother. Levee explains that his father, Memphis Green, "acted like he done accepted the facts of what happened," while he gathered the names of the white men involved. Memphis even smiled in the face of one of these white men and sold that white man his farm. Later, after he had sold the land and moved his family, Memphis returned and managed to kill four of his wife's attackers before he him-self was killed. Memphis's actions unite the power of the blues trickster with that of the revolutionary. Duplicitously, Memphis smiled in the face of a white man who had wronged him and his family deeply, all the while plotting his revenge. Present in Memphis's response to his wife's rapists is the inherent irony of the blues. In effect, his performance is again analogous to that of Baker's blues musician at the crossroads improvising on a theme. Memphis, through his actions, negotiates the excruciating pain of his African American experience.

Interestingly, in *Two Trains Running*, Wilson features a character again named Memphis who has also been abused and run off his land by a group of white men. After seeing his mule killed, his land burned, and his deed to his land denied by a white judge, Memphis decides to leave Jackson, Mississippi, to "call it a draw" and to head north for Pittsburgh. Much like the earlier Memphis, this Memphis in *Two Trains Running* has unfinished business that he must settle. He too plays the role of the blues musician at the crossroads. Faced with the onset of urban renewal and the plans for the demolition of his restaurant, Memphis refuses to accept the amount offered him by the city government for his property. Angered and insulted by the city's paltry offer of fifteen thousand dollars, Memphis, like a blues player improvising on a theme, creatively negotiating the pain of white oppression, determines to beat the city government at its own game and hires a white lawyer to plead his case. By hiring a white lawyer, he improvises on a theme, and the result is a settlement for thirty-five thousand dollars. After his victory, Memphis returns to the restaurant drunk and triumphantly singing the blues:

> We don't care what Mama don't allow
> We gonna barrelhouse anyhow.
> (*Two Trains*, 2.5.108)

Memphis, with an new awareness of his "blues voice" and his power to determine his own destiny, decides to return south, "to go back and pick up the ball" and reclaim his land.

Levee, in *Ma Rainey*, on the other hand, misinterprets his father's legacy and never discovers his blues voice. While his father plotted revenge with cunning duplicity, Levee approaches Sturdyvant with romantic naïveté. Levee defers to Sturdyvant because he believes that Sturdyvant has the power to make him a bandleader and a star. Sadly, Levee does not recognize the authority of black people over the blues song. Cutler attempts to explain this reality to Levee, citing Ma as an example: "The white man don't care nothing about Ma. The colored folks made Ma a star. White folks don't care nothing about who she is . . . what kind of music she make" (*Ma Rainey*, 2.78). Levee does not listen to Cutler's explanation. Unlike his father, Memphis, Levee allows his blues voice to be bought and controlled by the mechanisms of institutionalized racism. Memphis sells his land, but maintains his power of self-determination, his soul. Levee, on the other hand, internalizes his oppression and instead of acting out against Sturdyvant, he strikes out with fury against Toledo for the disrespect of stepping on his shoes. As Wilson explains, Levee transfers his "aggression to the wrong target."[41] The result reinforces the tragic implications of black-on-black violence, the senseless, self-destructive loss of black lives.

Floyd's misfortune in *Seven Guitars* likewise unfolds like a blues riff with passion and pathos. His story is reminiscent of the myths and legends of larger-than-life black bluesmen such as Buddy Bolden and Robert Johnson. Fiercely, Floyd believes that his future success depends on his deal with Mr. T. L. Hall, and he risks everything to return from Pittsburgh to Chicago. Desperate for money in order to redeem his guitar from the pawnshop, Floyd commits an armed robbery, and his accomplice is shot and killed by the police. As Floyd attempts to recover his stolen bounty from its backyard hiding place, Hedley, a mentally unstable West Indian inhabitant of the building where Floyd's girlfriend Vera lives, kills him.

In this moment, Hedley mistakenly believes that Floyd is the legendary musician Buddy Bolden. Bolden (1877–1931), a builder and part-time barber, cornet player, and bandleader in New Orleans, has been called the first man of jazz. Bolden was an innovator and an influential musician. His band became one of, if not the most popular street dance bands in New Orleans in the early 1900s. As a result, Bolden was dubbed the first "King" of New Orleans cornet players. He was said to play the cornet so loudly and with such force that he "blew the tuning slide out of his cornet and it would land twenty feet away."[42] For Hedley, Bolden is a sacred figure, a god. Throughout *Seven Guitars*, Floyd and Hedley play a game around a lyric to the song "I Thought I Heard Buddy Bolden Say," or "Buddy Bolden's Blues." This song was based on Bolden's own classic jazz dance tune "Funky Butt"[43] and was recorded by Jelly Roll Morton in 1939, nine years before the date in which Wilson sets *Seven Guitars*. It soon became a jazz staple. In keeping with Bolden's improvisatory conventions, Jelly Roll Morton and others constantly improvised the lyrics to the song in performance. At times the words were off-color and thus subject to censorship and not suitable for recording or publication at that time. Either Floyd or Hedley will begin to sing the lyrics, only to be corrected on the words by the other man.

> *Floyd:* "I thought I heard Buddy Bolden say . . ."
> *Hedley:* What he say?
> *Floyd:* He said, "Wake up and give me the money."
> *Hedley:* Naw. Naw. He say, "Come here. Here go the money."
> *Floyd:* Well . . . what he give you?
> *Hedley:* He give me ashes. (*Seven Guitars*, 1.3.23–24)

Their disagreement over the lyric reflects on the improvisational nature of the song and its oral transmission through time. It also symbolizes Floyd's and Hedley's divergent ideologies. While Floyd imagines Bolden as a self-serving fellow musician demanding payment, Hedley envisions him as a redemptive figure bearing monetary gifts and offering salvation.

Thus, when Hedley spots Floyd unearthing his stolen money, Hedley, drunk on moonshine, mistakenly imagines that Floyd is Bolden, finally returned to give him the money: "No, Buddy, give me the money. You say, 'Come here . . . here go the money.' Give it to me. It's my father's money. Give it to me" (*Seven Guitars*, 2.8.104). When Floyd refuses him, Hedley kills Floyd with a machete, repeating the black-on-black knife murder that ends *Ma Rainey*, another senseless loss of black life. In the earlier play, the murder of Toledo functions as a performance of tragic, unfulfilled promise, a loss of black activism that needs to be reclaimed through the triumph of the blues voice. Prior to his demise, Toledo continually preaches a doctrine of Black Nationalist consciousness: "As long as the colored man look to white folks to put the crown on what he say . . . as long as he looks to white folks for approval . . . then he ain't never gonna find out who he is and what he's about" (*Ma Rainey*, 1.29). In *Seven Guitars*, the representative of black militancy is Hedley, and it is he who kills the misguided bluesman, Floyd. Thus the tragic action is inverted. In Black Revolutionary plays of the 1960s such as *Slave Ship* by Amiri Baraka, the black revolutionary masses sacrificed the accommodationist Uncle Tom as a traitor to the cause. One could argue that similarly, Hedley sacrifices Floyd, who has failed to realize the message, power, and potency in his blues music. Yet Floyd is not simply a Judas. He is a blues musician with the potential for resistance. His loss, then, is a loss for the African American community and the liberatory project as whole.

In the final scene that serves as a coda to the play, Canewell, Floyd's friend and fellow musician as well as a rival suitor to Floyd's girlfriend, Vera, assumes Floyd's role and teases Hedley about the correct reading of the Buddy Bolden lyric. Again this is a repetition with revision. The implication is not only that Canewell has taken Floyd's place, but that he and Hedley share hidden knowledge, for Canewell now knows Hedley's role in the murder. Canewell asks, "What did he [Bolden] give you?" Hedley responds, "He give me this," and the crumpled money drops from his hands. The play ends with Hedley singing, "I thought I heard Buddy Bolden say . . ." (*Seven Guitars*, 2.9.107). The presence of the money serves as an ironic and cruel reminder of the power of capitalism and its futile energy. The endings of *Ma Rainey* and *Seven Guitars* are complex and confounding blues moments. Present in each of these final scenes is the ironic anguish of the blues wail.

Salvation through Song

Just as Wilson reveals the tragic implications of the failure to recognize the power of the blues, he also demonstrates the possibilities of redemption and salvation that are made possible through the active expression of one's blues voice. At the end of *Fences*, Cory Maxson returns home from the Marines on the day of his father Troy's funeral. He announces to his mother, Rose, that he cannot attend the funeral for the father, who threw him out of the house some seven years earlier: "[I] can't drag Papa with me everywhere I go. I've got to say no to him. One time in my life I've got to say no" (*Fences*, 188). Sitting on the steps, he encounters his half-sister Raynell for the first time. Their talk together turns into a moment of song as they share a blues ditty that their father taught them both:

I had a dog his name was Blue
You know Blue was mighty true
You know Blue was a good old dog

Blue treed a possum in a hollow log
You know from that he was a good old dog.
(*Fences*, 190–91)

In singing, they embody a collective memory and the oral transmission of history. The father passed the song, which he learned from his father, down to them. Despite their different mothers, their distance from each other over the years, the song symbolizes their shared legacy. Their separate memories and visions of their recently deceased father come together in this musical communion:

Old blue died and I dug his grave
I dug his grave with a silver spade.
(191)

Thus, within this interlude of song the past makes an indelible impact on the present, as memory and history congeal in this *lieu de mémoire* on the Maxson steps. The song is material, symbolic, and functional, a shared benediction for Troy but also a catalyst for reconsideration, reconciliation, and renewal. After the song is complete, Cory has changed his attitude toward the funeral. He tells Raynell, "You go on in the house and change them shoes like Mama told you so we can go to Papa's funeral" (*Fences*, 191). The song as a performative rite, as a cultural practice, brings past cultural traditions, the rememory of Papa, to bear on new circumstances—Raynell's late entry into the play, Troy's death, and Cory's reticence to attend his father's funeral.

In *King Hedley II*, Wilson uses music as personal memory, theatrical device, and force of history that promotes action and change. After Elmore and Ruby announce their engagement, she asks him to dance out in the backyard, and he refuses. Fresh from his refusal, she turns to her son, King, and begins to dance with him and to teach him how to waltz. They dance to imaginary music. (Relying on theatrical convention, George Gershwin's song "My Little Girl" played in the theater's speaker system for the Seattle production; Wilson's stage directions read, "The music plays softly in her head" [*King Hedley II*, 2.4.87].) The embodiment of the dance, the rememory of the music in her head, causes Ruby to think back: " 'The Mattie Dee Waltz.' That was the prettiest song. I never will forget that" (2.4.87). The song not only summons memory, but its singing as a ritualized cultural practice regenerates her will to survive, to persevere, and even to overcome. The Mattie Dee Waltz in jazz history was associated with Mary Lou Williams, a resident of Wilson's Pittsburgh who composed a "Waltz Boogie" in 1946. Williams was an important swing pianist, a prominent figure in New York bop of the 1940s and 1950s and was once regarded as the only significant female musician in jazz. Her achievement as a woman underscores Ruby's own defiance of her objectification in the male-dominated music industry. Through this invocation of the Mattie Dee Waltz, Wilson conflates the real and the figurative, memory and history.

For Elmore, the song and dance have a quite different effect. Seeing King, the son of his murdered rival Leroy, dance with Ruby conjures old jealousies. When Ruby boasts, "Leroy Slater taught me how to waltz. We used to waltz all over the country . . . me and Leroy used to waltz all over the country," Elmore barks, "Leroy was trying to play a riff on my tune. He didn't know I wrote the motherfucker!" (*King Hedley II*, 2.4.88–89). While dancing, King, the son, looks too much like Leroy, the father, for Elmore. The dance and invisible music cause Elmore to think back and then to reveal to the others the story of how he came to kill Leroy—a jazz aria he spews with rage, passionate self-interest, denial, and only tinges of regret. Ruby retorts, "I couldn't look at Elmore after I found out what he had done. Even though I loved him, it was a longtime before I could look at him. . . . Leroy Slater. A good man. I never will forget him" (2.4.96). Her unwillingness to release the memory of Leroy further enrages Elmore and causes him to unleash a guarded history that both devastates and initiates memory. At the end of his confession of murder, Elmore tells King that Leroy was his real father, destroying the illusion that his mother had maintained all his thirty-five years of life. This information brings new uncertainty to King, who believed his father was his namesake, the wild West Indian King Hedley. Elmore, like Hickey in O'Neill's *Iceman Cometh*, destroys the "life lies" that allow life, changing forever the world of King and Ruby. He stops the music.

At the end of the play, after Ruby has mistakenly shot and killed King in a vain attempt to protect him from Elmore's raised gun, she sings,

Red sails in the sunset
Way out on the sea

Oh carry my loved one
Bring him home safely to me.
(*King Hedley II*, 2.5.102)

Earlier in the play she sang this same **refrain**, recalling the happy days
of her career as a nightclub songstress. She remembers that this was
King's favorite song as a child—the "lullaby" she used to sing him to
sleep. Now she sings as if the power of the melody in memory can erase
the action that has just passed. The song as intervention functions when
words could only prove insufficient. She sings to numb the pain, to bear
the unimaginable horror of these events. Her refuge in song recalls
another moment in Wilson's chronicle when after Levee divulges his
harrowing memory of his mother's gang rape and father's murder, Slow
Drag, the bass player, sings a refrain from a blues song:

If I had my way
If I had my way
If I had my way
I would tear this old building down.
(*Ma Rainey*, 1.58)

Here the blues is again an index of the limitation of words. The brief
refrain articulates Levee's frustration and impotence in the face of his
mother's abuse, feelings shared by Slow Drag and other black men
caught within a situation in which they cannot physically respond; in
which they could not exercise enough capital to overpower the forces
against them. Song must suffice. Similarly, the words of Ruby's song—
"Oh carry my loved one to me. Bring him home safely to me"—emphasize a desire to reproduce what she can no longer affect: the reunion
with her son, his safekeeping. The song must again suffice. Present is a
blues moment of grief that "speaks the unspeakable."

Ruby's mourning song is another reflection of the multidirectionality
and multiple purposes of music within the Wilson cycle. At the same
time, this musical moment demonstrates the dynamic relationship
between music and time: Ruby's blues, Cory and Raynell's rendition of
"Old Dog Blue," Hedley's jamming on his one string, the men's rousing
version of "Ol' Berta" in *Piano Lesson* all operate in their own temporality, all amplified in the performative now. Wilson exploits the "magical"[44] possibilities of music to negotiate relationships of power, to tran-

scend and illuminate the meanings of the present, to impact, as well as to establish, community. Music as heightened and often ritualized cultural practice contains the potentiality for regeneration, for reaffirmation, and for, as Kimberly Benston notes, "reconsideration of narrative cause and consequence."[45] The music is at once historical and history in the making, inciting movement, action, and change. Because music is so integral to Wilson's articulation of an African American cosmology, the subject of music will return in the chapters to come. Music channels black rage and energy; it even transforms the very "madness" that has been a critical dynamic of race in America and is the central focus of the next chapter.

Chapter 2
Fools and Babes

A whole people of neurotics, struggling to keep from being sane. And the only thing that would cure the neurosis would be your murder. Simple as that. . . . Crazy niggers turning their backs on sanity. When all it needs is that simple act. Murder. Just Murder!

—*Dutchman*, LeRoi Jones

My first association with the August Wilson cycle came in the spring of 1989, when I was cast in the Studio Theater's production of *Ma Rainey's Black Bottom* in Washington, D.C. Because this was the second professional production of the play, August Wilson came in from Minneapolis to see it. It was a hit that ran for over twelve weeks, well into the swelteringly hot and humid D.C. summer. I played Ma's stuttering nephew Sylvester. Sylvester's and my shining moment occurs well into the second act, when after unsuccessfully stuttering through two previous attempts to record the intro to the title song, "Ma Rainey's Black Bottom," with Ma's coaxing he steps trembling up to the mike and produces a stammer-free rendition. "Alright boys, you done seen the rest . . . now, I'm gonna show you the best. Ma Rainey's gonna show you her black bottom" (*Ma Rainey*, 2.69–70). After performances, older black women would amble up to me and say "Son, let me hear ya' talk!" And I would explain that I really did not, in fact, have a speech problem.

Sylvester marks Wilson's first venture into a genus of character that becomes a repeated trope in his dramaturgy—one that he develops through Gabriel in *Fences*, Hambone in *Two Trains Running*, Hedley in *Seven Guitars*, and Stool Pigeon in *King Hedley II*. Paradoxically, in

Wilson's works it is the characters who appear mentally or physically impaired, besieged by madness, unable to grasp the reality of the world around them, who represent a connection to a powerful, transgressive spirituality, to a lost African consciousness and to a legacy of black social activism. With Sylvester this sense of both mental handicap and spiritual consciousness is nascent. Nonetheless, his act of delivering the song intro without stuttering is a moment of personal and collective transcendence that benefits the gathered community. As such, it serves as precursor to the redemptive acts and transgressive rituals performed by other figures in Wilson's subsequent dramas. In addition, as evidenced by Ma Rainey's gestures of accommodation and support toward Sylvester in the text (and even the comments of the older black women that hovered around me after performances), Sylvester's difference and deficiency does not isolate him from the community. Rather, others, women in particular, act to incorporate and nurture this difference as Wilson's mad figures operate in ways that reconnect their particular African American collective spiritually and psychologically to its history, to the African in African American experiences. Madness enables these characters both figuratively and literally to transfigure discord into harmony and to agitate for communal and cultural change.

Sylvester is the youngest character in *Ma Rainey* and thus perhaps also representative of the other part of the adage—"God looks out for fools and babes"—that inspires this chapter's title. The phrase implies that the innocence and irrationality of both fools and babes necessitates God's protection. Wilson's madmen, his "fools," however, are not so much looked out for as placed in a special relationship with God. They embody a godliness. "Babes," or children, become an increasingly significant element of Wilson's dramaturgy post-*Ma Rainey*; for Wilson children are a fertile soil in which the lessons of history can be planted. They model behaviors learned even as they act on their innocence. Questions of family, legacy and heritage, progress and development play out with these children, who affirm through their very existence the presence of the past. In Wilson's dramaturgy, these children and madmen may appear marginal figures, but repeatedly the marginal refigures the center. His fools and babes bring particular insights into the meanings of each work and the social and psychological need of African Americans to go backward in order to move forward.

"Irvin, I done told you . . . the boy's gonna do the part." Ma Rainey's Black Bottom, *Studio Theatre, 1986, with Harry A. Winter (Irvin), Caron Tate (Dussie Mae), Alfredine P. Brown (Ma Rainey), Nap Turner (Slow Drag), Harry Justin Elam, Jr. (Sylvester), Joseph Pinckney (Toledo), Bill Harris (Cutler), and Valdred Doug Brown (Levee). (Photograph by Joan Marcus.)*

Racial Madness

I begin by examining the relationship between the particular psychoses of Gabriel, Hambone, Hedley, and Stool Pigeon and concepts of racial madness in modern African American literature, criticism, and philosophy. Such an analysis will help to situate the meanings of these madmen within Wilson's overall project of African recuperation and African American regeneration. By racial madness, I refer to a trope that became operative in clinical practice, literary creation, and cultural theory in the modern period as artists, critics, and practitioners identified social and cultural roots for black psychological impairment. While I will ground racial madness within a particularly American context, I want to point out that Frantz Fanon, the Martinican psychiatrist-philosopher—whose seminal works of the 1950s and 1960s became manifestos for black revolutionary change in the 1960s and 1970s and re-emerged at the forefront of postcolonial studies in the 1990s—in his theory as well as his practice believed that the madness, the mental disorder and the melancholia of the colonial subject, was a direct product of the social and political circumstances of colonialism. As Francois Verges argues, Fanon's "psychology was a sociology of mental disorder" that linked the symptoms of madness to the cause of freedom.[1] Similarly, within modern America, racial madness has been inextricably connected to the abuses of racism and oppression as well as to the struggle for black liberation. My point here is not to pathologize blackness. Rather, by foregrounding this concept of racial madness, I want to recognize the relationship of, and work between, the clinical, the literary, and the philosophical, between the literal and figurative symptoms and significance of this dis-ease, always conscious of the cultural and the social orientation of this condition. Racial madness was and is not simply a mental condition, not simply a social one, but one that demands nevertheless a healing. Because of the complexities of the condition, this healing necessarily must conjoin the social and psychological and even the spiritual, and this I believe is where Wilson's madmen enter and what they attempt to accomplish.

In his seminal work *The Souls of Black Folk* (1903), W. E. B. Du Bois writes famously about the social and psychological predicament of American blackness. Writing at the same time as Sigmund Freud, Du Bois argues that the struggle to be both African and American requires negotiating a duality that can be debilitating.

> The Negro is a sort of seventh son, born with a veil, and gifted with second-sight in this American world—a world which yields him no true self-consciousness, but only lets him see himself through the revelation of the other world. It is a peculiar sensation, this double-consciousness, this sense of always looking at one's self through the eyes of others, of measuring one's soul by the tape of a world that looks on in amused contempt and pity. One ever feels this twoness—an American, a Negro; two souls, two thoughts, two unreconciled strivings; two warring ideals in one dark body, whose dogged strength alone keeps it from being torn asunder.[2]

Du Bois suggests that this double consciousness provides African Americans with a special and unique perspective on the American world, a "second-sight." Hortense Spillers posits that "Du Bois was trying to discover—indeed, to posit—an *ontological* meaning in the dilemma of blackness, working out its human vocation in the midst of overwhelming social and political power. It was not enough to be seen; one was called upon to decide what it meant."[3] For Spillers double consciousness requires a self-reflexivity on the part of black subjects as they consider who they are and how they are perceived within white America. The quandary of being at once both inside and outside American society can cause social and psychological tensions for black subjects. African Americans must constantly navigate their "twoness," "two thoughts, two unreconciled strivings; two warring ideals in one dark body," and this can prove maddening. Thus, double consciousness is a form of racial madness that defines and delimits African American subjectivity and directly impacts on modern African American cultural production. Sandra Richards argues that, through his twentieth-century dramatic cycle, August Wilson intends to "help African Americans more fully embrace the African side of their double consciousness."[4] Accordingly, Wilson's accentuation of the African could be construed as a response to the dichotomy, to the madness of double consciousness. And yet, I would argue, Wilson's madmen with their irreducible peculiarities, their particular neuroses that defy norms, suggest that resolution to the antimony of racial madness may not be simply a matter of emphasizing one side of double consciousness over the other. Rather, in and through their madness, Wilson reveals the complex interplay between the psychological scars of internalized oppression and the external damage due to racism that demand comprehensive strategies of healing.

Post–Du Bois, the questions of how to confront as well as how to define racial madness have continued to play out in political and cultural arenas. By 1948, the date in which Wilson sets *Seven Guitars*, ideas of racial madness and possible sociological and psychological treatments for it had become intricately intertwined with the so-called Negro Problem in America. While white supremacists believed that black inferiority made black people inherently insane, more leftist-minded racial critics, both white and black, argued that the conditions of oppression, racism, and restrictive prejudicial practices impressed on blacks a particular type of cultural neurosis. In her article "The Lunatic's Fancy and the Work of Art," Shelly Eversley notes that in April 1946, when the Lafargue Psychiatric Clinic opened in Harlem as the first clinic of its kind to offer treatment to indigent, mostly black clientele, it "rejected abstract notions of psychoanalytic neurosis to address what became understood as social and artificially induced crises."[5] Thus, through its clinical practice the Lafargue linked the psychological and the social and identified racism as both a social and psychological ill. Eversley points out that African American writers Ralph Ellison and Richard Wright were active supporters of the Lafargue Clinic. For Wright and Ellison, "schizophrenia," Eversley argues, becomes a metaphor that, not unlike Du Boisian double consciousness, "illustrates . . . what it means to live as contradiction, as both Negro and American."[6] Wright's black subject, Paul Gilroy observes, "is internally divided by cultural affiliation, citizenship, and the demands of national and racial identity."[7] In a powerful and harrowing moment of Ellison's classic *Invisible Man* (1952), the madness of the social environment leads Brother Tod Clifton to sell Sambo dolls on the corner. Social conditions of African American life place Clifton and the group of young Negroes on the subway train, observed by the Invisible Man, outside of history. "For they were men, outside of historical time. . . . They were outside the groove of history."[8] Plunged outside of history, recognizing the madness of his existence, Brother Clifton dies in disillusionment, while the Invisible Man comes to appreciate an alternative view to his earlier pseudo-Marxian perspective on historical progress.[9] Ellison's representation in *Invisible Man,* as well as that of Wright or Du Bois, is not that the race itself is insane, but that the conditions of modern African American life, the racism, alienation, and discrimination that black people face, induce a racial neurosis. Their argument is not one framed in Freudian psychoanalysis or one that fits neatly into white racist notions of black deviance but rather a social psychoanalytic approach professing that change within the social environment can affect the black psyche.

In a later, more radical reading of racial madness, LeRoi Jones's foundational text in modern black drama, *Dutchman* (1964), identifies a racial insanity fueled by years of racism and oppression to which the only solution is violent social change. The middle-class black protagonist Clay attempts to divorce himself from the madness of race in his final apocalyptic speech to his white nemesis-seductress Lula: "My people's madness, who needs it?"[10] Still, despite his own desire to disassociate himself from the black majority, Clay understands that this collective psychosis can only be exorcised through incendiary action, the massacre of whites.

> A whole people of neurotics, struggling to keep from being sane. And the only thing that would cure the neurosis would be your murder. Simple as that. . . . Crazy niggers turning their backs on sanity. When all it needs is that simple act. Murder. Just Murder![11]

Clay argues that madness is the relative state of modern black existence, but he rejects the more integrative social solutions, declaring that only murderous action will bring sanity.

If we take as background these modernist perspectives on racial madness, what happens when Wilson multiplies this madness through the creation of mentally impaired figures such as Gabe, Hambone, Hedley, and Stool Pigeon? Are they doubly mad or products of an even more fragmented consciousness? Does their madness within madness make them sane? My sense is that their particular madness places them in spaces removed from the normal trajectories of black difference and yet ones that enable their individual predicaments to reflect back on the black whole, to double double-consciousness in order to heal, to challenge, to renegotiate the collective black neurosis. Existing on the margins, outside behavioral norms and on the periphery of their play's central conflicts, fiercely particularized, idiosyncratic, and iconoclastic, they exemplify a subjectivity and interiority run amok. Wilson endows his more contemporary reading of racial madness with an awareness of history; most significantly, he perceives a potential for a cure by embracing the madness of black life in ways that prove regenerative.

Wilson's Madmen: Taking Madness Seriously

As a consequence of their particular "madness," Wilson's madmen evoke another sort of doubling: they are both culturally organizing and culturally organized. I classify their actions as *culturally organized* because they reflect specific cultural belief systems and practices. The ways in which they act and are acted upon visually codify Wilson's preeminent cultural project: the revelation of the African presence in contemporary African American identities. At once "outside of history," like Ellison's young Negroes on the train, they convey the significance of history and reinforce the impact of the past upon the present. I term these figures *culturally organizing* for their ability to explode and interrogate the meanings of madness. Their idiosyncratic presence and special spiritual powers within the structure of seemingly realistic plays expand traditional cultural limitations of the form and critique definitions of normalcy. Through his madmen, Wilson establishes a bridge between past and present, a way of connection to tradition even in the face of progress.

With each of these figures, madness largely results from symbolic confrontations with white power structures. These encounters cause ruptures and schisms for the characters that parallel primal scenes of loss, rupture, and schism within the experiences of Africans in America. As such, they become representations of collective African American social memories. Gabriel Maxson is a mentally disabled World War II veteran and brother of the central figure, Troy Maxson, in *Fences*. During the war, Gabriel was wounded and a metal plate was placed in his head. Following his impairment, the Army furnished him with some cash as compensation, but then left him on his own. Troy explains, "Man go over there and fight the war . . . messing around with them Japs, get half his head blown off . . . and they give him a lousy three thousand dollars. And I had to swoop down on that" (1.2.128). Gabe's fate reflects on the legacy of all the black servicemen who fought in World War II in the idealistic belief that they were keeping America safe for democracy, only to come home after the war to increased discrimination and second-class citizenship. Like these men, Gabe is alienated from his social environment. Paradoxically, Gabe's mental condition posits him in a space of alternative consciousness where he has a special spiritual mission to fulfill. He is beyond the threat of earthly events. Now, he fiercely believes he is the archangel Gabriel and chases hellhounds. Gabe claims, "I done died and went to heaven" (1.2.126). Significantly, the money the government provided Gabe after his war injury becomes the financing for Troy's home. "That's the only way I got a roof over my head . . . cause of that metal plate. . . . If my brother didn't have that metal plate in his head . . . I wouldn't have a pot to piss in or a window to throw it out of" (1.2.128). Thus Gabe's disability is materially connected to the well-being of his family.

Cheated out of his just compensation, a ham,[12] for painting the white butcher Lutz's fence, the character Hambone's mental condition in *Two Trains Running* has deteriorated so far that he only repeats variations of the phrase, "I want my ham." Nine and one-half years before the start of the play, Lutz hired Hambone to paint his fence. According to Memphis, the proprietor of the restaurant that is the site of play's action, "Lutz told him if he painted his fence he'd give him a chicken. Told him if he do a good job he'd give him a ham. He think he did a good job and Lutz didn't. That's where he went wrong—letting Lutz decide what to pay him for his work" (1.1.23). Memphis points to the fault in black capitalist strategies that depend upon a system of white hegemony to assess their worth. Inevitably, such dependencies result in exploitation. Hambone's peculiar, particularized plight parallels African Americans' unrequited demands for reparations for the wrongs of slavery. His unfulfilled expectations reflect on the historically promised, but never received, forty acres and a mule. Obsessed and possessed by his mistreatment, Hambone stands every day at the site of his indignity and demands from Lutz his just recompense: "I want my ham!"

While such obsessive behavior seems "mad," Wilson suggests that it implies a different level of consciousness, an unparalleled measure of commitment and a focused "sanity." Holloway, the wizened older regular at the restaurant, explains to Memphis that Hambone "might have more sense than any of us."

> We might take a chicken. Then we gonna go home and cook that chicken. But how it gonna taste? It can't taste good to us. . . . Every time we even look at a chicken we gonna have a bad taste in our mouth. That chicken's gonna call up that taste. It's gonna make you feel ashamed. . . . This fellow here [Hambone] . . . he say he don't want to carry it around with him. . . . That's why I say he might have more sense than me and you. Cause he ain't willing to accept whatever the white man throw at him. It be easier. But he say he don't mind getting out of the bed in the morning to go at what's right.
>
> (*Two Trains Running*, 1.2.30)

Thus, Holloway portrays Hambone's personal obsession as a singular effort against white hegemony and black complacency. The "bad taste in our mouth" brought on by accepting, cooking, and eating the chicken is in fact an internalized form of oppression, a racial neurosis that Hambone fights by returning each day to the originating site of rupture and confronting Lutz. Lost on the other characters until after his death is how Hambone's personal struggle against injustice reflects their own need for persistent, collective, revolutionary action.

In one startling moment of *Seven Guitars*, the wild West Indian Hedley disturbs the complacency of the gathered community onstage as he challenges them to recognize the need for proactive, communal struggle to protect against that time when "God ain't making no more niggers." Disturbed by the aimless chatter of the other characters about the noise caused by the neighborhood rooster, Hedley grabs the rooster from its perch, brings it into the yard, and in front of the others decapitates it. Hedley admonishes them,

> You want or you don't want, it don't matter. God ain't making no more roosters. It is a thing past. Soon you mark my words when God ain't making no more niggers. . . . You hear this rooster you know you alive. You be glad to see the sun cause there come a time sure enough when you see your last day and this rooster you don't hear no more. *(He takes out a knife and cuts the rooster's throat.)* That be for the living. Your black ass be dead like the rooster now. You mark what Hedley say. *(He scatters the blood in a circle.)* This rooster too good live for your black asses.
>
> (1.5.64)

Hedley's action shocks both the spectators onstage in Louise's backyard as well as those out in the theater audience. Having suspended their disbelief, theater audiences must still wonder whether he has killed an actual rooster or how this effect was accomplished, as blood spills from Hedley's knife onto the stage. His scattering of the rooster's blood in a circle functions as a ritual aimed at shaking the gathered community out of its passivity.

Continuously, in *Seven Guitars,* the West Indian Hedley rants and raves about black social action. He rages against the white power structure, but his cries go unheeded by the other characters. Wilson, however, wants the audience to recognize the truth, power, and prophecy in Hedley's words. As a West Indian immigrant, Hedley serves as an embodiment of the black diaspora, a "Black Atlantic" traveler. With Hedley the history and memory of the West Indies as a transport zone for the slave trade, the images of West Indian plantation slavery, the legacy of colonialism and sugar cane economies, the heritage of the native uprisings and Toussaint-L'Ouverture all congeal. These events constitute the site of his rupture, important sources of his madness and rage.

Hedley wants to be a "big man," free to determine his own fate. His name "King" Hedley is significant in this regard. With the name Wilson riffs on both notions of royalty and the madness in Hedley's head. At times people suffering from different forms of psychosis or hospitalized due to schizophrenia or other mental illness imagine themselves to be kings, queens, or figures of royal standing, power, and privilege in order to combat their fragmented sense of self or severely damaged self-image. Hedley suffers from such a psychosis and a troubled sense of self. Yet, most certainly his illness has racial and sociological roots. Hedley reveals that he once killed another black man because, says Hedley, "He would not call me King. He laughed to think a black man could be King. . . . After that I don't tell nobody my name is King" (*Seven Guitars*, 2.1.67). The symbolic implications of naming take on life and death import for Hedley. Similarly, the value of names and naming have been critical to African American identity, as the name for Africans in America has shifted through time from *colored* to *Negro* to *Black* to *Afro-* and *African American,* each one with real meaning and practical significance. Hedley is a black king, a mad king. Implicitly and explicitly, his name suggests incongruity and complexity. It signifies on concepts of sovereignty, royalty, power, and legitimacy. What is in a name and who can be king? Wilson riffs further on these questions and continues the line of "kings" with the title for his play of the 1980s and its central problematic figure, *King Hedley II.*

As noted in the previous chapter, Hedley the First's father named him King after legendary musician King Buddy Bolden, the first man of jazz and the first "King" of New Orleans cornet players. After repeated arrests, detentions, and struggles with mental illness, Bolden was committed to the Insane Asylum at Jackson, Louisiana on June 5, 1907 where he remained until his death twenty-four years later. Bolden was a heavy drinker, and his outbreaks of dementia often followed his abuse of alcohol. The connections among Bolden's music, his race, his lifestyle, and his insanity suggest parallels, or even a continuum, that links him to such tortured black geniuses as Thelonious Monk and Charlie "Bird" Parker. In each of these cases the music, the madness, the self-destructive behavior, the impacts of racism all intertwined. Despite or perhaps as a consequence of their musical virtuosity, the realities of being black and being an artist were overwhelming.

At times, Hedley too finds the pressures and madness of race overwhelming. He refuses at first to be tested for tuberculosis, believing that such doctors and such tests are a plot against the black man. Yet his paranoia and racial conspiracy theories echo with the truth of cases such as the Tuskegee Institute experiment, which in 1932 left black men untreated for syphilis in a U.S. government study on the effects of the disease. Hedley says, "Everybody say Hedley crazy cause he black. Because he know the place of the black man is not at the foot of the white man's boot. Maybe it is not all right in my head sometimes. Because I don't like the world. I don't like what I see from the people" (*Seven Guitars*, 2.1.67). Thus, Hedley implicitly connects his madness to sociological sources. He demonstrates a single-minded determination to restore the black man to his rightful position. This obsession eventually leads him to kill Floyd Barton, the central figure of the play. As Floyd attempts to recover his stolen bounty from its backyard hiding place, Hedley murders him. As previously discussed, in this moment of madness and misplaced rage, Hedley mistakenly believes that Floyd is the legendary musician Buddy Bolden.

The murder of Floyd Barton in *Seven Guitars* has a direct connection to the madness of the character Stool Pigeon in *King Hedley II*, set in 1985. With the latter play Wilson plunges characters and themes from *Seven Guitars* forty years into the future. In the second act of *King Hedley*, Stool Pigeon reveals to the title character that his real name is Canewell, a former friend of Floyd Barton's. At this point, those familiar with the earlier play recall that in the concluding moment of *Seven Guitars*, Hedley shows Canewell a fistful of crumpled bills from Floyd's bounty. This action serves as a confession of the murder by Hedley, the consequences of which the end of the play leaves open: Canewell may or may not keep secret Hedley's role in the murder. The answer remains unknown as the lights go down. *King Hedley II*, however, closes off conjecture. Stool Pigeon explains,

After Floyd was killed Hedley showed me the money. Told me Buddy Bolden gave it to him. That's when I knew. I say, "I got to tell." What else could I do? Ruby called me "Stool Pigeon" and somehow or another it stuck. I'll tell anybody I'm a Truth Sayer.

(2.1.62)

Stool Pigeon's madness results not merely from his act of informing the white authorities of Hedley's crime but from the rupture it causes as he is ostracized from the community and branded "Stool Pigeon."

Internal ruptures are the focus for the fateful vision of the African American community in the 1980s that Wilson presents in *King Hedley II.* Wilson depicts a black wasteland devastated by black-on-black violence and crime. Significantly, Aunt Ester, an absent spiritual force that figures prominently in *Two Trains Running* and that Wilson brings onto the stage in *Gem of the Ocean,* a woman as old as the black presence in America, dies of grief in *King Hedley II.* Her black cat dies as well. The set for the April 2000 production at the Seattle Repertory Theatre imagined an inner city devastated by a holocaust of external neglect and internal disregard. The characters live in the shell of former buildings. The backdrop reveals the crumbling brick and worn-out remains of tenements. The lively backyard of some forty years earlier in *Seven Guitars* is now in a state of fragmented ruin. This "postmodern" apocalyptic set symbolizes the conditions Wilson perceives as endemic in black America during the 1980s, a community destroyed by systematic abandonment, internalized oppression, self-destructive violence, and in need of spiritual and social regeneration. Wilson's 1980s play out as a period of loss and rupture, not just in terms of black lives but of history and collective memory. The lessons of black suffering, terror, and survival have been forgotten and the way into the future blocked as a result.

Stool Pigeon, not unlike his predecessors, Gabriel and Hedley, prophesies a day of judgment in which God will right the wrongs of the earth. Stool Pigeon's faith is a syncretic one. For him God is a "Bad Motherfucker." He repeats this mantra and warns the others of God's ability to bring devastating fires of retribution. Stool Pigeon is also a symbolic repository for lost history. Obsessively he saves newspapers, piling them so high that he can no longer fit into his own house. Mister asks him, "Why you save all them newspapers? What you gonna do with them?" Stool Pigeon replies, "See I know what went on. I ain't saying what goes on . . . what went on. You got to know that. How you gonna get on the other side of the valley if you don't know that?" (*King Hedley II*, 1.2.27). Stool Pigeon suggests that you cannot move into the future without knowing the past. Through his preservation of the newspapers, he holds onto history and protects the knowledge of what went on before.

In a gesture that enrages his neighbor Ruby, but one that subverts existing rules of power and privilege, Stool Pigeon repeatedly removes the covers of trash cans so that the neighborhood dogs can eat from them. Symbolically, this act opens up to those without access the spoils of the garbage cans. Using the metaphor of food, Stool Pigeon's benevolence reveals the hierarchies present in the rules of our social order as he provides the "underdog" with sustenance. Ruby and the others object on more practical and personal grounds: the dogs overturn people's property rights. In the Seattle Repertory Theatre production, director Marion McClinton blocked a continuing territorial war over garbage cans between Ruby and Stool Pigeon. He removed the lids in one scene; she in the next recovered them. The animosity expressed by Ruby toward Stool Pigeon reflects the fragmentation present within Wilson's picture of the black community in the 1980s. It also reveals how the single-minded determination of madness can undermine normative controls.

Wilson uses the obsession of Hambone, his inability to conform to normal expectations of verbal communication in *Two Trains Running* to emphasize the difference between rhetoric and reality, to demonstrate the need for concrete social change. At one point Sterling, the young and rambunctious, recently released ex-con attempts to teach the madman Hambone the adage "Black is beautiful" and then the phrase "United we stand, divided we fall." In each case, after learning and repeating these new phrases, Hambone returns to his signature line: "I want my ham!" One interpretation of Hambone's regression to old ways is that Hambone's fragile psyche cannot take on new information and so he resorts to what he knows and that with which he is comfortable. Yet for Hambone, his stand against the butcher Lutz and his desire for a ham as just compensation represent a real, concrete cause, while the words "Black is beautiful or "United we stand" have no real, active value for him. They remain at the level of rhetoric. This scene, then, comments on the need of African Americans not simply to mouth global strategies of unity and reform but to work specifically and collectively on a local level for change.

Hedley's obsession with black liberation and with being a big man at first seems only rhetoric. His singular focus, like that of Hambone or Gabriel before him, enables him to connect with the suppressed and oppressed African song of freedom in ways "a normal or sane mind" could not. As with Gabriel and Stool Pigeon, Hedley's messianic prophecy and spiritual faith syncretically blends the African and Christian.

> The Bible say it all will come to straighten out in the end. Every abomination shall be brought low. Everything will fall to a new place. When I get my plantation I'm gonna walk around it. I'm going to walk all the way round to see how big it is. I'm gonna be a big man on that day. . . . I tell you this as God is my witness on that great day when all the people are singing as I go by . . . and my plantation is full and ripe . . . and my father is a strong memory . . . on that day . . . the white man not going to tell me what to do no more.
>
> (*Seven Guitars*, 1.3.24)

Ironically, the historic site of black enslavement, the plantation, now becomes the environment for Hedley's mission of black liberation. With Hedley's vision of the plantation, Wilson offers an intertextual linkage to, and revision of, William Faulkner's *Absalom, Absalom!* where the white character Sutpen builds a plantation out of nothing on the backs of "wild Haitian Negroes."[13] But Hedley is not mentally stable, and his plantation dreams appear harmless but unattainable, the wayward musings of a madman.

Through his figuration of Hedley and similar madmen, Wilson ponders the conditions under which we take madness seriously. In the climactic moments of *Seven Guitars*, Hedley, blinded by cheap booze and mistaken assumption, kills Floyd with his machete in a blues moment of tragic, ritualized violence, as Floyd stands before him, resplendent in a white suit, a beacon of light. In this scene, the "drunk" madman Hedley becomes a threat. In inebriation, he exhibits a very serious madness; he takes actions that he would not otherwise undertake and moves madness, beyond thought or rhetoric into concrete deeds. Hedley's deed, his sacrifice of Floyd, must also be read as a repetition and revision of his earlier slaying of the rooster at the end of act 1. Now Hedley kills Floyd, the musician who has betrayed black communality and dis-served the legacy and the power of the blues. Hedley's signifying act functions not only as an admonition to others who would so transgress, but as a corrective for Floyd's sins; a corrective that can only be carried out by the highly charged, emotionally disruptive, and disturbed actions of this madman. Blinded by moonshine, Hedley brings a clarity, a higher vision. Wilson suggests here and elsewhere that madness can slice through the ordinary in life toward an alternative vision of reality, a different sense of blackness. Madness offers not simply an altered consciousness or a freedom to perform in ways normally not permissible, but the clearest articulation of a challenge to be black and whole, a challenge that others in Wilson's cycle are at times not willing to face. Wilson's madmen, through activities that break barriers of normalcy—from Hambone's single-minded mantra to Hedley's drunken act of murder to Stool Pigeon's manic hoarding of the news—call for a radical alteration in systems of power. With their acts of madness comes the possibility of contagion, the potential to infect others who will then act for black liberation and regeneration.

Madness, Death, and Spiritual Healing

Significantly, in *Seven Guitars* lessons learned from madness come with a death, as Wilson draws a connection between madness, death, and dying. In death, Wilson's madmen function as a conduit for healing, providing a benediction for the gathered community. Accordingly, Wilson suffuses the mourning for the death of Hambone at the end of *Two Trains Running* with a call to action and a cacophony of sound. As the other characters listen to Memphis plan for his future, the crash of breaking glass and a whirl of a burglar alarm are heard. Then, the young rebel Sterling enters bleeding but carrying a ham stolen from Lutz's window, a blood sacrifice for Hambone's casket. Rather than asking Lutz for reparation, Sterling claims for Hambone that which was long due. His act and Hambone's death unite the community in cele-bratory revolution. Reminiscent of black revolutionary dramas by Jones and others in the 1960s that concluded by inciting their spectators to participate in communal sounds of revolt, Wilson wants his audiences to leave chanting, "I want my ham!" With his death we also learn that Hambone "had so many scars on his body. . . . All on his back, his chest . . . his legs" (*Two Trains Running*, 2.3.91). Thus, Hambone bears the material legacy of the horrors of slavery. His madness is a modern response to that legacy.

At the conclusion to *Fences*, Gabriel through sound also links the black past to the African American present in a moment of ritual and spiritual possession. Gabriel summons his special faith to open Heaven's gates on the day of his brother Troy's funeral. His actions proclaim a new day for Troy and the Maxson family. Prior to opening Heaven's gates, Wilson writes that Gabriel endures "a trauma that a sane and normal mind would be unable to withstand" (*Fences*, 2.5.192). Thus only his special mental state can "heal" the cultural dis-ease of the Maxson family. Gabe's supposedly limited capacity translates into a strength. When Gabe's horn fails, he dances and sings in what Wilson calls an "atavistic signature and ritual" (*Fences*, 2.5.192). These cultural practices connect Gabe back to his African ancestors and push him forward into a spiritual transcendence that enables him to open the gates of Heaven. Gabe's performance is a symbolic and functional *lieu de mémoire*. His actions (w)right history, as they reinforce the impact of the past on the present and provide a benediction for Troy and the Maxson family.

The concluding moment of *King Hedley II* continues this trope of the redemptive power of madness, as Stool Pigeon in the face of seemingly insurmountable tragedy calls out for God's renewal. "Thy Will! Not man's will! Thy Will! You wrote the Beginning and the End! Bring down the Fire!" (2.5.103). This exhortation follows the violent death of King Hedley II at his own mother's hands, another senseless black death. Yet Ruby's accidental murder of King is also epic and ancient as it recalls and inverts Orestes' matricide in Aeschylus's *Oresteia*. However, no furies seep out to haunt and follow Ruby; no Areopagus acts to resolve the line of killing. Still, there is a cosmic justice present, and Ruby's murder of King does end a pattern of senseless black-on-black violence. The shooting of the son by the mother who brought him into the world stops the violence because unlike murders discussed previously within the play, this one cannot provoke retribution. There can be no subsequent act of revenge. The grief is too deep, too final.

In this bleak scene, a world seemingly devoid of hope, as Ruby collapses on the ground and King's wife Tonya runs screaming into the house, Stool Pigeon performs his ritual. Previously, following the death of Aunt Ester and her black cat, Stool Pigeon had buried the cat in the backyard and enacted rituals over it, repeating and revising blood sacrifices seen throughout the Wilson historical cycle. "All you need now is some blood. Blood is life. You sprinkle some blood on there and if she ain't used up her nine lives Aunt Ester's coming back" (*King Hedley II*, 2.2.69). Significantly, as Wilson's stage directions command, King dies over the grave, and his blood consecrates the ground. Standing over the body of sacrificial King, Stool Pigeon sounds a chant that unites the Christian and African as he extols God to act. "The Conquering Lion of Judea! Our Bright and Morning Star! I want your best! See Him coming! We give you our Glory!" (*King Hedley II*, 2.5.103). Stool Pigeon calls on ancestors as he calls for "The Conquering Lion of Judea," the name by which Hedley refers to himself in *Seven Guitars* and that King repeats in *King Hedley II*. The idea, then, is that Stool Pigeon is calling out a God who looks like him, who understands the history of black struggle and survival and who can and will respond to black needs. As the lights go down to end the play, Wilson's directions indicate that "the sound of a cat's meow is heard." The sound of the cat signals the success of Stool Pigeon's efforts, of King's sacrifice; it trumpets the potential rebirth of Aunt Ester and thus renews hope for the African American future. Stool Pigeon's madness is transformative. God has heard Stool Pigeon's plea, and the past renews the present.

The direction that Stool Pigeon and each of these mad figures takes beckons toward what Paul Gilroy refers to as the revolutionary or eschatological apocalypse or Jubilee.[14] During slavery times, the notion of the Jubilee, a Judgment Day when the terrors of slavery would be overcome, offered slaves hope in something after slavery, an afterlife, salvation. Faith in an eschatological transcendence in the future enabled the slave to survive and struggle in the present. Wilson's madmen and their ritualized actions similarly point to a secular spiritual revelation in which past and present conjoin, directing African Americans to a future of social and cultural change. Within this ritual action, madness is not exorcised, but rather embraced for its potential to effect change and healing. It alters the stakes of realism. The madness must be taken seriously.

Children and Lessons Learned

Because Wilson's work vitally concerns the cultural legacy passed from one generation to another, children have profound value, as they inherit cultural patrimony from their parents and ancestors. On and through his children, Wilson builds strategies of re-membrance that bond immediate members of the plays' families as well as the greater African American community. And yet the representation of children in Wilson is not static; children do not simply reap "the sins of the father," but act on them and even revise them. Thus, "babes" in Wilson's cycle, like his "fools," are symbolically capacious. While Wilson's mad figures operate as culturally organized and cultural organizing agents who endow the present with figurative and literal connections to the past and visions of the future, the children in Wilson's dramas function simultaneously to reveal the past, to shape the present, and also literally to represent the hopes and dreams of the future.

The seven-year-old Raynell, the product of Troy's illicit affair, enters in the final scene of *Fences* and produces powerful reverberations of change; she is the living manifestation of Troy's past infidelities and also the signifier of his eventual redemption. The intrusion of this new character during the play's denouement is a deliberate breach of the accepted conventions of realistic play construction. Wilson uses her appearance to convey the importance of legacy but also the potential for growth and progress. Significantly, Raynell's entrance not only occurs on the day of her father's funeral, but in the year 1965, in the midst of the Civil Rights era, a period of intense struggle and new opportunity for African Americans. Raynell's emergence at this precise moment brings a "ray" of sunshine that hearkens a brighter tomorrow for the Maxson family and for black America. The scene opens with Raynell watching and poking a stick at her recently planted garden, waiting for it to grow. "It don't look like it never gonna grow. Dag!" (*Fences*, 2.5.183). At the time of Troy's funeral, his "ending," she hopes for new beginnings. "You just have to give it a chance. It'll grow," her mother reminds her. Growth happens inexorably; it happens when you are not even looking; it can come up on you suddenly. In fact, Raynell uses her own growth as an excuse not to wear her new shoes to the funeral:

Raynell: Mama, can't I wear these shoes? Them other ones hurt my feet.
Rose: Well, they just gonna have to hurt your feet for a while. You ain't
said they hurt your feet when you went down to the store and got them.
Raynell: They didn't hurt then. My feet done got bigger.

(*Fences*, 2.5.187–88)

Humorously, Raynell notes that growth has its own sense of time. As
demonstrated by this passage, children are elastic, in constant change
and flux.

Earlier in the play, the baby Raynell functions as the catalyst for life-
changing decisions and new self-realizations for Rose. After the death
of Raynell's mother, Alberta, Troy brings the baby home and asks Rose
if she will help him to care for the "innocent" baby. In one of the most
powerful moments of the play, Rose consents to take this child in need
into her home, even as her heart breaks over Troy's betrayal of their
marriage and their intimacy.

Okay, Troy . . . you're right. I'll take care of your baby for you . . . cause
. . . like you say . . . she's innocent . . . and you can't visit the sins of the
father upon the child. A motherless child has got a hard time. From right
now . . . this child got a mother. But you a womanless man.

(*Fences*, 2.3.173)

Through her act of accepting Raynell, Rose asserts agency and redefines
her relationship with Troy. She addresses the need to protect the innocence of the child in order to enable its growth. With children, the passage suggests, there is potential for a different order, and maternal intervention and its particular gender dynamics have the power to interrupt
Troy's hegemony. But while Rose challenges Troy's patriarchal authority, she also evidences traditionalism as she assumes the role of mother.
Earlier in the second act, when Troy confesses his infidelity, Rose
admonishes him by recalling her own childhood: "And you know I ain't
never wanted no half nothing in my family. My whole family is half.
Everybody got different fathers and mothers . . . my two sisters and my
brother. Can't hardly tell who's who" (*Fences*, 2.1.162). Based on her
own experience Rose perceives a need for continuity and coherence in
the family, a need to be black and whole. What is at stake are larger
questions of cultural identity and even the survival of the African American family. While Rose's act is personal, it has an even greater cultural

"I had a dog his name was Blue." Fences, *TheatreWorks, Lucie Stern Theatre,* 2000, *with Cyril Jamal Cooper (Cory) and Rashida "Cocoa" Bryant (Raynell). (Photograph by David Allen for TheatreWorks.)*

significance, as the baby Raynell is a conduit for change but also for reconstituting the family.

While the matrilineal order, Rose's adoption of Raynell, enables growth in *Fences*, Berniece's, the mother's, overprotection in *Piano Lesson* retards the child's, Maretha's, cultural development. Paradoxically, Berniece, like Rose, wants to save her daughter from "the sins of the father." Plagued by her own ghosts, Berniece never tells her daughter about the ghosts that reside within the piano and the history of the markings that adorn it. Yet when Boy Willie discovers Maretha's ignorance, he scolds his sister for not revealing the history of the piano to her daughter:

> You ain't even told her [Maretha] bout that piano. Like that's something to be ashamed of. Like she supposed to go off and hide somewhere about that piano. You ought to mark down on the calendar the day that Papa Boy Charles brought that piano into the house. You ought to mark that day down and draw a circle around it . . . and every year when it come up throw a party. Have a celebration. If you did that she wouldn't have no problem in life. She could walk around here with her head held high.
>
> (*Piano Lesson*, 2.4.90–91)

The significance that Boy Willie ascribes to the piano's history is analogous to the position of prominence that Wilson believes slavery must achieve in African American cultural life. Wilson laments that instead of black Americans celebrating the slave legacy, for black Americans it is too often a site of shame: "the fact of slavery is something that blacks do not teach their kids—they do not tell their kids that at one time we were slaves. That is the most crucial and central thing to our presence here in America. It's nothing to be ashamed of. Why is it, after spending hundreds of years in bondage, that blacks in America do not once a year get together and celebrate the Emancipation and remind ourselves of our history?"[15] In *Piano Lesson,* the carved piano is inscribed history, and when Boy Willie earlier reveals to Maretha the family's struggle to obtain it, he not only passes on the family's legacy, he affirms the collective need to know the history of slavery and all its pain. Later, as Boy Willie prepares to return to his southern home, he warns his sister, "If you and Maretha don't keep playing that piano . . . ain't no telling . . . me and Sutter both liable to be back" (2.5.108). As Boy Willie implies, cultural preservation necessitates a vigilance and consistency in order to prevent usurpation by white specters such as Sutter—the former owner of the piano whose ghost returns in an attempt to reclaim it. Boy Willie also suggests that cultural transmission involves embodied practice, Maretha's actual playing on the piano. Her playing constitutes what Joni L. Jones calls "bodily knowing"; through her actual performative practice, "physical elements of culture" are inculcated.[16] It is Maretha's playing the piano that will maintain the linkages to the past on into the time to come.

While Maretha's embodied performance becomes a marker of cultural identity and collective memory, I think it is important to remember Bert O. States's well-known remarks on the phenomenology of the child in performance: "Who has ever seen a child on stage without thinking, 'How well he acts for a child!' . . . The point is not so much that they are children but that they are conspicuously *not* identical with their characters. As a consequence the medium becomes the message. The form winks at the content."[17] In other words, the presence of children on stage is always metatheatrical, as the audience is continuously aware of the child actor playing Maretha or playing Raynell as well as the character. Wilson's *Joe Turner* in its construction of Herald Loomis's eleven-year-old daughter, Zonia, and Reuben, the boy who lives next door to Seth's boardinghouse, accents this relationship between the child and the role, contracting and at times extending the gap between. Zonia's and Reuben's scenes take place in a liminal playing area that is theirs alone, in the backyard that separates Seth's boardinghouse from the property of Reuben's grandfather. This "betwixt and between" environment mirrors the liminality of the "blues matrix" boardinghouse. Significantly, Reuben appears only to Zonia—no one else in the play sees him—affirming his metatheatrical status[18] and further insuring that these children exist in a space that is at once outside and inside the world of the play and within and without the world of the adults. Reuben and Zonia, two children on the verge of young adulthood, play at being grown, at dating, at having an understanding beyond their years of the cycle of life. Similarly, the child actors in the roles, by the very nature of their performing in an "adult production," need to take on a maturity, focus, and discipline beyond their years; they play at being grown up, while playing children who play at being grown up. Zonia and Reuben must share a first kiss that, as Wilson writes it, is a rather nervous but exciting moment of experimentation for both of them. It is equally a fraught moment for the actual child actors, who generally are also at the age where boys and girls keep their distance, even as their interest has been roused, and so the audience observes the actors' own trepidation over this moment, which adds to its poignancy.

Paul Carter Harrison notes that Reuben and Zonia act as a chorus underlining the play's messages about growth and progress, comings and goings.[19] Early on, as Reuben watches from a hiding place, Loomis eyes his daughter with concern about her impending development into young womanhood. "You growing too fast. Your bones getting bigger every-day. I don't want you getting grown on me. Don't you get grown on me too soon. We gonna find your mamma" (*Joe Turner,* 1.1.230). Loomis worries about his ability to continue to care for Zonia—they share one room at Seth's. Later, Loomis's anxiety over her new growth is part of his rationale for returning Zonia to her previously missing mother, Martha, to chart a new course for her progress. "Whatever I know I tried to teach her. Now she need to learn from her mother whatever you got to teach her. That way she won't be no one-side person" (*Joe Turner,* 2.5.286). Herald wants her to be black and whole, to gain from her mother a roundedness. But Zonia, afraid of the change that will come with this separation from all she has known, cries out desperately, if it is her growth that troubles her father, she will not grow. "I won't get no bigger! My bones won't get no bigger! They won't! I promise! Take me with you till we keep searching and never finding" (*Joe Turner,* 2.5.286). In this moment, rather than desiring to be an adult, the prepubescent Zonia reverts to being the child, and the audience feels her despondency at the impending disunion from her father. Her words contain both futility and irony. In the world of the play that is constructed on and constricted by the lines of the text, the beginnings and endings that Wilson has drawn, Zonia will not grow. She is eternally prepubescent; for the child actor the future is less certain. In addition, Zonia's desire to keep "searching but never finding"—a reference to a continued state of liminality—stands opposed, not only to Loomis's fervent and currently realized drive to find his wife and a starting place, but also to Wilson's overall project to situate African Americans in time and space by connecting past, present, and future. Zonia wants to stop time or at least to reorder it, and Wilson, too, wants to move our understanding of time beyond linearity toward a more cyclical concept in which the past, present, and future coexist. Here, then, in this moment, in the performative now of the theater, in the parting of father and daughter and the reunion with wife and mother, time comes full circle but does not repeat, and thus growth, continuity, progress all are refigured.

Wilson's children learn about the inexorability of change as well as the presence of the past. Faced with the uncertainty of life after the death of his equally young friend, Eugene (Eugene was the name of a childhood friend of painter Romare Bearden, whose painting *Mill hand's Lunch Bucket* inspired Wilson's *Joe Turner*), Reuben has ignored Eugene's dying request to release his pet pigeons and instead keeps them as a memorial.[20] As a consequence, a ghost from the past returns. Much as in *Piano Lesson,* spirits resurface when promises, legacies, inheritances are not properly venerated. Miss Mabel,[21] Seth's deceased mother, comes from the dead as an intermediary for Eugene and beats Reuben in retribution. "She says, 'Didn't you promise Eugene something?' Then she hit me with her cane. She say, 'Let them pigeons go.' Then she hit me again. That's what made them marks" (*Joe Turner,* 2.4.276). Here in the stories and remembrances of Reuben, as in the incantations and belief systems of Wilson's madmen, the ancestors have a tangible presence. It is through the innocence and marginality of these figures that Wilson challenges understandings of the real. Reuben is literally marked by history, and this brings him a form of "bodily knowing." Only by letting go of the past can Reuben gain control of the present and move into the future. Zonia later explains to Reuben in their last scene together that her present must involve movement. "He [Herald Loomis] say we got to leave on Saturday" (*Joe Turner,* 2.4.278). In contrast to her later desire to continue her nomadism, she now expresses regret that they are always moving on while getting nowhere. Neither the significance nor the senselessness of this activity is lost on her. Reuben's words in response give her a starting place and a hope for the future. He kisses her a second time and then leaves her with the promise, "When I get grown, I come looking for you" (*Joe Turner,* 2.4.280). Wilson employs black grammatical vernacular and puts Reuben's words in the present rather than the future tense—"I *come* looking for you" rather than "I *will come* looking for you"—semantically making the future present. In its simplicity, Reuben's oath reaffirms the value of their time spent together as well as the significance of progress: "When I get grown," he says. What he offers is a circular progression, a repetition and revision of endings and beginnings that is at the heart of this play and of Wilson's (w)righting of history.

The Sacrificial King

I want to close by turning to the man-child title character of *King Hedley II*, King, whose journey catalyzes the issues of innocence and development, madness and legacy examined in this chapter. Through King, Wilson reveals what happens to dreams deferred, to hopes unfulfilled, to the power of the past unrealized in the present. Tragically, King Hedley II is a toxic combination of heredity and environment; the sins of the father are, in fact, visited upon this son. His mother, Ruby, has named him after King Hedley, the man she slept with when young and pregnant by another man. King, the son, naively believes Hedley to be his real father, as Ruby has not told him differently. Consequently, the son lives in what he perceives to be his father's footsteps. He carries along with him his "father's" anger with the plight of African Americans and his militant distrust of white people. At the end of the first act, King rails against the devaluation of black worth in America: "It was all right when they ain't had to pay you. They had plenty of work for you back then. Now that they got to pay you there ain't no work for you. I used to be worth twelve hundred dollars during slavery. Now I'm worth $3.35 an hour. I'm going backwards. Everybody else moving forward" (*King Hedley II*, 1.3.55). King's frustration with the system leads him to rebel. However, he rebels through criminal activity, not through constructive efforts at social change. He does not know how to channel his rage into effective action. While he possesses the same insurgent spirit that consumed Hedley in *Seven Guitars,* he is also a product of an urban environment that has thwarted his potential and stunted his revolutionary growth. "King" the title character is placed in a world that is decidedly unkingly. Wilson creates an ironic portrait of royalty and a kingdom steeped in the depressed circumstances of the 1980s urban milieu, where black poverty, despair, and cultural devastation are the norm. Sadly, King represents a generation of black children unable to thrive in their kingdoms in the self-destructive 1980s.

Wilson connects King, the man-child, to images of children and tropes of inheritance found in his other plays to underscore this message of generations lost. Like Raynell in *Fences,* King has a garden that he worries over. At the beginning of *King Hedley II,* he plants seeds and constructs a flower garden for his wife Tonya in the infertile soil of his backyard. While Rose teaches Raynell patience and encourages her dream of future blossoms, King's mother, Ruby—a mother he disowns—warns him that flowers will never grow there, "You need some good dirt. Them seeds ain't gonna grow in that dirt" (1.1.4). Tellingly, this repetition and revision of mother and child expresses the decidedly different socioeconomic circumstances—from the turbulent possibilities of social change in the 1960s to nihilistic cynicism of the 1980s—the ground now has "too many rocks" to enable black growth. Yet and still, King persists because, as he explains to his mother, "This the only dirt I got. This is me right here" (1.1.4). King identifies with this dirt and recognizes how its ability to foster life symbolizes his own ability to prosper despite the constraints and limitations of his surroundings. We never see the fruit of Raynell's garden or whether it, in fact, grows. In *King Hedley,* on the other hand, King's garden actually sprouts through the hard earth at the end of the first act. Clearly such a special effect causes considerable mental strain and artistic anguish for the designers and technical directors that mount this play. Still, the image of buds miraculously blooming in the hard, rocky dirt reaffirms that even in this barren environment, hope is possible.

When Elmore, Ruby's former boyfriend and the man who murdered King's real father over forty years before the action of the play, accidentally steps on King's garden, it emphasizes that these small buds have little protection against powerful outside forces that crush them. King explodes. Reminiscent of Levee's enraged, violent reaction to Toledo's stepping on his shoe in *Ma Rainey's Black Bottom,* or Herald Loomis's crazed outburst in response to the Juba dance and religious ceremony that ends the first act of *Joe Turner,* King erupts in his own moment of madness. Like these other men, King overreacts due to his own internalized demons. King believes a part of him has been violated, and that he must fight back:

What you doing! You stepping on my seeds! Everybody always stepping on me! *(He grabs up a handful of dirt.)* Look! Look! There! It was coming up! That's mine! I planted that there! Everybody talking about it wouldn't grow. Talking about get some good dirt. Look there! This is good dirt! It was growing and you stepped on it! Look at that dirt! *(King*

"This the only dirt I got." King Hedley II, *Seattle Repertory Theatre, 2000, with Marlene Warfield (Ruby) and Tony Todd (King Hedley). (Photograph by Chris Bennion.)*

drops to his knees. He grabs the dirt with both hands and tries to cover himself with it.) This is good dirt! My dirt! Look at it! This is good dirt! . . . *(He buries his face into the dirt, pushing it into the ground as though trying to replant himself.)*[22]

Unlike the other *King Hedley II* passages, which come from the published version, the stage directions quoted above come from Wilson's first draft of *King Hedley II* and are particularly telling. In subsequent drafts, King does not cover himself but only tears at the dirt in anger and frustration. The act of covering himself, however, ritualistically and literally connects King to the dirt, "the ground on which he stands." If this urban soil represents the essence of his being, his effort "to replant himself" denotes a desire not simply to return to the earth but to start again, to grow and bloom anew, to recapture the innocence of childhood that has been lost. "Everybody always stepping on me!" he exclaims, reacting as victim divorcing himself of responsibility for his fate. Eventually, King puts up a barbed wire fence around his garden to protect it, an excessive response to be sure, and a powerful symbol of the times, 1980s America, in which fences, gates, and metal detectors sprang up in communities, in homes, even in schools to protect us and our children from each other. As Bono remarks in *Fences*, "Some people build fences to keep people out, others to keep people in" (2.1.157). Ironically, King employs the same material, barbed wire, that has historically been used to confine people of color in prisons and prison camps. Moreover, he does not recognize the ways in which he himself has been internally held in place, mentally imprisoned.

Unlike Maretha, who learns the value of her playing the piano, or Reuben, whose beating leads him to free Eugene's pigeons, King does not move to an embodied practice or bodily knowing. He does not know how to act on his legacy. At one point in *King Hedley II*, Stool Pigeon gives the machete that King Hedley I used to kill Floyd Barton to King Hedley II, the rightful heir, as his inheritance. Just as Boy Willie shares with Maretha the story of the piano in *Piano Lesson*, Stool Pigeon tells King the machete's history. Through presenting the machete to King, Stool Pigeon/Canewell "closes the book" on a cycle of black-on-black senseless violence and the personal trauma of suffering and blame that it causes him. However, for King, the machete provides not closure but a conduit that opens up questions of belonging, heritage, destiny. He tells his friend Mister, "This was my father's machete. Stool Pigeon give it to me. Say this the machete that killed Floyd Barton. This is the machete of the 'Conquering Lion of Judea.' This is mine" (*King Hedley II*, 2.1.63). When Mister asks him, "What you gonna do with it," King can only reply, "I don't know" (2.1.63). The violent history inscripted on the machete places demands on King that he does not yet comprehend. King wants to understand what his birthright is and just how he lives up to his name. Where is his kingdom? Like Shakespeare's Hamlet or Prince Hal, Wilson's King desperately wants to know how, in a world rocked by chaos, can he follow his father's legacy and yet remain true to himself.

King's sense of questioning, his innocence with respect to his "kingly" heritage, is dashed by Elmore, who reveals to him that Hedley is not his real father; rather, Leroy, the man Elmore killed and served jail time for, is King's true father. Through this revelation, Elmore kills King's father a second time. Devastated and further dislocated and alienated by the news, King seeks revenge. With the ground under his feet now shaken by Elmore, he draws a circle in the dirt with his machete. He marks out a territory, a small "kingdom," and invites Elmore to play craps with him within it. This circle becomes a place for ritual enactment of life and death import. As the combatants enter the space, Mister intones from the sideline, "blood for blood King." The madman Stool Pigeon attempts to make King realize the potential madness of his actions and the possibilities that the world outside holds for him. "You got the Key to the Mountain. You can go sit on Top of The World" (*King Hedley II*, 2.4.100). Despite the mixed metaphor of key and mountain, Stool Pigeon's inducements recall King's own personal history as well as the vision that Hedley had of his son, a messiah who would someday have a kingdom and bring change. Without full cognizance of its significance, King repeatedly asks other characters if he has a halo around his head, something he has seen in a dream. Earlier in the play, retrospective dialogue reveals that King as a child mowed the lawn of Aunt Ester, who gave him a golden key chain, the proverbial "Key to the Mountain" to which Stool Pigeon refers. Aunt Ester's gift sanctions the importance of King's destiny as prophesied by Hedley and symbolized by the apparition of the halo. And yet Stool Pigeon's words, much like those of Hedley in *Seven Guitars,* fall on deaf ears. King does not understand how to act on this legacy or how he can claim the "Keys to the Mountain." At first, King threatens Elmore's life within the circle and scares Elmore to death—holding the machete up to his throat—but does not kill him. In a ritualized act of forgiveness, he lets the machete drop. Wilson explains, "His forgiveness of Elmore is the key to the mountain through forgiveness—so it gives birth to a new tradition that's based on forgiveness and reconnecting to that new tradition."[23] Rather than continuing acts of murder that have stretched from Hedley's killing Floyd through Elmore's killing Leroy until this present date, King puts down his weapon. Symbolically, he acts against the past, the sins of the father, rather than accepting them, and he forges a new tradition. Elmore, however, does not see it within this light; rather, King's threat shames and shocks him. It threatens his manhood and grounding much in the way Elmore has removed the ground under King's feet. Elmore strikes back by pulling his gun on King. The end is the most tragically violent moment in a Wilson play to date. In an effort to save her son's life, Ruby accidentally shoots and kills King.

King's death is both an ending and a beginning. He falls on the grave of Aunt Ester's black cat and his blood seeps onto the grave, symbolically blessing the ground, the same rocky soil he claimed for his garden, enabling Aunt Ester to be reborn. King is now literally the chosen one who is sacrificed in order to prepare the way for the regeneration of the greater community, for the good of those who live on. His death is a repetition and revision of the sacrifice of the Christian messiah on the cross, who, according to doctrine, died for the sins of mankind and whose blood is now ritualized as the Communion, blessing those who partake. King, too, dies for our sins, and his death offers new life. As a ritualized act presided over by Stool Pigeon, King's sacrifice serves as a beacon of hope promising a new tomorrow against the bleak background of tragic loss and unfulfilled promise.

Wilson himself functions with a kind of creative madness that renegotiates the meanings of the African American past and the madness of race. His theater calls for a cultural healing of the dis-ease present within social fabric of America. Madmen and children, fools and babes who exist on the margins of society hold a "key to the mountain" through their special access to God. Wilson (w)rights them into moments of centrality in which their actions—Reuben's final promise to Zonia, Gabe's dance of redemption—symbolically comment on and even direct the collective community toward a better future. While Wilson's cycle offers fools and babes who begin from a place of alternative consciousness, it most profoundly reveals men and women dislocated in time who need to reckon with their own personal demons and confront internal scars of oppression so that they can move to a different space of understanding. Their individual struggles to be black and whole have collective impact and meanings.

The next two chapters examine how issues of masculinity and femininity inform this journey toward self-determination. The world Wilson depicts is decidedly male. And yet within his malecentric focus, the communal interactions of men and women are vital to the fruition of Wilson's re-evolutionary project.

Chapter 3
The Woman Question

As Fanon says, "Today I believe in the possibility of love, that is why I endeavour to trace its imperfections, its perversions." Dialogue makes love possible. I want to think critically about intellectual partnership, about the ways black women and men resist by creating a world where we can talk with one another, where we can work together.
—bell hooks, "Feminism as a Persistent Critique of History"

Writing on Frantz Fanon, bell hooks argues that "Radical subjectivity, as Fanon perceives it, is registered in the recognition of that longing to be free. This desire is seen only as present in the hearts of men. Reciprocal recognition, then, is always about men desiring men. It is a love affair between black men and white men."[1] Wilson could be said to place similarly the struggle for freedom most principally in the hearts of his male characters, as the white father remains a constant unmarked presence in his drama. What then of black women? Could we or should we, conjecture that black women in Wilson function solely to disrupt men's homosocial bonding and quest for liberation?

Simply put, women are not the focus of Wilson's project. Wilson has been accused by critics—including me in other publications[2]—of constructing women who, in his male-dominated dramatic vision, not only exist in subordinate positions but also operate solely in reaction to men and are defined and confined by these relationships. Such a position, however, I now maintain is simply too reductive; the woman question in Wilson is much more complicated. Still, this is a critique of which Wilson himself is well aware. In a 1996 interview with Nathan L. Grant, Wilson discusses his ability to create well-rounded representations of women:

It probably has to do with the fact that I'm a man. I do create some black women characters and try to be honest in their creation, but it's hard to put myself in their space. I don't know. . . . It's very hard to do. For instance, Risa in *Two Trains Running*—I felt I was right in having her refuse to be defined by her genitals, and I felt this was a blow for self-definition by having her define herself as other than a body by cutting her legs. But I couldn't go beyond that into making some heavier interior psychology of it. Not that I didn't want to, I guess, but I don't know it.[3]

Wilson's comments are telling on several fronts, not just in his admission of his limitations, but in his desire to represent black women who want to define themselves and realize their own subjectivity. Interrogating the roles of women within Wilson's history project does, in fact, suggest ways in which women must negotiate interlocking systems of racial and gender oppression. I do not mean to imply that Wilson's world is not malecentric or that his works should escape feminist critiques. What I do want to explore is how Wilson's women operate within the constraints of their particular sociohistoric circumstances as well as within the above-mentioned, self-declared constraints of Wilson's craft.

In Wilson's (w)righting, the domestic becomes a site that is both problematic and enabling for female characters. While Jill Dolan has argued that the genre of realism is "a conservative force that reproduces and reinforces dominant culture relationships,"[4] Wilson's dramatic structure with its rituals, musicality, and lyricism defies certain conventions of domestic realism even as it works within other constraints of the genre. At times, the operation of Wilson's women within the domestic correlates with Angela Davis's interpretation of the domestic in slavery. According to Davis:

> Domestic life took on an exaggerated importance in the lives of slaves, for it did indeed provide them with the only space where they could truly experience themselves as human beings. Black women, for this reason— and because they were workers just like men—were not debased by their domestic functions in the way that white women came to be. . . . In the infinite anguish of ministering to the needs of the men and children around her . . . she was performing the *only* labor of the slave community which could not be claimed by the oppressor.[5]

Within the domestic sphere, as Davis notes, black slave women were able to steal away time for themselves and their family. They could

"Maybe you ought to go up to Chicago and find you a man." Seven Guitars, *Goodman Theatre, 1995, with Michele Shay (Louise) and Viola Davis (Vera). (Photograph by Goodman Theatre.)*

imagine themselves as subjects rather than as property, and so nurturing their own families within this sphere could be read as an act of resistance. Translated to the postslavery world of August Wilson, the domestic sphere, the location for a character such as Rose in *Fences*, need not be understood solely as a constraining space. His representations of women in the context of the domestic can serve not only to reaffirm "dominant culture relationships," but also to critique them. Yet I must sound a note of caution; even as they express patriarchal resistance, Wilson's women also conform to conventional gender hierarchies in ways that complicate their construction as well as their interpretation. As I will argue in this chapter, their contradictory positions in relationship to men, their lack of voice and their insufficient character development, can also undermine his women's potential to articulate agency or female empowerment.

At the close of this chapter, however, I will read closely points of contact and love between men and women with the hypothesis that the communion of men and women is critical to Wilson's overall project of African American regeneration. For black women placed within Wilson's world of men, there would seem space for little else than interaction with the men and involvement with their particular plights. The women mediate, negotiate, enable, and inform the migratory politics and emancipatory initiatives of Wilson and his men. Only with and through exchange, connection, and interaction with women can Wilson's men find freedom and self-determination. At points, Wilson finds, as I will explore in this chapter, the places of loving liberatory communion, places, as bell hooks says, "where black women and men in particular, would dialogue together."[6]

Blueswomen

I begin my investigation of Wilson's women with the blues, not simply because of their prominence in Wilson's dramaturgy, but also because of the critical role that the blues have played in articulating desire, sexuality, and subjectivity for African American women. Wilson, as noted in the first chapter, discovered the blues listening to black female blues singer, Bessie Smith. Smith and her compatriot Ma Rainey, as Angela Davis points out in *Blues Legacies and Black Feminism*, offer us a privileged glimpse of prevailing perceptions of love and sexuality in postslavery black communities in the United States. Both women were role models for untold thousands of sisters to whom they delivered messages that defied the male dominance encouraged by mainstream culture. . . . By so doing, they redefined women's "place." They forged and memorialized images of tough, resilient, and independent women who were afraid neither of their own vulnerability nor of defending their right to be respected as autonomous human beings.[7]

Like Davis, feminist critics Hazel Carby, Hortense Spillers, and Michele Russell have turned to the blues as a site of black feminist expressive resistance. According to Carby, "The blues women did not passively reflect the vast social changes of their time; they provided new ways of thinking about these changes, alternative conceptions of the physical and social world for their audiences of migrating and urban women and men, and social models for women who aspired to escape from and improve their conditions of existence."[8] Understanding Wilson's women in relation to feminist theories of the blues provides a methodology for recognizing the ways these women express agency within the limitations of male dominance. Through application of blues theory, I will explore where Wilson's women evoke blues-like self-determination and participatory consciousness sharing.[9] Reading the blues can connect the personal struggles of Wilson's women to the wider social reality as well as to the political and communal objectives of Wilson's overall project.

In *Ma Rainey's Black Bottom,* Wilson's fictionalized representation of legendary blues figure Gertrude Pridgett "Ma" Rainey, appears the prototypical example of feminist assertiveness found in the blues. From her first entrance onto the stage, Wilson's Ma establishes her independence and control. Despite gender and racial dynamics and difference, she commands her band members as well as the white record producer, Sturdyvant, and her white manager, Irvin. The actual Ma Rainey in her personal history and recording career continually challenged the conventional limits and expectations of gender. Rather than being subjugated to a limited role as just a singer with the band, she became the dominant force in her musical group, the bandleader. She alone decided how the music would be played and when she would record and perform. As the leader of her own band, Ma Rainey displaced the traditional positioning of women within the music industry's hierarchy. Recognizing that the purpose of the recording session is to record her voice and her music, Wilson's Ma does not allow herself to be objectified but uses her position as a desired musical commodity to legitimize her authority. She reminds Irvin, "What band? The band work for me! I say what goes!" Her resistance to subjugation extends to spaces outside the music studio. Ma's late entrance into the first act comes as a result of institutional racism and her refusal to be treated as "just another nigger" by a white policeman, who accosts her after a minor traffic accident. Repeatedly and insistently she shouts to Irvin as she enters the studio with the arresting officer, "Tell him who I am!" Her declaration of self, her demand for Irvin to inform her accuser of her unique status and identity, testifies to her independence and self-determination.

Wilson uses actual blues music to reinforce Louise's construction as a woman with a "blues spirit" of independence in *Seven Guitars*. As we first encounter her, Louise sings a bawdy blues song that Wilson's stage directions note "is a much-needed affirmation of life" (1.1.1). The song, sung in the aftermath of her neighbor Floyd Barton's funeral, may, at first, seem antithetical to the mood of solemn mourning commonly associated with such occasions. On second glance, however, her singing and her choice of songs reflect the dichotomous nature of the blues, a form that can at once contain both the tragic and the comic. Moreover, the sexual desire expressed within the song celebrates the physical body, the corporeal appetite. In the wake of interring the body of Floyd, the song serves as a form of resurrection for his spirit. In fact, the play, which functions through a series of flashbacks, literally resurrects Floyd in the next scene, and we subsequently learn the circumstances of his demise. Here in this first moment of sadness, the sexual license, the humor and innuendoes, the transcendence of social and cultural taboos present in Louise's song acts as life-giving agent that enables the characters to escape, at least temporarily, their grief.

> *Louise:* Anybody here wanna try my cabbage
>   Just step this way
> Anybody here like to try my cabbage
> Just holler Hey. . . .
> *Red Carter:* Hey!
> *Louise:* I gave some to the parson

> And he shook with glee
> He took a collection
> And gave it all to me . . .
> (*Two Trains Running*, 1.1.1)

The lyrics to the song express the subversive, liberatory potential of the blues as sung by black blueswomen. Louise, just removed from Christian funeral services presided over by Reverend Thompson, who "sound like he reading from the bible even when he ain't," vamps about giving some to the parson. The woman blues singer, according to Hazel Carby, "had no respect for sexual taboos, for breaking through the boundaries of respectability and convention. The comic does not mellow the assertive voice, but, on the contrary undermines mythologies of phallic power, and establishes a series of woman-centered heterosexual demands."[10] In these lyrics, the woman not only exercises her freedom to give some to the parson but also invites of her own free will others to try "her cabbage." As with blueswomen, Louise's sexual vitality functions as communal reaffirmation in the face of pain, suffering, death. She calls the community back to life and to pleasure in this world.

Like Wilson's Ma Rainey, Louise is not attached to any man but works for herself and depends on no one else for her survival. In fact, Louise maintains a fierce commitment to her freedom from love relationships with men that bind and restrict. She tells her friend and neighbor Vera, "I don't need me no love. I'm forty-eight going on sixty. Hedley's the closest I want to come to love . . . and you see how far that is" (*Seven Guitars*, 1.4.31). She and her boarder Hedley share an antagonistic but caring bond. Louise goads him, looks out for him, and occasionally feeds him, but there is no sense of physical intimacy or sexual love. When Hedley offers her his services as a man, Louise admonishes him, "I don't need none that bad. I got me a thirty-two-caliber pistol up there. That be all the man I need" (1.3.19). Symbolically, Louise establishes control of her own desire by appropriating the phallic pistol. At the same time, the gun serves as real protection against unwanted advances by men. Davis notes that the blues of black women feature a scarcity of references to marriage and domesticity but rather accentuate "the contrast between the dominant cultural construction of marriage and the stance of economic independence black woman were compelled to assume for their own survival."[11] Wilson constructs Louise similarly as an unmarried woman free from any conventional financial dependence on men.

Even before the action begins in *Two Trains Running*, Risa, the one female character, engages in a radical blues-like expression of self-definition and sexual autonomy from men. In a singular blues moment, frustrated by men who deny her humanity by observing her body as sex object, Risa takes a razor and scars her legs, seven scars on one leg, eight on the other. Holloway, an older black man and daily visitor to the restaurant where Risa works, interprets her self-mutilation for the other male characters:

> I know Risa. She one of them gals that matured quick. And every man that seen her since she was twelve years old think she ought to go lay up with them some where. She don't want that. She figure if she made her legs ugly that would force everybody to look at her and see what kind of personality she is.
>
> (1.2.32)

Risa later reiterates Holloway's contention: "That's why I did it. To make them ugly" (2.4.99). In accordance with the role that Angela Davis defines for sexuality in the blues of Bessie Smith and Ma Rainey, Risa's revolt against objectification represents an explicit articulation of sexual politics.[12] By scarring her legs, Risa literally "deconstructs" herself as sexualized commodity. She defies traditional expectations and exists outside cultural codes of femininity. She subverts what Jill Dolan identifies as traditional representation, in which the female body "is imaged within representation only as the site of male desire."[13] Her employer, Memphis, with disdain proclaims:

> A man would be happy to have a woman like that except she done ruined herself. . . . She ain't right with herself . . . how she gonna be right with you? Anybody take a razor and cut up herself ain't right. . . . Something ain't right with a woman don't want no man. That ain't natural. If she say she like woman that be another thing. It ain't natural, but that be something else. But somebody that's all confused about herself and don't want nobody . . . I can't figure out where to put her.
>
> (1.2.31–32)

Although unintended, Memphis's words support the effectiveness of Risa's feminist strategy. No longer is she viewed simply as sexual object or a possession for "some man to lay up with." Her scarification and the corresponding reaction by men emphasize the interlocking systems of women's oppression and objectification.[14]

In the December 1991 production of *Two Trains Running* at the Kennedy Center in Washington, D.C., and the subsequent 1992 Broadway production, the staging by director Lloyd Richards and the movement and speech patterns created by actor Cynthia Martells emphasized Risa's rebellion against objectification. Martells, as Risa, moved and spoke extremely slowly. While the men talked and debated around her, demanded her services and made overtures toward her, Martells, as Risa, continued to move at her own rhythm. Even as Memphis ordered her about and demanded that she hurry, her Risa never stirred from her deliberate pace, but responded with quiet defiance. Perhaps most significantly, Martells's first languid cross from behind the restaurant counter to a downstage right table grounded in the spectator's mind the painful, visual image of the scars on her legs.

Risa's scarification also calls attention to Western beauty standards that have historically valorized fair skin, blue eyes, and long blonde hair, while denigrating dark skin and kinky hair. As Patricia Hill Collins in *Black Feminist Thought* maintains, "Current standards of beauty require either/or dichotomous thinking: in order for one individual to be judged beautiful, another individual—the Other must be deemed ugly."[15] In African tradition, standards of beauty are markedly different. In certain African tribes such as the Tiv of northern Nigeria, scarification is a rite of religious and social significance. Scarification renders women of the Tiv tribe beautiful, thus inverting Risa's belief that by scarring her legs she makes herself ugly. If we consider Risa's action in such an African context, beauty is shown to be a social construct rather than a physical reality.

In Wilson's representation and in her actual life, Ma Rainey's self-presentation not only calls attention to measures of beauty but to issues of sexuality and desire. By traditional Western measures, Ma Rainey would have been perceived as an unattractive woman and yet, as Sandra Shannon notes, "Those who truly connected with her ethos were not distracted by what critical Northern blacks and whites perceived as her physical ugliness."[16] Through her performance, Ma Rainey transformed beauty conventions and situated herself as a desiring and desired subject. As the black female blues singer asserts control over the

"Woman, you everything a man need." Two Trains Running, *Center Stage Theatre, 1994, with Keith Glover (Sterling) and Rosalyn Coleman (Risa). (Photograph by Richard Anderson.)*

content and form of her song, she equally declares control over her own sexuality. Hortense Spillers notes, "She is in the moment of performance the primary subject of her own being. Her sexuality is precisely the physical expression of the highest self-regard and, often, the sheer pleasure she takes in her own powers."[17] Ma Rainey's body in performance signified not the limitations of stereotypes but the possibilities of self-definition. Always adorned in lavish gowns and extravagant gold jewelry, Ma Rainey became known for her flamboyance. Through her performance the image of the heavyset black woman as mammy figure was subverted and transformed into a symbol of sexuality and style. Wilson asks that his Ma display equally regal adornment onstage: "Ma Rainey is a short heavy woman. She is dressed in a full-length fur coat with matching hat, an emerald green dress, and several strands of pearls of varying lengths. Her hair is secured by a headband that matches her dress. Her manner is simple and direct, and she carries herself in a royal fashion" (*Ma Rainey*, 1.38). Yet, while the real Ma Rainey reached the peak of her performing career in her forties, Theresa Merritt, an actress in her sixties, played Ma in the original Broadway production. Subsequent productions have replicated this pattern in casting.[18] My point here is not to make the ageist suggestion that senior citizens cannot exude sensuality, but rather to point out the way that the stage performance can play a significant role in how Ma is understood. The Merritt version accentuated Ma's bombast and sauciness while downplaying her sexuality. Thus, the stage production has the potential to constrain Ma's expression of autonomous, liberated sexuality found in black women's blues.

In her personal sex life, the real Ma Rainey refused to conform to traditional gender expectations. She was a bisexual with acknowledged lesbian relationships. According to Daphne Duval Harrison, "Rainey's and Bessie Smith's episodes with women lovers are indicative of the independent stance they and other blues singers took on issues of personal choice."[19] Her lesbianism and the public knowledge of it further testified to Ma Rainey's personal revolt against male hegemony and her ability to survive outside male domination and societal norms. Wilson opens up the possibility for the representation of Ma's lesbianism by having her lover Dussie Mae accompany her to the recording session. Although he has Cutler describe Dussie Mae as "Ma's gal," Wilson includes no stage directions or dialogue that compel Ma and Dussie to express lesbian desire.[20] Here, then, within performance is space for what Sandra Richards refers to as "absent potential":[21] "Thus, the unwritten, or an absence from the script is a potential presence implicit in performance."[22] The actresses in the October 2000 production of the play, directed by Luther James, at the Lorraine Hansberry Theatre in San Francisco—Michele E. Jordan as Ma and Olive Groves as Dussie Mae—through their physicality left no doubt as to the relationship between Ma and Dussie Mae. The performance contains the potential for actors and directors to explore, within the gaps and silences of the written text, the freedom of the blues that Ma Rainey embodied in her real life.

Decidedly more overt than the physical exchanges between Ma and Dussie Mae is the sexual embrace shared by Dussie Mae and Levee that is written into the script. Protected by the privacy of the downstairs band room, they exchange a passionate kiss. Their stolen embrace emphasizes Levee's fateful defiance of Ma Rainey's authority. Yet equally significant, Dussie Mae jeopardizes her financially stable lesbian relationship (Ma has supplied her with money and clothing) for a extremely tenuous but conventional heterosexual tryst with Levee. Implicit is a privileging of the heterosexist norm. The sexual desire expressed by Dussie Mae and Levee reflects back on and dilutes Ma's potency despite the historic efforts of the real Ma Rainey to resist the authority of heterosexist paradigms and male power and privilege.

Ma Rainey, a woman, is not the primary subject of Wilson's *Ma Rainey's Black Bottom*. As a model of blues assertiveness and cultural resistance, she is dichotomously empowered and silenced. Placing Ma Rainey's chaotic entrance late in the first act draws the audience's attention to her, but it also provides Wilson with the time to establish interest and involvement in the lives of the band members who await Ma Rainey's arrival. Shannon explains, "Ma Rainey's tardiness also serves as a means of equalizing her role in the play with those of her band members: She becomes one who *interrupts* rather than instigates the ongoing action of the play."[23] The construction of the set further emphasizes the collective voice of the band, while limiting the presence and power of Ma Rainey. Ma Rainey remains above, on the surface, in the recording studio. In the band room below, the domain of the men, the drama simmers.[24] When Ma Rainey enters this environment, she *interrupts* the men. In the stories and conflicts of these men, she cannot act. Sandra Richards asks,

> [W]hy is the play called **Ma Rainey's** *Black Bottom*? The obvious answers are, of course, that Ma is the head of this fictional band of musicians, and that the historical figure around whom this drama revolves did indeed record a song with such a title. But they are insufficient when one realizes that Ma is one of the least visible characters in the play, and that the celebrated storyteller August Wilson has given her no particular story to relate.[25]

Another answer to Richards's query is that the play's title invokes not Ma herself but the song's double-voicedness and coded meanings, which suggest the position Ma and the other black musicians find themselves in with respect to issues of identity, race, racism, commodification, and the music industry of the 1920s. When Ma and her band sings, "They say your black bottom is really good, Come on and show me your black bottom, I want to learn that dance" (*Ma Rainey*, 2.70), the comedy as well as the sexual innuendoes are evident. But Ma also expresses within the song a specific coded defiance of her white manager, Irvin, and the white studio chief, Sturdyvant, who control the recording session.[26] She shows them her black bottom. Still, Ma lacks the authority of a signature monologue that voices her inner sentiments in the ways that the male figures are enabled to speak their personal histories. The structure of the play itself removes her from the discourse of men and the final decisive action. Ma and her entourage leave before the final traumatic moment that ends in Levee's misguided murder of Toledo. She exits as she entered, in a flurry, after exhibiting a final degree of blues-inspired autonomy and delaying signing the required release for Irvin and threatening to make her "records some place else."

Similar to Wilson's dichotomous representation of Ma Rainey, Risa's blues defiance in *Two Trains Running* is principally silenced even as it is accented by her self-scarification. To adopt Patricia Hill Collins's terminology, Risa is an "outsider within" the male world of Memphis's restaurant.[27] Risa's location within the restaurant's labor system, but outside the male network of conversation and associations provides her with a unique perspective on the men as well as her own subordination. On Broadway, Martells's exaggerated movement pattern—an exercise perhaps of the play's absent potential—rendered Risa's silence visible and emphasized her removal as woman from the men's topic of discourse. Risa does exercise a degree of control over the men through one particular code of conduct in Memphis's restaurant that correlates with the liberated sexual politics of black women's blues. Whenever the men need sugar for their coffee, they must ask Risa, and she brings it to them. Observing this behavior one day, newcomer Sterling asks her, "How come you don't give nobody no sugar? You make them ask for it." Risa responds, "I give it to them. All they got to do is ask. West ask for sugar and half the time he don't use it" (*Two Trains Running*, 1.3.50). Every time the men ask for sugar, they have to acknowledge her presence, and Risa delivers the sugar in her own time. This subtly subversive act is analogous to Ma's demanding a Coke from Irvin before she will continue with the recording session in *Ma Rainey's Black Bot-*

tom. Recognizing the duration and limits of her power, she insists that the men wait for her and record on her time. In each case, the women seek to personalize and control time. Still, in *Two Trains Running,* the allusions to sexuality in the sugar exchange are thick and compelling, for sex, like sugar, can be understood as a commodity to be dispensed. Risa's actions structure a protocol for men's behavior: they cannot take but must ask and thereby acknowledge her consent. "I give it to them. All they got to do is ask." She defines a potential power in the act of giving that confronts sexual orthodoxy and male hegemony. This interpretation of Risa's sugar management resistance, read within the larger picture of a Risa who has scarred her legs in order to interrupt the circuit of male desire, further emphasizes that Risa wants to be understood on her own terms. Yet within the constraints of Memphis's restaurant, Risa's expression of this desire must come largely through her nonverbal expression.

In *Seven Guitars,* a play that in terms of chronological dating precedes *Two Trains Running,* but in Wilson's personal trajectory was written afterwards, the women, Vera and Louise most particularly, have more voice than either Risa or Ma within the male-dominated discourse. During one of the few occasions in Wilson's dramaturgy where women converse with other women, Louise shares her opinions on men in general, and Floyd in particular, with Vera. While she acknowledges that Vera loves and wants to believe in Floyd's invitation to accompany him to Chicago, Louise warns her that, "Floyd don't mean nobody no good. He don't even mean his own self no good. How he gonna mean you any good?" (*Seven Guitars,* 1.4.31). Her words prove prophetic, as Floyd's desire for individual stardom ultimately destroys not only his own life but leads to his betrayal of Vera's loving trust. Louise's interaction with Vera in this scene parallels the dynamics found in the performance of call-and-response "advice songs" in which black blueswomen shared their feelings and problems with other women as the audience would vociferously respond. Angela Davis writes:

> These [advice] songs implicitly emphasize the dialectical relation between the female subject and the women within which this individuality is imagined. In an aesthetic realm, these songs construct a women's community in which individual women are able to locate themselves on a jagged continuum of group experiences.[28]

The communion between women in blues performance became a place of collective strength and *communitas*[29] where women through the collective could summon their individual resolve to resist oppressive conditions and destructive relationships. Present in the backyard as Louise and Vera prepare food together and converse is community and communion of women, a rarity in Wilson. Louise uses their time together to bolster Vera's layers of self-protection. "What I'm trying to tell you is, don't let no man use you up and then talk about he gotta go. Shoot him first" (*Seven Guitars*, 1.4.32). Louise again invokes the appropriated power of the phallic gun. Then in a blues-infused inversion, she tells Vera, "Maybe you ought to go up to Chicago and find you a man" (1.4.32). I call this humorous retort blues infused because, as in black women's blues, it asks Vera to move from sexual object into the position of sexual subject responsible for her own desire. Rather than accepting conventional gender roles and power dynamics, Louise suggests that Vera assert her own individuality and operate outside culturally determined modes of female conduct.

Wilson draws on the blues and its gendered performances in structuring the economic relationships between the men of *Seven Guitars* and Vera and Louise. He states, "One of the things I know I got from Bessie Smith's song was that women were always stable. The women had their houses, the apartment. They let the men come. They had the key. There was—I don't know—there must be five of Bessie Smith's songs when she asked for her key back."[30] Both Louise and Vera are employed as domestics. Vera and Louise's financial stability contrasts with the black male characters, Floyd and Canewell, who are arrested for vagrancy, lack work, and have no place of their own. Vera and Louise, on the other hand, are fiscally responsible for the properties that they rent from Bella—who also figures in the dialogue of *Fences* as the owner of the neighborhood grocery store that Troy frequents in lieu of the A&P. Floyd stays with Vera, while Canewell, who lived previously with Lulu Barton, is now staying with a woman on Clark Street. "I'm drifting right now, but I ain't gonna be drifting long. . . . She just some old gal. I'm just helping her out with the rent" (*Two Trains Running*, 1.3.28). The economic condition of the characters speaks to a historical reality of that time; gender differences structured distinctive patterns for African Americans in employment.[31] More specifically, these circumstances enable Vera and Louise to exercise degrees of autonomy and to to maintain associations with men that are not based on financial dependence. When she observes Floyd chastising Canewell for not taking his hat off in *his* house, Vera interjects and makes it abundantly clear to Floyd, "It ain't your house. Let's get that straight first, if it's your house, give me twenty-five dollars for the rent" (*Seven Guitars*, 1.3.26).

Particularly cautious of Floyd's attention and intentions, Vera is twice the victim of a blues trope common in Wilson's cycle as well as in the history of black women's blues, the "my man has left me blues." Prior to the action of the play, Floyd left her and went with another woman to Chicago. He now comes back to her with the request that she accompany him on the return trip. Hazel Carby points out that in African American women's blues, the lamentation of being left behind is a repeated theme associated with the experience of migration.

> Migration for women often meant being left behind: "Bye Bye Baby" and "Sorry I can't take you" were common refrains of male blues. In women's blues the response is complex: regret and pain expressed as "My sweet man done gone and left me dead," or "My daddy left me standing in the door," or "The sound of the train fills my heart with misery."[32]

The blues afforded black women a space to articulate and to commiserate the experiences of being left behind. Vera, perhaps because of her position of stability and economic independence, is able to voice her hurt, indignation, and feelings of betrayal to Floyd on his reappearance.

> You never showed me all those places where you were a man. You went to Pearl Brown and you showed her. . . . After I would lay myself out on that bed and search my body for your fingerprints. "He touched me here." Floyd touched me here and he touched me here and he touched me here and he kissed me here and he gave me here and he took me here and he ain't here he ain't here he ain't here quit looking for him cause he ain't here he's there!
>
> (*Seven Guitars*, 1.2.14)

With blueslike vulnerability, Vera expresses her own sexual desire, her recollection of being touched as a woman. She challenges Floyd's betrayal of intimacy when he leaves rather than risk revealing to her "all those places where you were a man." Vera's iteration of the word "here" in its excess and amplification summons the active presence of memory with her body as text, as *lieu de mémoire*. And yet, as she remembers their past in the real presence of Floyd, the memory cannot supplant the void made present by his absence. The repetitions and revisions in Vera's monologue replicate patterns of linguistic inversion found in the black women's blues as they reflect on the gendered consciousness of the ambiguities of love and loss.

Prior to their entrance into *Joe Turner's Come and Gone*, the characters Molly Cunningham and Mattie Campbell were equally victimized by the "my man left me blues" and now look for solutions in the present. Mattie's husband, Jack Carper, has left her without explanation, and Molly relates that she "Come home one day and he [her husband] was packing his trunk. Told me the time comes for even the best of friends must part. Say he gonna send me a Special Delivery some old day" (2.1.260). Wilson recalls this image of a man packing his trunk in *Seven Guitars*, where Canewell explains that in his current living arrangements he keeps his trunk packed. Vera, knowing that Floyd is present, responds, "That's what the problem is now. Everybody keep their trunk packed. Time you put two and two together and try and come up with four . . . they out the door" (1.3.28). Mattie confides that Jack Carper, her husband, caught what Bono in *Fences* calls the "walking blues," "Ain't said nothing. Just started walking. I could see where he disappeared. Didn't look back. Just kept walking" (*Joe Turner*, 1.1.224). In the case of Mattie, Mollie, and Vera the men are free to move on, to travel, while the woman are left singing the blues.

Both Mattie and Molly diverge from the conventional image of the woman left behind and venture north themselves. Their trip north to Seth's Pittsburgh boardinghouse in 1911 comes at the inception of the Great Migration that changed forever the demographics of black America, as millions of African Americans headed north in search of a promised land of increased opportunity. Yet the process of migration for black men and women held very different meanings, means, and potential dangers. The methods of travel negotiated by men, such as hopping on freight trains, were not as accessible for most women. In addition, the cultural expectation was that women would stay home and mind the family in the absence of their men. Wilson explains, "And so you get the idea of men moving from place to place and the women are stable. There's a reason for that, and it's historically connected to slavery and our experiences after that."[33] Because of the restrictions on movement in slavery, in emancipation blacks were all the more anxious to travel, to explore, and to leave behind the conditions that they had known. The dominant gender ideology, however, still imagined that a woman's place was in the home, and as a result, the singular black female migrant was the exception rather than the rule. Carby notes, "The movement of black women between rural and urban areas and between southern and northern cites generated a series of moral panics. One serious consequence was that the behavior of black female migrants was characterized as sexually degenerate and thereby socially dangerous."[34] Consequently, both Mattie and Molly, alone without men, traveling north, would be deemed loose, promiscuous women who could threaten the stability of the community. Mattie disassociates herself from such a label by maintaining that the reason for her peregrinations north is solely to recover the man who left her, Jack Carper. She enlists the help of Bynum, the binder of souls, to find her husband. Molly, unlike Mattie, determines not to wait for her former man or any man, saying that "one's just as good as the other" and trusting nobody but "the good Lord above." In their travels north, both Molly and Mattie struggle with personal, historical, and cultural expectations of gender.

Like Molly and Mattie in *Joe Turner*, Berniece in *Piano Lesson* is not only a victim of the "my men left me blues" but also a woman who has migrated north following her loss. Three years prior to the action of the play, Berniece's husband Crawley was gunned down by the sheriff in Sunflower County, Mississippi, as he attempted to help Berniece's brother Boy Willie retrieve previously stolen lumber. Still mourning the loss, Berniece and her daughter Maretha left the south and came north to Pittsburgh. The trope of women losing men, of men leaving women, recurs throughout the text of *Piano Lesson:* Berniece's mother, Mama Ola, lost her husband, Papa Boy Charles over the piano; Doaker, working aboard the railroad, consistently leaves the women who await him on his various stops; Wining Boy left his wife Cleotha, years earlier. While the "my man left blues" are implicit in Berniece's position of mourning, she—unlike black women blues singers that Carby identifies—will not express her blues voice and refuses to play the family's piano until the final climactic moment of the play.

Berniece's perspective on her own fate as well as on the family's history are colored by gender. While Boy Willie acknowledges the legacy of his father as a motivating force, Berniece pays homage to her mother.

She presses Boy Willie to recognize their mother's role in the tragic history of the piano: "You always talking about your daddy, but you ain't looked to see what his foolishness cost your mother" (1.2.52). Berniece, as she reflects on her mother, represents and defends the world and worth of women because she believes that women's suffering and sacrifice have been devalued in the traditions and rituals of the patriarchy. And yet Berniece, a widow, keeps the memory of her deceased husband, Crawley, alive. She has resisted involvement with any other man since her husband's death. Avery, a rejected suitor, presses Berniece, "How long you gonna carry Crawley with you, Berniece? It's been over three years. At some point you got to let go and go on" (*Piano Lesson*, 2.2.67). Berniece responds, "I know how long Crawley's been dead. You ain't got to tell me that" (2.2.67). Berniece's refusal to release the spirit of Crawley, coupled with her particular, painful memories of the suffering that her mother endured, paralyze her and make her unwilling to embrace fully the family's past and move on with her life.

Consequently, Berniece is a figure of conflict and contradiction who both acknowledges and ignores the impact of the past on the present. While Berniece is the protector and progenitor of the family's cultural heritage, the piano, she will not play it. It rests in her house, and she has determined to keep it there. In her persuasive arguments for securing the piano and thwarting Boy Willie's efforts to sell it, Berniece relies upon the history, the legacy of familial sacrifice, both maternal and paternal, that have carried the piano to its current resting place. For Berniece, selling the piano would desecrate her parent's memories. Doaker explains, "that why we say Berniece ain't gonna sell that piano. Cause her daddy died over it" (1.2.46). At the same time, however, Berniece seeks to avoid the memories of the past. She is fragmented and dislocated from her southern roots and wants to maintain this dislocation. It is this position that Wilson seeks to critique in *Piano Lesson*: "the question was, 'Can one acquire a sense of self-worth by denying one's past?'"[35] Through the action of the play, Wilson answers this question, as Berniece comes to reconnect with the past so that she and her family might be freed from the negative psychological and sociological forces that haunt their present.

Wilson believes that the historical context within which he sets *Piano Lesson* affects his representation of Berniece and her expression of gendered resistance. "Originally I had Berniece in *Piano Lesson* utter some

"*You all had this planned. You and Boy Willie had this planned.*" Piano Lesson, *Yale Repertory Theatre, 1987, with Starlette DuPois (Berniece) and Lou Myers (Wining Boy). (Photograph by Gerry Goodstein.)*

very feminist ideas. These were not ideas that were even in the world that she would have been aware of in 1936. I had to take them away from her."[36] While I understand Wilson's desire to not be either anachronistic or presentist in his construction, I must note that assertions of feminist resistance are not always time bound but that their meanings and function are constituted not only in their time but in how they are interpreted in the present. As evidenced by their citation in this chapter, the songs of Bessie Smith and Ma Rainey of the 1920s that inspired Wilson's interest in blues have been equally rediscovered by black feminist critics in the 1980s and 1990s as a site of black feminist agency. Feminist interpretations of these blueswomen of the 1920s reveal how they worked within the limits of their historical moment to express autonomy and to defy accepted gender constructions. My reading of Berniece is that her desire for self-definition finds complications not simply because of her historical context but the contradictions of her relationality to men. While her blues lament rails against male domination—"You [Boy Willie], Papa Boy Charles, Wining Boy, Doaker, Crawley . . . you're all alike. All this thieving and killing and killing. And what it ever lead to"—it equally contains the heartache and the longing for men lost to violence. At issue always with Wilson's women, even those like Berniece, who express the autonomy and assertiveness of black women's blues, is their relationship to and even need for a man. It is a paradox that Wilson seems to recognize,[37] and yet does not step outside of, in his depiction of women.

Needing a Man

On the whole Wilson's representations of women operate within a heterosexual paradigm—the notion that a woman needs a man—and thus any re-definition of women's place can succumb to the pressures of conventional cultural politics. At different points in *Joe Turner,* both Mattie and Molly become involved with Jeremy, a confident and ingratiating young boarder at Seth and Bertha's Pittsburgh boardinghouse. For Mattie, Jeremy offers the possibility of stability, a replacement for her missing husband. For Molly, the attraction to Jeremy is not security, but adventure, as he presents her with an opportunity to travel under more legitimized circumstances, not as a solo woman but as a couple. While Jeremy moves Mattie into his room at the boardinghouse, he asks

Molly to leave the boardinghouse with him and "travel around and see some places." In his wooing of Mattie and Molly, Jeremy appeals to their particular circumstances and uses male privilege to his advantage. He first tells Mattie:

> A woman like you need a man. Maybe you let me be your man? . . . A woman can't be by her lonesome.
>
> (*Joe Turner*, 1.1.226)

He later informs Molly before they go off together:

> A woman like you can make it anywhere she go. But you can make it better if you got a man to protect you.
>
> (2.1.262)

In his rap to both women, Jeremy insightfully fuses the personal with larger social concerns. He seizes upon how each woman sees herself in relation to the historically and culturally programmed requirement that a woman be with a man. With Mattie, he recognizes her emotional need for a man as well as the economic struggles she faces as a single black woman. With Molly, he addresses her understanding of practicality and codes of morality, that a woman traveling with a man has better prospects than a single woman. Still, Molly does exercise some agency when she sets down critical ground rules for her companionship with Jeremy:

> *Molly:* Molly don't work. And Molly ain't up for sale.
> *Jeremy:* Sure, Baby. You ain't got to work with Jeremy.
> *Molly:* There's one more thing.
> *Jeremy:* What's that, sugar?
> *Molly:* Molly ain't going South.
>
> (*Joe Turner*, 2.1.263)

Through her negotiated conditions, Molly asserts and protects a degree of her autonomy. Like the blueswomen whose songs de-romanticize love, Molly—who like Risa controls the sugar—strips Jeremy of any illusions of her gendered subordinance. While she accepts her need for a man, she does so on her terms.

In *Piano Lesson*, set over thirty years later than *Joe Turner*, Wilson has Berniece, at first, stand in opposition to this dictum that "a woman needs a man to be complete." When Avery chastises her for pushing him away and not accepting his love, she responds:

> You trying to tell me a woman can't be nothing without a man. But you alright, huh? You can just walk out of here without me—without a woman—and still be a man. That's alright. Ain't nobody gonna ask you, "Avery, who you got to love you?" That's alright for you. But everybody gonna worry about Berniece. "How Berniece gonna take care of herself? How she gonna raise that child without a man? Wonder what she do with herself. How she gonna live like that?" Everybody got all kinds of questions for Berniece. Everybody telling me I can't be a woman unless I got a man. Well, you tell me, Avery—you know—how much woman am I?
>
> (*Piano Lesson*, 2.2.67)

Berniece decries the double standard of social acceptability that is applied to single men and single women. She questions the traditional perception of women as defined solely by and in relation to men. And yet, after warding off Avery, Berniece succumbs to the charms of Boy Willie's friend Lymon. They share an unexpected, but passionate, embrace. In fact, in an early draft of *The Piano Lesson*, Lymon and Berniece, after they caressed, went upstairs to bed together. The existing scene between Berniece and Lymon contrasts sharply with the earlier scene between Berniece and Avery, for Berniece and Lymon exhibit a sexual attraction unseen in her relationship with Avery. Avery tries to "unsex" Berniece and paint her as frigid in order to explain her denial of his suit. Her kiss with Lymon, however, shows that Berniece is still able to exercise and act on desire. Yet, after their encounter, neither Berniece nor Lymon ever expresses the rationale for their unlikely embrace. Without articulation, their brief passion dissipates the impact of Berniece's earlier protest. Following directly after the tête-à-tête with Avery, this scene suggests a contradiction in Berniece, that she does in fact need a man; Avery is just not the right one. With Berniece therefore, and for that matter Wilson's other women, the question is how and to what degree they are able to achieve self-definition given their relationship to the men in their lives. How are they defined in terms of, and limited by, their relationship with men?

Perhaps the most confounding example of the complex, complimentary, and contradictory conjunction of women and men in Wilson occurs in *Seven Guitars,* when Ruby, forty years younger than she is in *King Hedley II,* sleeps with the mad West Indian Hedley. At this moment, Hedley, as Wilson describes him, is "feverish with lust" (*Seven Guitars,* 2.5.89). Yet, Hedley grounds his appeal to Ruby not simply in sexual need but in a confluence of race, spirituality, and masculinity.

> The black man is not a dog! He is the Lion of Judah! He is the mud God made his image from. . . . I am a man, woman. I am the man to father your children. I offer you a kingdom. . . . I offer you to be Lily of the Valley. To be Queen of Sheba. Queen of the black man's kingdom.
>
> (*Seven Guitars,* 2.5.88–89)

Hedley sees his power and his identity wrapped up in his image of manhood and his ability to pass on his legacy, to produce an heir. His sexual desire conjoins with his concern for racial uplift and vision of a black messiah. Somehow the young, already pregnant, seemingly self-interested Ruby decides to lie down with the now sex-crazed, formerly just crazed Hedley: "She lifts her dress and gives herself to him out of recognition of his great need" (2.4.90). Read simply, the gesture seems to reflect a malecentric dramaturgy that depicts women solely in relation to men. Where is the character development for Ruby to make this decision? It is, in fact, an act of madness, an act that seems out of sorts with the character we have seen. Is it perhaps a hysterical response? After all, what normal woman would lie down with a figure so deranged with lust?

Ruby's act, let me suggest, however, is not simply the design of Wilson's malecentrism but an expression of practical agency within the constraints of her circumstances. The language of the stage directions is particularly significant here: "She lifts up her dress and gives herself." The "giving of herself" does not connote passive submission but rather needs to be read by critics as well as actresses undertaking the role as an active choice. Her giving of herself presumes self-possession, individualism, and subjectivity that can find representation in performance. This scene, in how the director constructs it and the way the actress as Ruby enacts it, is "wonderfully charged with potential."[38] Sandra Richards writes:

> Some feminists might wonder why I would choose to cover up or to fix the chauvinist appropriation that Wilson has written. My response to

both is to refer once again to an African-American folk aesthetic that understands as a generating motive and values as an ideal in performance, the potency and heightened emotion arising from a dense interlock of competing energies. Thus, the unwritten, or absence from the script, is a potential presence implicit in performance.[39]

The "dense interlock of competing energies" that Richards describes is equally present in any effective mounting of the Ruby/Hedley scene and can work against reading this as simply a chauvinist moment. Absent from Wilson's dialogue or even from the revealing stage directions for this scene is any notation of the time it should take Ruby to respond to Hedley or how she should use her body and gestures to embrace him and "give herself to him." How the actress conveys Ruby's thought pattern and her rationale for action can be telling. Equally significant, within the script itself, there is also evidence of Ruby's own rationale and determination that stands opposed to readings of her as silenced compliant woman. For Ruby, too, has needs that this act of lying down with Hedley serves, and she too gets what she wants:

> I'm gonna tell him it's [i.e., her baby is] his. He's the only man who ever wanted to give me something. And I want to have that. He wants to be the father of my child and that's what this child needs. I don't know about this messiah stuff but if it's a boy—and I hope to God it is—I'm gonna name it after him. I'm gonna name him King.
>
> (*Seven Guitars*, 2.7.95–96)

Impregnated by another, Ruby chooses Hedley as the father for her child. While Hedley speaks of transcendent visions, she responds to practical needs, to a child coming into the world without a father. Through this act she subverts conventions of legacy and paternity and usurps the domain traditionally staked by men, the seed of heredity, the power of masculinity. She names both the father and the son. In what René Girard refers to as "triangular desire,"[40] Ruby mediates between Hedley and the unborn child. As mediator of desire she enables Hedley to realize his vision, without subscribing to the patriarchal terms of it. Still, the incendiary sexual politics of this scene, of Ruby the young and vibrant mother-to-be consensually bedding the crazed and crusty Hedley, make this a complex and contradictory moment that demands close reading.

Mothers and Wives

Through Rose Maxson in *Fences* and Tonya in *King Hedley II*, both wives and mothers, Wilson examines the interconnections as well as the distinctions in these roles as personal, cultural, and familial tensions converge. Because the positions of wife and mother are particularly relational—each depends on a presence of another, be it husband or child respectively, for definition—one question for this chapter is where within these inherently dependent roles there is space for Rose or Tonya to define herself. Central to *Fences* is the struggle of mother and father over the raising of the son, Cory. In *King Hedley II*, the parents argue over the issue of abortion. While Troy wants his son to keep his job at the A&P, to learn a marketable skill, and to stay away from sports, Rose wants Cory to have the opportunity offered him by a college football scholarship. Embittered by how racism thwarted his own development in professional baseball, Troy intends to protect his son from this same eventuality. "The white man ain't gonna let him get anywhere with that football. I told him when he first come to me with it" (*Fences*, 1.1.111). Rose on the other hand believes that "times have changed" since Troy played baseball, that football is means to an end for Cory—"he ain't talking about making no living playing football. It's an honor to be recruited" (1.1.111). During the last scene of the first act, Rose boldly directs Troy to perform on his son's behalf: "And next week . . . when that recruiter come from that school . . . I want you to sign that paper and go on and let Cory play football. Then that'll be the last I have to hear about that" (1.4.146). Rose's aggressive defense of her son in the face of his father's stubborn will attests to her desire for Cory to have the freedom to pursue his dreams. Yet, her dictates to Troy still depend on his authority as the man of the household. He is the one who must sign the papers. She can only enjoin him to act. Later, we learn that, in fact, Troy has operated on his own and informed Cory's coach that his son will no longer play on the team.

Unlike Rose, Tonya, in the 1980s, is not beholden in the same ways to the patriarchal will of her husband, King. She pays a preliminary visit to the abortion clinic solely of her own volition. Her desire not to bring another child into this world, to exercise control over her body, stands

"Your daddy's a big man. Got these great big old hands. But sometimes he's scared." Fences, TheatreWorks, Lucie Stern Theatre, 2000, with Gloria Weinstock (Rose) and Anthony J. Haney (Troy). (Photograph by David Allen for TheatreWorks.)

in direct opposition to the wishes of King. Still in their negotiations of these familial conflicts, both Tonya and Rose experience epiphanies of self-discovery that compel them to act, to assert their will and to change.

As the action of *Fences* soon displays, the definitions of wife and husband that Troy and Rose have built for themselves provide a problematic codependency. Each Friday Troy hands over his paycheck to Rose. As he relinquishes this element of economic control in the opening scene, Troy complains to his compatriot Bono, "You see this Bono? Now I ain't gonna get but six of that back" (1.1.120). This public demonstration of acquiescence to Rose's domestic authority, even as it reveals the compromises of marriage and conveys Rose's control over the household finances, affirms her dependence on him in his role as husband and breadwinner. She must await this symbolic act of his turning over his paycheck to her.[41] Rose's duties as wife extend to the bedroom, where Troy exercises a similar command. Holding Rose in his arms, Troy announces to Bono his husbandly machismo, "See this woman, Bono? I love this woman. I love this woman so much it hurts. I love her so much . . . I done run out of ways of loving her. So I got to go back to basics. Don't you come by my house Monday morning talking about time to go to work . . . 'cause I'm still gonna be stroking!" (1.1.121). Troy touchingly yet crudely declares his love and sexual desire to which he expects his wife to comply. He is "still gonna be stroking." As husband and father, Troy provides for his family and expects them to respond to and obey him as a result.

And still, Troy maintains that his existence with Rose has restricted him. When he explains his sexual affair to Rose, he does so by reflecting on the burdens of marriage and fatherhood: "I'm responsible for it. I done locked myself into a pattern trying to take care of you all that I forgot about myself. . . . It's not easy for me to admit that I been standing in the same place for eighteen years" (2.1.163–65). Troy rationalizes his affair with Alberta, by implying that he needed her to affirm his masculinity in the face of difficult social pressures. "She gives me a different idea . . . a different understanding of myself. . . . Then when I saw that girl . . . she firmed up my backbone" (2.1.163–64). His manhood has been diminished by a system of white hegemony in which "you born with two strikes on you before you come to the plate" (2.1.164). Originally, he felt he beat this system and secured his manhood through marrying Rose and fathering Cory: "I fooled them, Rose, I bunted.

When I found you and Cory and a halfway decent job . . . I was safe"
(2.1.164). Then, needing more, he seeks out Alberta.

Rose, however, maintains that marriage demands such sublimation.
She has eschewed her own desires and needs and castigates him for not
doing the same.

> But I held onto you, Troy. I took all my feelings, my wants and needs, my
> dreams . . . and buried them inside you. I planted a seed and watched and
> prayed over it. I planted myself inside you and waited to bloom. And it
> didn't take me no eighteen years to find out the soil was hard and rocky
> and it wasn't never gonna bloom. But I held onto you, Troy. I held you
> tighter. You was my husband. I owed you everything I had. Every part of
> me I could find to give you. And upstairs in that room . . . with the dark-
> ness falling in on me . . . I gave everything I had to try and erase the doubt
> that you wasn't the finest man in the world. And wherever you was going
> . . . I wanted to be there with you. 'Cause you was my husband, 'cause
> that's the only way I was gonna survive as your wife.
>
> (2.1.165)

Rose's poetic and poignant diatribe reveals how she has suppressed herself and her identity to be Troy's wife. Wilson's choice of words and
imagery here is particularly telling, for in reversal of conventional gender assignations, Rose states that she attempted to impregnate Troy. He
is the womb in which she, in a misguided attempt at agency, planted
herself and "waited to bloom." It is an act of self-erasure, and yet she
perseveres only to discover that Troy is barren. His own specific circumstance coupled with the sociological forces of oppression that he
endures as a black man render him infertile. While Rose attempts to
flower through Troy, Troy seeks to find himself through an extramari-
tal relationship; both prove equally unsuccessful.

Rose's opposition to her husband Troy and acceptance of his baby
Raynell eventually does enable her to bloom and to find new self-awareness, but, tellingly, her sense of self-definition comes with the recognition of her own complicity within the relationship. Her final assessment
of their marriage, delivered to Cory in the last scene functions to reconcile her psychological separation from Troy, as Rose emphasizes her
own resignation to "what life offered me in the way of being a woman"
(*Fences*, 2.5.190). She confides:

> That was my first mistake. Not to make him leave some room for me. For
> my part in the matter. But at that time I wanted that. I wanted a house

that I could sing in. And that's what your daddy gave me. I didn't know to keep up his strength I had to give up little pieces of mine. I did that. I took on his life as mine and mixed up the pieces so that I couldn't hardly tell which was which anymore. It was my choice. It was my life and I didn't have to live it like that. But that's what life offered me in the way of being a woman, and I took it.

(2.5.189–90)

For a black woman in 1957, marriage required compromise and quite often a loss of self. Rose reflects on this historic truth experienced by many black women; she calls attention to the limitations of gender roles and implicitly critiques the patriarchal system that created these restrictions. Yet Rose also accepts blame for the choices she made.

In *King Hedley II,* Tonya's decision to abort also emerges with her realization of her own liability for her current circumstances. With *King Hedley II,* Wilson says he "wanted to deal with the so-called breakup of the black family," and using his depiction of Tonya's dilemma of impending motherhood, he works within and beyond another powerfully pejorative stereotype, that of the black teenage mother.[42] Tonya, a mother at age seventeen, now not only finds herself a grandmother at age thirty-five, as her seventeen-year-old daughter Natasha has given birth, but once again pregnant. The context for her crisis of motherhood is Pittsburgh 1985, a time when the percentage of black teen mothers increased as the number of young black boys dying on the streets to gun violence escalated. As Patricia Hill Collins notes,

> In the 1980s, the entire community structure of bloodmothers and othermothers came under assault. Racial desegregation as well as the emergence of class-stratified Black neighborhoods greatly altered the fabric of Black civil society. African-Americans of diverse social classes found themselves in new residential, school and working settings that tested this enduring theme of bloodmothers, othermothers, and woman-centered networks. In many inner city, working-class neighborhoods, the very fabric of African-American community life eroded when crack cocaine flooded the streets.[43]

Patricia Hill Collins defines "othermothers" as women "who assist bloodmothers by sharing in the mothering responsibilities."[44] Both Ma Rainey and Risa at times function in this capacity. Ma's concern for and promotion of her stuttering nephew Sylvester—who she insists will perform the recorded introduction to her song "Ma Rainey's Black Bottom"—in the face of his seeming inability to complete the task, stand in stark contrast to her peremptory, dismissive attitude toward the white men, Irvin and Sturdyvant. Despite her boss Memphis's objections, Risa welcomes the "madman" Hambone into Memphis's restaurant; she nurtures him, feeds him, and even clothes him. Collins points out that othermothers have been central to the tradition of black motherhood and critical to maintaining community-based networks of child care. As Collins indicates, social, cultural, and environmental pressures in the 1980s abraded the historically established networks of black motherhood. For Tonya, her own particular concerns about motherhood are exacerbated by the urgencies of the time, her understanding that mothering takes time and her feeling that she has continually lost time: "Look at Natasha. I couldn't give her what she needed. Why I wanna go back and do it again? . . . I look up, she ten years old and I'm still trying to figure out life. Figure out what happened. Next thing I know she grown. Talking about she a woman. Just 'cause you can lay down and open your legs to a man don't make you a woman" (*King Hedley II*, 1.2.38–39). Through Tonya's poignant monologue stating her opposition to motherhood at thirty-five, Wilson bemoans the tragedy of "babies making babies." Tonya lacked the knowledge and experience to give Natasha what she needed. By the time Tonya recognizes and acknowledges her lack as a mother, Natasha herself is with child. Tonya determines to end this cycle, despite her husband King's opposition, by aborting the baby that she now carries.

Tonya's decision to abort functions as a signifying revision of two memorable mothers in African American theater history, Rachel in Angelina Grimke's *Rachel* (1916) and Ruth in Lorraine Hansberry's *Raisin the Sun* (1959), in which women use decisions about impending motherhood to resist poverty, racism, and oppression. In *Raisin*, Ruth, aware of the overwhelming economic pressures on her family, considers abortion in order to save her family for fear that she and her husband could not care for another mouth. Tonya's threatened abortion is equally intended not to condemn her family but to rescue it. Her own situation with her husband, King, like that of Ruth and Ruth's husband Walter, is on tenuous ground. Natasha's father is currently in prison, and Tonya knows that King could easily end up there as well. In *Raisin*, Walter learns about Ruth's intentions not from Ruth herself but from Mama Younger, who rises to her daughter-in-law's defense, Tonya, however, directly confronts King and justifies her planned abortion. "Why? . . . . Why I wanna go back and do it again? . . . I ain't having this baby . . . and I ain't got to explain it to anybody" (*King Hedley II*, 1.2.38–39). Tonya asserts subjectivity in ways that Ruth does not, and forces into the forefront issues more subtly expressed in *Raisin* concerning the social and ethical responsibilities of black motherhood.

Tonya's actions, like those of the title character in *Rachel,* which gained notoriety when first produced in Washington, D.C., in 1916 for its explicitly propagandistic message, foreground significant moral questions surrounding the personal act of giving birth to a black child.[45] Bolstered by her knowledge of the lynching of her father and her brother's inability to find work commensurate with his education, Rachel Loving decides that, rather than bring black children into a life of racist oppression, she will not marry or have children. Similarly, in *King Hedley II* Tonya's justification for abortion testifies to the dangers of raising black children in a world where their innocence is constantly threatened and little value is attached to their lives. "I ain't raising no kid to have somebody shoot him. To have his friends shoot him. To have the police shoot him. Why I want to bring another life into this world that don't respect life? I don't want to raise no more babies when you got to fight to keep them alive" (1.2.39). Tonya like Rachel recognizes that one way to end the violence against black children is to stop having black babies. Hers is a politicized decision that reflects on the *power* within black motherhood. As Patricia Hill Collins writes, "viewing motherhood as a symbol of power can catalyze Black women to take actions they otherwise might not have considered."[46] Through Rachel's action, playwright Grimke sought to appeal to white mothers to raise their awareness of the suffering incurred by black mothers and to enlist their aid in the struggle against racism.[47] Wilson is not so much interested in reaching white mothers but in emphasizing the tragic loss of black life and the need not only for empathy but for action.

If I think of the 1980s, I think it started somewhere around '84 or '85, you had this rash of these young kids with guns out there killing one another. I think of Washington, D.C., with 500 and some murders in one particular year. That's more than one a day. I was in D.C. I'd pick up the paper—four people got killed and the next day three people. Hell, I was scared to come out of my hotel. It was very much a part of the eighties. If I ever wanted to write a play about eighties, I didn't want to write about the kids, but I wanted to somehow deal with that.[48]

Wilson, rather than "write about the kids," confronts their mothers and how they figure within the cycle of black loss. In her powerful monologue Tonya, as mother and mother-to-be, uses the power of her position to voice passionately the urgent need for black people themselves to take decisive action to end the violence.

Although Tonya and Rose express a liberating self-awareness and a sense of responsibility for and power over their own social circumstances, these assertions, in Wilson's dramaturgy, are always in tension with events that demand social conformity or that result in the assumption of more conventional positions of black femininity. Tonya's decision to resist the cycle of black children born into violence does not reach enactment, nor do she and her husband get to struggle through their impasse, as King is accidentally shot and killed by his own mother, Ruby. The death of the son by the mother offers ironic commentary on Tonya's proposed abortion and the senselessness of black-on-black violence. Worried about her ability to control her life, Tonya finds herself in a world out of control, and she now must play the role of the grieving black widow, a role seen too many times in black urban enclaves during the 1980s. Rose, as Kim Marra argues, is ultimately "fenced in" by her gender.[49] While Rose spiritually distances herself from Troy, she does not leave the marriage; rather, the church becomes her surrogate. Hill Collins maintains that institutions such as the church can be "contradictory locations" where black women not only find religious affirmation, but also "learn to subordinate our interests to the allegedly greater good of the larger African-American community."[50] Rose conjoins her church work with her devotional mothering of her adopted daughter Raynell. And so her new psychological freedom from her husband becomes channeled into traditionally gendered avenues and behaviors. The relationality of these women in particular and Wilson's women more generally, the ways in which they interact with men, continually informs their choices and inhibits self-expression.

Women and Men, Love and Resistance

And yet, in Wilson's cycle, women through their loving communion with men play a critical role in his project of African American social renewal. A relationship between women and men that is founded on love can prove mutually beneficial and can provide the catalyst for both personal and collective change. In the epigraph to this chapter, bell hooks theorizes a way that love, interaction, dialogue can act as forms of resistance: "I want to think critically about intellectual partnership, about the ways black women and men resist by creating a world where we can talk with one another, where we can work together." Resistance here does not entail just physical opposition to injustice, but internal and psychological evolution, collective struggle and mutual communication toward a common goal. In a scene from *Two Trains Running*, directly following an embrace between the wayward young warrior Sterling and the independent-minded Risa, Wilson has Holloway extol the virtues and responsibilities of love. "Love got a price to it. Everybody don't want to pay. They put it on credit. Time it come due they got it on credit somewhere else" (2.5.103). As expressed by Holloway, love exacts a price that for some is too expensive. And yet, Wilson's dramaturgy reveals that the cost of love is not a singular burden, but one that requires collective effort.

This spirit of collaborative love is something that the character Rena asks of her live-in boyfriend and the father of her child, Youngblood [Darnell], in *Jitney*. When Darnell, whose nickname "Youngblood" was Wilson's own as a young man, confesses that he has taken her baby food money in order to secure the down payment on a house, Rena responds, "You bought a house without me! . . . You gonna surprise me with a house? Don't do that. A new TV maybe. A stereo . . . a couch . . . a refrigerator . . . okay. But don't surprise me with a house that I didn't even have a chance to pick out."[51] Rena demands an equal voice in their lives together. "I'm not asking you to do it by yourself. I'm here with you. We in this together" (2.1.74–75). Rena's vision of male/female relations, she implies, is one involving serialized joint decision making, not grand but unilateral gestures of love—especially those predicated on masculine notions of gift giving in which women are involved merely as the recipients of men's largesse. Youngblood's planned surprise of a new house represents not love and understanding, but rather a way to control and limit Rena's involvement. What she advocates instead is not simply the right to participate but a space of shared communication, like that articulated by bell hooks, where black men and women can dialogue together. Rena does not diminish Youngblood's self-worth as they argue, even as she chastises him for not including her in his deci-sion-making processes: "You supposed to know what's important to me like I'm supposed to know what's important to you . . . If we don't know what's important to one another and learn to share that then we can't make it" (*Jitney*, 2.1.75, 77). As a consequence, Youngblood is not only able to appreciate her critique, but to grow. Because Rena only appears in two scenes within the play, Wilson risks presenting her as a polemical mouthpiece or as a gendered cliché rather than as an individ-ualized character, and one can again claim she exists only in relation to Youngblood and solely to enable his growth. Moreover, Rena chal-lenges Youngblood's authority on particularly gendered terms as a mother. This is made especially poignant by the fact that Youngblood's assumptions about what and how to give her something comes at the expense of her wanting to give to their child. Yet, I would argue that Rena effects their mutual understanding and renewal. Rena's words and her loving confrontation with Youngblood carve out a space for herself and equally provide Youngblood with the ability to evolve and to accept Rena differently. They recommit to their partnership and reach a place of mutual agreement and love: "I want you baby . . . I told you that. You already my pride. I want you to be my joy" (*Jitney*, 2.1.77).

In *Piano Lesson*, Berniece exhibits a different kind of loving resis-tance that symbolically both frees and connects her to the past, that even serves as a catalyst for new understanding. After her brother Boy Willie pursues the ghost of the white landowner Sutter upstairs, Berniece, searching desperately for some way to aid her brother in this confrontation, sits down at the piano she has avoided for so long. According to Wilson, "as much as Berniece and Boy Willie battle, as much as they appear disharmonious, Berniece is forced to play the piano to save Boy Willie and to support his struggle with Sutter. When she does that they become one. When the conflict within the society at large—white society—comes in, then the people unite on the basis of their commonality of culture."[52] Berniece's previous neglect of the piano, her unwillingness to confront the ghosts of her past, threatens the current stability of the Charles family and allows the ghost of Sutter to return and contest them for ownership of the piano and the possession of their "songs." Thus, it is only when Berniece returns to the piano that the ghost of Sutter can be exorcised. While Boy Willie's "man-to-man" battle with Sutter's ghost happens offstage, Berniece's engagement with her demons occurs visibly before the audience as she sits down at the piano. No longer is the play's focus on the men of the Charles family. Berniece's vulnerability and insecurities, her own particular courage to defend her family through loving resistance, take center stage. She plays a song that explicitly calls on family, her ancestral spirits for assistance, "Mama Ola, I want you to help me" (*Piano Lesson*, 2.5.107). Through this embodied performance, she reconnects with the past and develops a new understanding of the family's legacy. Correspondingly, Boy Willie also arrives at a new appreciation of the value of the piano and the need to keep it within the confines of the family. Through this performance of loving resistance, brother and sister come together in harmony to symbolically defeat the psychological forces of white oppression.

Resurrecting Mama

A different communion of women and men, which has a profound impact on the characters' psychological trauma, repeatedly plays in the desire of Wilson's black sons to resurrect their absent mothers. For these troubled men, the departed mother represents unfulfilled promises. They deeply experience her loss and must confront the sense of impotence and culpability that surrounds the circumstances of her departure. Levee in *Ma Rainey* confides to the other band members his horrific memory of being forced as a child to watch his mother raped by a gang of white men. This act removed her psychically from him, and he is tragically tormented by guilt for his inability to defend her. In *Jitney*, both Becker and his boy, Booster, must carry with them the loss of the wife and mother, who died of unbearable grief after Booster was sentenced to life in prison for murder. They blame each other for her passing, and this intensifies their own separation from each other. Troy's recollection, in *Fences,* of his mother is a story of abandonment and alienation. In one of his backyard tales, he imparts to Bono and Lyons that his mother left his siblings and him as a child because she was no longer able to endure his abusive father: "She run off when I was about eight. She sneaked off one night after he had gone to sleep. Told me she was coming back for me. I ain't never seen her no more" (*Fences*, 1.4.148). Forced to confront his father alone, Troy feels both betrayal and ambivalence at his mother's departure; he too misses his mother. In *Seven Guitars,* the central figure Floyd longs for his deceased mother and visits her grave with the hope to someday mark it with a real gravestone. He confides to the other men, "If I could hear my mother pray again, I believe I'd pray with her. I'd be happy just to hear her voice again. I wouldn't care if she was cussing me out. They say you don't miss your water till your well run dry. If I could hear my mother's voice again I never would say nothing back to her" (1.5.49–50). Floyd wants to fill the present with the past, to displace the void of lost time. As a grown man now, he will be the perfect child and not "say anything back" to his mother. Somehow bringing her back will promote psychic healing and will absolve him of any blame for her going away. Yet, while he knows that a new gravestone can mark the memory of his mother and that he can celebrate her through his visits to the cemetery, he recognizes that he cannot see her in life again. Her materiality is lost. How then to fill the void, the loss of the mother? How then to confront the shared impotence at this loss? How does this need for psychic recovery of the mother impact the son's assertions of black masculinity?[53]

The desire for the mother is a struggle not simply to reclaim the past but to find meaning in the present. Hortense Spillers, theorizing about the particular condition of the mother in African American history and culture, argues, "It is the heritage of the mother that the African-American male must regain as an aspect of his own personhood—the power of 'yes' to the 'female' within."[54] Spillers posits that the "condition of the mother"—the slave law that made all children born to a slave mother inherit her condition irregardless of the baby's father—as a legacy from slavery puts the African American man and mother into a special and unique connection. As a result of the "condition of the mother," black mothers became the repositories of blackness. Spillers perceives the residue of this past in contemporary African American culture where single mothers raise sons and pass facets of their identity on to them. The boys learn of manhood through the mother. Spillers maintains that "the black American male embodies the *only* American community of males which has had the specific occasion to learn *who* the female is within itself."⁵⁵ And yet within such an economy the mother must risk her own disappearance as the boy becomes a man or, as Spillers puts it, must take "the could-be fateful gamble against the odds of pulverization and murder, including her own."

Too often, the absenting was forcible, as black mothers in slavery and its aftermath were literally taken away from their sons. In *Ma Rainey,* the mother suffers a powerfully symbolic and material erasure. She is raped, and Levee's sense of impending manhood is eclipsed because he cannot fight to defend her; too young and too small to act decisively, he is forced to watch until he picks up his father's hunting knife and tries his "damnedest to cut one of them's throat! I hit him on the shoulder with it. He reached back and grabbed hold of that knife and whacked me across the chest with it. That's what made them stop. They was scared I was going to bleed to death" (*Ma Rainey,* 1.57). They stop because of his vulnerability—he is too weak, they see the blood and fear his death—not because of his masculine potency. Levee is jettisoned into a more profound recognition of his racial identity in this violent usurpation of his black mother by a gang of white men, and he remains haunted by this event and the continued command of white men over black lives. Levee lives after his slashing because his mother, despite her own pain, carried him "two miles down to the Furlow place and they drove me up to Doc Albans. He was waiting on a calf to be born, and he say he ain't had time to see me. They carried me up to Miss Etta, the midwife, and she fixed me up" (*Ma Rainey,* 1.58). Turned down by the white doctor treating a pregnant cow—a further testimony to the value ascribed to black life—Levee is saved by the black midwife, who must constantly negotiate between black mothers and sons. Significantly, all the images Levee describes in this scene—Doc Albans waiting on the calf, Miss Etta the midwife—concern birth, and Levee is in effect born again through these events in which his mother both acts and is acted upon. She then disappears from his narrative. He turns to discuss his father's revenge, but the trauma of these events lingers in his memory. If in Wilson's work and in Spillers's thesis black manhood survives, where is the space for the black woman?

Spiller's argument is that a space of the feminine must be discovered *within* the black man. Historically the black man, denied the traditional measure of masculinity, work, wages, authority, has been repeatedly effeminized by white hegemony. Thus, the demands for black equality emanating from the Civil Rights movement in the 1960s were frequently situated within masculinized declarations; "I am a Man!" Spillers does not speak to this type of feminization by external forces. Rather what she calls for, and what I believe Wilson's dramaturgy suggests, is a turning inward, struggling against oneself to locate a point of engagement and healing that is at once personal, cultural, and familial. For Wilson's men the remembrance, need, and longing for the mother are evidence of a desire for a reconnection to a lost personal and collective past. They must come to terms with impotence, with anger and blame as they work to recover the mother. While not negating the impact of the father's legacy on Wilson's sons, the heritage of the mother calls the sons back to unfinished business.

Chapter 4
Men of August

To the real question, how does it feel to be a problem? I answer seldom a word.

   And yet, being a problem is a strange experience,—peculiar even for one who has never been anything else, save perhaps in babyhood and in Europe. . . . The history of the American Negro is the history of this strife,—this longing to attain self-conscious manhood, to merge his double self into a better truer self. In this merging he wishes neither of the older selves to be lost.

—W. E. B. Du Bois, "Of Our Spiritual Strivings,"
The Souls of Black Folk

In *The Souls of Black Folk,* W. E. B. Du Bois raises this incendiary question that Wilson's investigation of black men in his twentieth-century cycle provocatively revisits: "How does it feel to be a problem?" Wilson's examination of black masculinity not only references Du Bois's historical query, but reflects the contemporary politics of representation that inform black male subjectivity. Remarking on his own inscription within demonizing representations, Trey Ellis notes, "We [black men] have become the international symbol for rape, murder, robbery, and uncontrolled libido."[1] In a similar vein, Patricia J. Williams intones, "with the agency of Reasonable or Average Black Men being pretty completely blockaded from the script of the great American dream, black men's social lot is made far grimmer for having been used as the emblem for all that is dangerous in the world, from crime to disease."[2] In a vicious cycle, for black men the emblematic status as "all that is dangerous" too often becomes internalized and then egested in self-destructive behaviors that reinforce the pejorative characterization of black male deviance and difference. Accordingly, Wilson's representation of black men addresses their historical stigmatization within American society as well as their internalized oppression. In his foreword to a book on black masculinity, Wilson notes: "And now the only duty our young men seem ready to imagine is to their maleness with its reckless display of braggadocio, its bright intelligence, its bold and foolish embrace of hate and happenstance."[3] His comment suggests that young black men self-inflict these demonizing representations.

In response, Wilson marshals representation to promote a view of black men that operates in contradistinction to the mainstream perception of black men as a problem. Part of Wilson's project is to re-present black masculinity so that it becomes a site of self-determination, pride, self-respect, and historical consciousness. The loss of historical awareness, Wilson believes and his (w)righting implies, has led to a self-destructive image of black masculinity, the devaluation of black life and the escalation of black-on-black violence. Rather than imaging their maleness within these limits and "reckless displays," Wilson's express purpose is to reform the representation and therefore the perception of black masculinity. He writes,

> What we lack is the ability to give the ideas and images we have of ourselves widespread presence, to give them legitimacy and credence in the same manner in which the debasing and degenerating images that provide other Americans with a basis for their fear and dislike of us are legitimized by constant repetition through myriad avenues of broadcast and dissemination.[4]

Evident here is his cognizance of the politics and power of representation and a desire for African Americans to control the representational economies that impact not only how they are read but how they read themselves.

Wilson's attempt to reimagine black masculinity implicitly points to the troubled and troubling risk of representing masculinity as a monolithic identity category. Homi Bhabha, quoting Herbert Sussman, observes that masculinity "is a 'problematic in which the governing terms are contradiction, conflict and anxiety.'"[5] The term *masculinity* comes extremely loaded and invariably involves dynamics of power, privilege, and sexuality. The insertion of *black* before the term *masculinity* must complicate it by foregrounding the dimension of race in relation to manhood, positing that they both inform each other. Conse-

"I ain't got no money. I'm trying to get some." Piano Lesson, *Yale Repertory Theatre, 1987, with Lou Myers (Wining Boy), Rocky Carroll (Lymon), Samuel L. Jackson (Boy Willie), and Carl Gordon (Doaker). (Photograph by Gerry Goodstein.)*

quently, our understanding of black masculinity and its representations in Wilson's twentieth-century cycle depends on investigating the interactions between race and gender, and the ways that his black men operate within existent socio-economic structures and internalized constraints that impinge on their ability to act or, as David Marriott suggests, even to dream.[6]

Fathers, Sons, and Bigness

I begin with a discussion of fathers and sons because of the weight that Wilson assigns to this relationship, with its transmission of legacy and primogeniture—conventions that historically apply to men—and with its power to model masculinity. Marriott posits that the "problematic" status of black manhood is a critical inheritance of sons from their black fathers:

> Hence the mark that the black father leaves, a mark that is both ineffaceable and irremediable. Typed, in the wider culture as the cause of, and cure for, black men's "failure." His father's apparently lost, and untellable, life is the story that the son must find and narrate if he is to begin to understand how and why, blackness has come to represent an inheritable fault.[7]

Marriott argues that because of their particular heritage, African American sons have historically experienced a driving need to discover and tell their fathers' story. Correspondingly, for so many of Wilson's male characters—from Cory's struggle with larger-than-life Troy, to Booster's battle with his father Becker in *Jitney*—the ability to move onward in life depends upon the complex redemption of their fathers, both present and absent. Wilson's personal history with the two father figures in his life—August Kittel, the German baker who fathered Wilson and his five siblings and David Bedford, the step-father and troubled ex-con who became a prototype for Troy Maxson in *Fences*—parallels this central theme.

The playwright's invocation of this troubled and troubling father in his dramas engages and revises narrative tropes common to American domestic realism. The redefinition of family in American family drama and the reordering of the problematic father figure are critical factors in Wilson's overall strategy of African American re-evolution. Charles R. Lyons notes that "the problematic father becomes a staple of American realism as evidenced by *Long Days Journey into Night, All My Sons, Death of a Salesman* and *The Glass Menagerie*."[8] In each of these plays the stability of the family, the sons in particular, is threatened by the earlier transgressions of the fathers. The common narrative result is the fragmentation and dysfunctionality of the family unit. The family members must suffer psychologically as well as materially as a result of the father's actions. Lyons situates Sam Shepard's three "family" plays, *Buried Child, Curse of the Starving Class,* and *True West,* in relation to this dramatic continuum. He argues that these three plays "articulate the processes of exorcising the presence of the father, and assimilating his energy by appropriating self-consciously both the aesthetic conventions of realism and the archetypal paradigms in which we perceive the relationships of fathers and sons."⁹ Wilson's dramaturgy however, alters this trajectory. While his plays repeat the narrative trope of the problematic father, they do not attempt to absent the father or to vilify him for the family's tragic demise. Instead, even as they reveal the faults and frailties of the father, the underlying objective is to reconcile and restore the position of the patriarch within the fabric of the family, precisely because the black father seems so apparently lost. Historically in America, black men have systematically been absented from the systems of power, wealth, and privilege that control, construct, and maintain the American capitalist patriarchy. They have had little voice in their representation and have existed as property, absented by legislation, even from their humanity. Starting with the premise of black absence, Wilson considers how we can recuperate the black father as a presence in images of masculinity. In addition, Wilson conceives of the family not as a nuclear unit as in *Death of a Salesman* or *Long Day's Journey into Night,* but rather as the extended family unit, common to African American culture.

Wilson's recovery of black masculinity through the problematic patriarch finds particular manifestation in *Fences.* Wilson claims that he "started *Fences* with the image of a man standing in his yard with a baby in his arms."¹⁰ Beginning with this picture, Wilson sought to subvert the dominant culture's representations of African American men as irresponsible, absentee fathers. Wilson creates Troy Maxson, a larger-than-life figure, who feels an overwhelming sense of duty and responsibility to his family. Ironically, it is around his concepts of duty and responsibility, however, that the character of Troy is problematized. Troy's worldview is myopic. With an impenetrable resolve, he perceives familial values only from his perspective. Troy's self-involved concept of familial duty and responsibility prevents him from seeing the harm he causes, the pain his decisions inflict on other family members.

Through a series of retrospective stories performed by Troy, Wilson reveals that Troy has been warped by resentment of the forces of social and economic oppression, and thus in turn he also becomes a warping presence for his son. Troy came along before Jackie Robinson broke the color line in professional baseball and therefore—despite his prodigious talents that he unabashedly describes—he never had the opportunity to play in the major leagues. "There ought not never have been no time called too early! . . . Come telling me I come along too early. If you could play . . . then they ought to have let you play" (*Fences*, 1.1.112). Wilson also uses Troy's oracular moments of retrospection to disclose the influence that his prior relationship with his own father now exacts on his relationship with Cory. "Sometimes I wish I hadn't known my daddy. He ain't cared about no kids. A kid to him wasn't nothing. All he wanted was for you to learn how to walk so he could start you to working" (1.4.147). Troy relates how he was physically beaten by his father and forced to strike out on his own. "Right there is where I became a man . . . at fourteen years of age" (1.4.148). During the course of the play, Cory must undergo a similar rite of passage into manhood. Repeating the family history, Cory physically confronts his father, is beaten by Troy and forced to leave his father's house. The altercation is represented as a distinguishing mark of coming of age but in its repetition of behavior patterns by father and son also suggests the son is irrevocably caught in the cycle of history.

Wilson again tackles the question of ambivalent paternal legacy in his second Pulitzer Prize–winning play and his second family drama, *The Piano Lesson*. According to Wilson, "The real issue is the piano, the legacy. How are you going to use it?"[11] It is around the piano that the past's impact on the present is contested. From the outset of *Piano Lesson*, as Boy Willie attempts to persuade his sister of the inherent logic of his vision for the piano, he invokes the spirit of his father as an element in his persuasive strategy. His absent father is another problematic patriarch of sorts, and the family must decide how to best honor his memory. Boy Willie maintains, "If my daddy had seen where he could have traded that piano in for some land of his own, it wouldn't be sitting up here now. He spent his whole life farming on somebody else's land. I ain't gonna do that."[12] The father was absented from their lives after an act of resistance, when he removed the piano from the home of the white landowner Sutter. Boy Willie perceives himself as following in his father's footsteps, and sees farming as the "family business." In addition, he imagines himself in a position to right the wrongs of racism that restricted his father's economic and social mobility. He believes that he is now able to purchase land that his grandfather worked as a slave and where his father toiled as a sharecropper, an option that was never available to his father. Caught up in an agrarian vision of the American capitalist dream, Boy Willie associates the acquisition of wealth and property with masculinity. He argues fiercely to Berniece that selling the piano and buying Sutter's land is an assertion of manhood that his father would understand. "Now, the kind of man my daddy was he would have understood that" (*Piano Lesson*, 1.2.51). The rite of passage appears modeled and warranted by the father, but Boy Willie misunderstands the transmission of the father's legacy.

Boy Willie seeks to capitalize literally on his father's legacy, which includes his father's prior interactions with white men; in contrast, Hedley in *Seven Guitars* carries with him a distrust for and a resistance to white power systems as a consequence of lessons learned from his father. Through retrospective dialogue, Hedley reveals that he questioned his father's complacency in the face of white oppression: "I go home and my daddy he sitting there and he big and black and tired taking care of the white man's horses and I say, 'How come you not like Toussaint L'Ouverture, why you do nothing?' And he kick me with him boot in my mouth" (2.4.86–87). Haunted by this memory of disparaging his father and his father's violent response, Hedley seeks his father's forgiveness, but his father dies before he can give it. In a rant that testifies to the black man's lack of value within the white social system, Hedley angrily reports that his father, who was farrier for the white doctor, died while waiting for the same white doctor to attend him—as with the slashed young Levee in *Ma Rainey,* wherein a white doctor also fails to aid a black man. Hedley relates how some time after his father's death, his father appeared to him in a dream: "Then my father come to me in a dream and he say he was sorry he died without forgiving me my tongue and that he would send Buddy Bolden with some money for me to buy a plantation" (*Seven Guitars,* 2.4.87). The absent father becomes present in this vision, as a critical element in the delusions of grandeur and redemption that Hedley passionately clings to and that motivate his eventually tragic actions.

Obsessively, Hedley desires to prove himself a "big man" in his father's eyes. "I always want to be a big man. Like Jesus Christ was a big man. He was the son of the Father. I too. I am the son of my father" (*Seven Guitars,* 2.1.67–68). Hedley's notion of "bigness" conflates racial liberation, economic prosperity, spirituality ascendancy, and even masculine bravado as he sees himself one day as the "King" of a large plantation or at least the father of son who like a black Moses would "lead the black man out of bondage" (*Seven Guitars,* 2.1.68). Wilson repeats and revises this concept of bigness—with its implicitly sexualized reference to the size of the phallus—as a metaphor for masculinity in the interactions of fathers and sons throughout the cycle. On one hand, the metaphor is rather simple, when one is young and small, the father is big, even figuratively outsized due to the son's adoration. Bigness represents a matter of perspective then, not actual size. In Wilson's drama, as the son grows into manhood, the son must eventually displace the father by cutting him down to scale. In *Fences,* both Troy and Cory stand up to their fathers only when they no longer fear these formerly towering figures. The confrontation with the father not only thrusts them into manhood but prompts them to constantly negotiate with the father's absence and presence within their own sense of self.

Unfortunately the father is often diminished in relation to the son because of his abasement before the "white" man. The prodigal son Booster in *Jitney,* in keeping with Hedley, Troy, and Cory, first imagines his father as big and wants to be just like him. "I would just look at you and wonder how you could be that big. I wanted to be like that. I would go to school and try to make myself big" (1.4.56). Then, as with Hedley, his vision of his father changes when he sees how his father reacts to his mistreatment by a white man.

> You came out on the porch and he [Mr. Rand] started shouting and cussing and threatening to put us out on the street where we belonged. I was waiting for you to tell him to shut up . . . to get off our porch. But you just looked at him and promised him you would have the money next month. Mama came to the door and Mr. Rand kept shouting and cussing. I looked at mama . . . she was trying to get in the house . . . and I looked at you . . . and you had got smaller . . . The longer he shouted the smaller you got. . . . When we went back to the barbershop you didn't seem so big no more. You was the same size as everybody else. You was just another man in the barbershop. That's when I told myself that if I ever got big I wouldn't let nothing make me small.
>
> (1.4.57)

In Booster's young eyes, his father's size is racially indexed: at first, larger than life within the race—amongst the other black men in the barbershop—and then, conversely shrunken in relation to the white landlord. After the encounter with the landlord, back in the barbershop, the father becomes not simply resized but reduced to "just another," in Booster's words, diminished to the size and status of all the other black men in the barbershop. Writing on Frederick Douglass's *Narrative*, Gwen Berger notes that there persists "a homoerotic structure that requires enslaved African-American men to first identify with, then to desire, and to always fear white men."[13] Operating in a post-slavery economy, observing the downsizing of his father, Booster revises Berger's logic. He not only does not identify with the landlord, he does not desire or even fear him. Rather, the process of his father's emasculation galvanizes Booster's refusal to allow anyone to "make him small" as he rises into manhood.

In contradistinction to his father, Booster attempts to achieve bigness through co-optation of white license. First, he becomes involved with a white girl: "Then when I met Susan McKnight and found out her daddy was the vice-president of Gulf Oil . . . that's when I got big. That made me a big man" (*Jitney*, 1.4.57). Booster believes that his association with this white girl brings him status and power through her whiteness. However, this is not actually an achievement of bigness but a phantasm, as Booster's relationship with the white girl is always and already tenuous due to their unequal access to wealth and to the historic tensions of this interracial association. In dating this white woman, the nineteen-year-old Booster steps into a historically charged and critically overdetermined space of black men and white women and interracial desire, a space "heaped with myth," as Amiri Baraka (LeRoi Jones) notes in *Dutchman*, which outlines the seduction and destruction by the white Lula of the black Clay. When caught in the act of lovemaking by her father, the girl believes her own economic access is threatened and invokes the racist and historically destructive image of black male as deviant, sexual predator, an image she knows her father is more than willing to accept. She exercises her historic privilege: she cries rape. Wronged but enlightened by this false accusation, Booster walks onto the porch of his white mistress, pulls out a pistol, and murders her. Wilson reverses the inaction of Baraka's Clay in *Dutchman*, who dies at the hands of the white temptress, Lula. With his gun, the potent symbol of the male phallus, in his hand, Booster fires in attempt to reclaim his masculinity, a self-image deflated by her lie. Booster explains to his father:

> Then when she told that lie on me that's when I woke up. That's when I realized I wasn't big from the inside. I wasn't big on my own. When she told that lie it made me small. I wanted to do something that said I wasn't just another nigger . . . that I was Clarence Becker. I wanted to

make them remember my name. And I thought about you standing there and getting small and Mr. Rand shouting and Susan McKnight shouting out that lie and I realized it was my chance to make the Beckers big again.

(*Jitney*, 1.4.57)

Booster believes that by breaking the rules of the white power structure, by striking back against its oppression, he can become big. His act, however misguided, is one of resistance against the laws, the mores, the social institutions of the white patriarchy, even as it seems to fulfill the white myth of black male deviance.

Like the appropriately named protagonist in Richard Wright's classic novel *Native Son* (1940), "Bigger" Thomas, whose sense of importance in the world grew after his murder and decapitation of white heiress Mary Dalton, Booster presumed his own stature would swell to bigness through this violent outburst, that boldly declared he was not "another nigger." In Wright's *Native Son*, Bigger's murder of Mary, his dissection and burning of her body, his subsequent ransom plan all similarly constitute acts that express his frustration at his exclusion as a black man from the American power system—acts that ultimately incarcerate and yet fleetingly liberate him. Paradoxically, only through these destructive deeds does Bigger claim to find some meaning in life. Before his execution Bigger passionately confesses to his lawyer Max with new awareness, "What I killed for must've been good. It must have been good! When a man kills it's for something. . . . I didn't know I was alive in this world until I felt things hard enough to kill for 'em."[14] Bigger's words announce a new consciousness. His feeling alive as black man in this white world comes directly after he kills a white woman. Still, even as Wright's figure of Bigger metaphorically strikes out against the symbols of white rule and its limits on black masculinity, he also reinscribes the image of the black man as uncivilized violent brute that must be caged and controlled. This image of Bigger Thomas has subsequently morphed into the Willie Horton ads in George Bush's 1988 presidential campaign and to a darkened representation of O. J. Simpson on the cover of *Time* on the eve of his trial of the century in July 1995. Suzan-Lori Parks in *The Death of the Last Black Man in the Whole Entire World* (1989–92) comments on the expanding image of the black brute Bigger Thomas in her creation of the character "And Bigger and

Bigger" who desires simply to "return to the book from whence he came."[15] Booster too wants to return from whence he came, to the love of his father. So he seeks out his father, wizened after his prison sentence. He now understands that his murderous act does not bring bigness, nor does it contradict the image of him as black criminal, but rather reaffirms his danger and his deviance.

Booster and other Wilson young men, his native sons and misguided warriors, repeat and revise Bigger Thomas's position as both victim and victimizer within the particularly American politics of representation. In his treatise "How Bigger was Born," Wright explains that he had encountered many Bigger Thomases in his life, men who innately sensed the injustices of the social system that constricted their opportunities and who then struck out against it through violence or sullen rage. For Wright, Bigger is a product of his time, a "native son" with an absented father, desirous of the advantages that America holds for its sons but unable to achieve them. "He is product of a dislocated society; he is a dispossessed and disinherited man; he is all of this, and he lives amid the greatest plenty on earth and he is looking and feeling for a way out."[16] For these Bigger Thomases, according to Wright, the desire for "a way out" finds expression in their isolation from other blacks and their resentment of whites; it becomes manifested in outbursts of violence or other forms of resistance. However, their rebellion is nascent, lacking in sophistication and social awareness and thus not fully articulated or carried out. "I am not saying that I heard any talk of revolution in the South when I was a kid there. But I did hear the lispings, the whispers, the mutters which some day, under one stimulus or another, will surely grow into open revolt unless the conditions which produce Bigger Thomases are changed."[17] Wright muses, "Who will be the first to touch off these Bigger Thomases?"[18] Wilson asks a similar question with his young men whom he calls his "warrior spirits," and to varying degrees they express self-awareness and powers of self-determination that he again connects to their interpretation of the father's fraught legacy.

Sterling of *Two Trains Running* is just such a young warrior in search of direction, and of the proper articulation of his revolutionary energies. Like Bigger Thomas and Booster, Sterling finds momentary glimmers of bigness through crime. He states that robbing a bank "made me feel strong too. Like I had everything under control. I did until they arrested me" (1.3.48). Sterling understands the unequal distribution of power and the burden that earlier generations of black men had to endure and as a consequence desires a different outcome for himself. Corresponding to Wilson's other young warriors, he learned these lessons through his observation of the father figure in his life. Although an orphan, Sterling lived in a foster home where he witnessed the lifestyle of Mr. Johnson:

> He get up every morning at six o'clock. Sunday too . . . Now what he got?
> . . . He got a raggedy house with some beat-up furniture. Can't buy no house cause he can't get a loan. Now that sound like a hard working man. Good. Clean. Honest. Upright. He work thirty years in the mill and ain't even got a union card. You got to work six months straight. They lay him off for two weeks every five and a half months. He got to call the police after he cleanup the fish market so they can let him out of the building. Make sure he don't steal anything. What they got? Two pound of catfish? There got to be something else. I ain't sure I want to do all that.
> (*Two Trains Running*, 2.4.100–101)

Sterling paints Mr. Johnson as a man of responsibility and integrity whose ability to achieve for his family is severely limited by the constraints placed upon him by white hegemony. Sterling within the world of black America 1969 is not willing to compromise himself in this same manner. He wants something more. Yet Sterling, like Wright's Bigger Thomas, does not possess sufficient political awareness to move his concerns into a strategy of activism. While he attends Malcolm X rallies, his politics have not evolved beyond rhetoric into action.

Wilson highlights the differences between the rhetoric and reality of politics in an encounter Sterling has with an older "father figure," Memphis, the restaurant owner. Memphis disparages Sterling for his attendance at a Malcolm X rally and his support of "black power niggers."

> I don't know how these niggers think sometimes. Talking about black power with their hands and their pockets empty. You can't do nothing without a gun. Not in this day and time. That the only kind of power the white man understand. . . . These niggers around here talking about they black and beautiful. Sound like they trying to convince themselves. You got to think you ugly to run around shouting you beautiful. You don't hear me say that. Hell, I know I look nice.
> (*Two Trains Running*, 1.2.42–43)

Memphis attacks the advocates of black power for not understanding the actual mechanisms of power and for not developing concrete strategies to effect change. Paradoxically, Memphis uses rhetoric similar to that pronounced by the Black Power movement to denounce it: "You can't do nothing without a gun. Not in this day and time. That the only kind of power the white man understand." In Memphis's strategy, however, he proposes not violent overthrow but self-determination, a strategy of meeting force with force in order to control black destiny. By the play's end, Sterling begins to find direction for his energies, rage, and desire. His final act of breaking Lutz's window and stealing a ham for Hambone's casket serves as a symbol of moving beyond talk to active black resistance. Ironically active black resistance takes the form of fulfilling white fears of black degeneracy.

In *King Hedley II,* the title character, another one of Wilson's misguided young warriors, strikes out in the 1980s, in a world seemingly devoid of meaning, in a rage-filled attempt to define himself. He too seeks to follow after the man he believes to be his father, Hedley, another patriarch with a problem endemic to the African American family so historically sundered by slavery. Repeating both the cycle of black-on-black violence and the desire for size and value, King relates that he, like his surrogate father Hedley, killed another black man, Pernell, because he too wanted to be a big man. According to King, "That's why I killed Pernell. If you get to the bottom line . . . I want everybody to know that King Hedley II was here. And I want everybody to know, just like my daddy, that you can't fuck with me" (1.3.58). His mother, Ruby, reveals the similarity between King the son and Hedley the surrogate father who murdered another black man—one who refused to call him King. "King just like Hedley. Hedley had his own way about him. He wanted to be somebody and couldn't figure out how" (2.3.78). King has the desire to swell and grow into his own identity but is thwarted by social limitations.

One of the ways King tries to "figure out how" to make himself somebody is by controlling how his racial body is read. To King, murdering Pernell served as revenge for the long, unattractive scar that Pernell cut into the side of his face. The scar marks King, further highlighting his black difference. If black men are symbolically and physically marked by a white society that demonizes their color and visibility, then King is hypervisible, hyperproblematic through the powerful signifier that is his scar. As such the act of killing Pernell brings meaning to the scar and ironic commentary on his inherently marked, inherently deviant, ontologically criminal status. "But I figure that scar got to mean something. I can't take it off. It's part of me now. I figure it's got to mean something. As long as Pernell was still walking around it wasn't nothing but a scar. I had to give it some meaning" (*King Hedley II*, 2.2.74–75). And yet even if the act of killing Pernell brings the scar meaning, it exposes King's insecurities and abject status that run much deeper than the surface. King rages against a world that has devalued him, a world in which he cannot discern the meaning of his father's legacy or achieve the measures of masculinity. It is this anxiety that drives Hedley to crazily appeal to Ruby to father his child. Correspondingly, King—desperate to find a compensatory sign of his manhood—turns to the biological, the malecentric authority of paternity. He tells his wife Tonya that fathering a child will confirm his place in the world and his continuance. But Tonya, fearing the inherent dangers of bringing another black boy into a chaotic, senseless, violent environment, plans an abortion. King finds his position all the more desperate and dislocated when Elmore reveals his true birthright, that Hedley is not his real father.

While the sons crave radical bigness and social upheaval, their fathers find that the responsibility of and providing for family are measures of masculinity that demand compromises and compel alternative expressions of resistance. Evidencing the generational difference between his strategy of black survival and that of his son, Becker perceives his inaction in the face of his shouting white landlord, his complacency with his mistreatment by the white mill workers union, not as accommodationist, but rather as necessary responses that enable him to maintain his position and to provide for his family. Booster protests that his father should be proud of him for "being a warrior. For dealing with the world in ways that you didn't or couldn't or wouldn't," but Becker vehemently responds, "you trying to say that it's all my fault because I didn't knock Mr. Rand on his ass so I could keep a roof over your head. So you wouldn't have to sleep in the street, in the cold and snow" (*Jitney*, 1.4.57). Placating the white patriarchy, Becker maintains, has made it possible for him to perform the masculine role of breadwinner and to fulfill his obligations as father to his family. The time is not right, he argues, for another response.

For the fathers Becker and Troy, the fragility of their own masculinity within the white patriarchy complicates their dreams of their sons' development. Like other fathers, they want their sons to have a better life, and yet they also ironically keep their sons small. Rose confides to Cory that his "daddy wanted him to be everything he wasn't . . . and at the same time he tried to make you into everything he was" (Fences 2.5). Embittered by his experiences with racism in baseball, Troy determines to prevent his "boy from getting hurt over playing no sports." At the same time, Cory's possible success in sport has the potential to diminish Troy's own achievement, and so Cory's later attack, that Troy was "[a]fraid [Cory] was going to be better," stings with a ring of truth. The son's growth reflects on the father and puts the father's own precarious manhood at risk. Quoting James Baldwin, Marriott maintains that " 'If one cannot risk oneself, then one is simply incapable of giving.' Giving, like dreaming, then becomes an art of risk for some black men."[19] Wilson's father's struggle with the giving and the "art of risk." On his son's return from prison, Becker, still battling to reconcile with his own relation to the white power structure, cannot give his son the forgiveness and love he desires. Earlier, rather than chance eviction, Becker explains that he endured Mr. Rand's abuse with the faith that someday when grown Booster would fight his battles for him. The public shame of Booster's murderous act instead makes him feel small and causes him to disown his son—perhaps when his son needs him most. With their own masculinity at risk, the desire to protect the fathers' status comes in conflict with the need of the sons for the fathers' validation.

Thus, the continued process into manhood for both Cory and Booster means confronting the psychological scars left from his father. Buffeted by his father's seeming dismissal of his chance to meet with a college football recruiter, Cory asks his father, "How come you ain't never liked me?" Troy responds,

> Like you? . . . You about the biggest fool I ever saw. It's my job! My responsibility! You my flesh and blood. Not cause I like you! Cause it's my duty to take care of you. I owe a responsibility to you! Let's get this straight right here . . . before it go along any further . . . I ain't got to like you. . . . Don't you try and go through life worrying about if somebody like you or not. You best be making sure they doing right by you.
>
> (1.3.137)

Without sentimentality, Troy attempts to educate Cory about the harsh realities of his world.[20] Troy's experiences as a black man, coupled with the lessons he has learned from his father, have taught him that even family relationships are not bound by kinship or affection but duty and responsibility. Unfortunately, his message bruises and scrapes Cory below the skin even as it works to harden his exterior. Wilson compounds Cory's internal anguish in the final scene between father and son, when Cory, no longer in fear of his father, stands up to him, is beaten by him and forced to leave his father's house. During the battle, Troy disavows Cory's status as his son: "Nigger! That's what you are. You just another nigger on the street to me!" (2.4.180). Both men hurt each other more with their cutting words than with their fists, but even more harmful is Troy's refusal of his son through this appeal to the racially pejorative epithet "nigger."

Booster's encounter with his father, Becker, in *Jitney* is equally bruising. As each man expresses his own loss, his own particular sense of the past and perspectives on their relationship, each fails to communicate with the other or to achieve any reconciliation. The son reaches out to a father that neglected him in a time of particular need and misunderstanding, but his father cannot reach back. Echoing Troy, Becker tells Booster, "You are my son. I helped to bring you into this world. But this moment on . . . I'm calling the deal off. You ain't nothing to me, boy. You just another nigger on the street" (*Jitney,* 1.4.60). These words not only signify on Troy's rebuke of Cory in *Fences,* but are earlier stated by Booster when he explains that in his act of murder he "wanted to do something that said [he] wasn't just another nigger" (Jitney 1.1.57). In each case the position of "another nigger on the street" is one of racial anonymity. It is a space that is powerless and without any access to the privileges of family. "Another nigger" status is a construction, even a phantasm, constituted by actions and perceptions of those actions. "Another nigger," then, is an absence, a lack not included within the particular world of Troy or Becker. It is a site of denial and repudiation of the ties that bind.

Wilson, however, moves Booster and Becker beyond "another nigger" status to a different understanding of their own identity, their shared connections, and toward an alternative perception of masculinity. Their rapprochement does not occur face to face, and yet the communication is dialectic. Each learns lessons from the other: as the father's spirit lives on in the son, Booster learns (his)tory. Jolted by his reunion with his son, Becker decides that he can no longer wait on the future, but in 1977 must fight now for change against the forces of urban renewal.

> I told myself that's alright my boy's coming. He's gonna straighten it out. I put it on someone else. I took it off of me and put it on someone else. I told myself as long as I could do that then I could just keep going along and making excuses for everybody. But I'm through making excuses for everybody including myself. I ain't gonna pass it on. I say we stay here.
>
> (*Jitney*, 2.2.85)

Becker decides to act for himself, to be his own man and not to compromise his position. Booster too evolves in his understanding of his father and his appreciation of his father's stature. After he learns of Becker's sudden death, Booster, the ex-con son, immediately turns to answering the telephone at the gypsy cab station. He symbolically and defiantly assumes his father's position. Becker and Booster are able to forgive and let go even as they hold on to memory. The distance built up over twenty years of imprisonment dissolves. Tragically this resolution comes without their having the opportunity to tell each other of their mutual forgiveness. The influence of the father once battled, mentally if not physically overcome, still remains an indelible part of the son.

Cory attempts to escape from his father, to "say no just once" to this overwhelming authority by refusing to go to his father's funeral:

> Papa was like a shadow that followed you everywhere. It weighed on you and sunk into your flesh. It would wrap around you and lay there until you couldn't tell which one was you anymore. That shadow digging in your flesh. Trying to crawl in. Trying to live through you. Everywhere I looked, Troy Maxson was staring back at me . . . hiding under the bed . . . in the closet. I'm just saying I've got to find a way to get rid of that shadow, Mama.
>
> (*Fences*, 2.5.188–89)

The words he uses to explain this desire to his mother, Rose, are hauntingly reminiscent of ones Troy employs to describe the power of his father: "part of that cutting down was when I got to the place where I could feel him kicking in my blood and knew the only thing that separated us was a matter of a few years" (1.4.149). Rose impresses on Cory

"Hey Pop . . . I just stopped by to say hi. See how you doing." Jitney, Center Theatre Group, Mark Taper Forum, 2000, with Paul Butler (Becker) and Carl Lumbly (Booster). (Photograph by Craig Schwartz.)

that he has no other recourse but to work with the legacy left him by his father. "That shadow wasn't nothing but you growing into yourself. You either got to grow into it or cut it down to fit you" (2.5.189). To translate this sartorial metaphor of the father's shadow to the historical situation of black people in America: the heritage of slavery is one that can also not be escaped but must either be embodied or resized. Wilson writes in a poem that precedes *Fences*:

> When the sins of our fathers visit us
> We do not have to play host.
> We can banish them with forgiveness
> As God, in His Largeness and Laws.
> *(Fences, 95)*

The message is that we can effect change and learn from the past even as we are shaped by it. The spirit of love and forgiveness represent a different sort of size and bigness and when put in place can represent an alternative view of masculinity. Wilson's cycle suggests that the tensions between father and son that contribute to the anxieties of black masculinity must be addressed by confronting the past, finding room for forgiveness as well as resistance, re-membering the "father's story" in ways that allow one to hold on but also to let go.

The Politics of Prison

The experience of prison is another recurring theme in the Wilson cycle that marks the problematic stature of Wilson's black men. Prison becomes virtually an offstage site for the rite of passage into black masculinity. Upon his arrival on the scene in *Two Trains,* Sterling announces to the gathered community of regulars at Memphis's restaurant, "I just got out the penitentiary." Troy tells his son Lyons in *Fences* that he and Bono met and cemented their friendship while in prison. Later Lyons must receive a special release from "the workhouse," where he is doing time for passing bad checks, in order to attend his father's funeral. Boy Willie, his uncles Doaker and Wining Boy, as well as his friend Lymon in *Piano Lesson* all have spent time on the Parchman Prison Farm, just as in *Seven Guitars* Floyd, Canewell, and Red have all done time in the workhouse. In a humorous tautology Canewell, a "typically" lazy, worthless black man, finds himself arrested and jailed for the racial crime of "laziness and [they] give me thirty days" (1.3.23). Wolf relates in *Two Trains Running* that he would "Give you a dollar for every nigger you find that ain't been to jail . . . I been to jail. Stayed down there three months. They kept me down there in the county jail for three months. Ain't done nothing but walk down the street" (1.3.54). Incarceration for these men is not only unjustified but inevitable and inescapable, an element in their common development.[21]

Prison in Wilson's work is part of the greater system of white hegemony that constrains and seeks to control black men. Michel Foucault in *Discipline and Punish* discusses Jeremy Bentham's architectural concept of a Panopticon, a system in which each prisoner could be watched by a central observer in a tower but the prisoners could neither see each other nor the central observer.[22] The central observer therefore functions as a powerful unmarked, absent presence maintaining the order within the prison and surveying everything and everyone within sight. While the observer is invisible, the prisoners are marked and visible. Foucault argues, "Visibility is a trap,"[23] but visibility for black men becomes racialized. Indeed, the hypervisibility of black men, inside as well as outside of prison, makes them all the more subject to systems of patriarchal surveillance and authority. Frustrated by his unwarranted arrest, Wolf concludes in *Two Trains Running* that as a result of this experience he "learned to watch where I was going at all times. Cause you always under attack" (1.3.54). Attacked by and trapped within this system of constant white surveillance, the power, access, and agency of black men becomes severely restricted. The white producer and manager economically govern the recording session in *Ma Rainey*. The white-controlled city government in *Two Trains Running* even has the ability through the laws of eminent domain to seize Memphis's property. At issue for Wilson's black men is whether they internalize this white hegemony or, as Toledo puts it in *Ma Rainey*, whether they become "spooked up with the white man" (1.56). Also in question is how they confront the "mark" of incarceration, a different form of forced servitude that brands them as delinquent "leftovers from history." The "de-markation" of prison stamped upon these men by the white patriarchy becomes something that Wilson's men must strive to overcome; they must struggle to beat the system.[24]

The notion of freedom here is critical because prison represents the opposite of freedom: One is free in inverse relation to one's imprisonment. If part of Wilson's project in defining a liberatory masculinity is to construct a place where black men are in fact free, then a critical question is how they can remove the vestiges, the markings of prison, once outside of its walls and constraints. Are black men within the general society still systematized, watched, and controlled by a "panoptic" unseen white observer, as they are within the prison walls? Are they truly free? To what degree do Wilson's men specifically and African Americans more generally still bear the scars of the imprisonment of slavery? Within each historical period of his cyclical plays Wilson recontextualizes his answer to these questions. His responses confront the external manifestations of white patriarchal control as well as the myriad of ways black men have internalized their oppression.

Through symbolic acts of rule breaking, Wilson's men assert their masculinity and attempt to throw off the negative stigmatization of enslavement. In his first-act narrative history of the piano, Doaker reveals that years after slavery, Papa Boy Charles, Berniece's and Boy Willie's father, remained obsessed with the thought of reclaiming the piano from the Sutter family. "He be talking about taking it out of Sutter's house. Say it was the story of our whole family and as long as Sutter had it . . . he had us. Say we was still in slavery" (*Piano Lesson*, 1.2.45). While no longer physically bound to the slave master, Wilson argues through Doaker that African Americans can remain spiritually and psychologically imprisoned by the dominant culture unable to express or discover their inherent "African-ness." Thus, the Charles' reclamation of the piano becomes a declaration of self-determination. Moreover, it is a particularly malecentric act, undertaken by the Charles men against the power of the white patriarchy and the white Father-in-Law, the absent/present figure of Sutter, who eventually materializes in the play as a ghost. The women, Mama Ola and Berniece, find very different gendered patterns of resistance. By stealing the piano, these men beat the system and assert a counterclaim on what constitutes ownership and the rights of property. This declaration is not without consequences, as it results in the death of Papa Boy Charles, who is set on fire in the boxcar of the train called the Yellow Dog by a white mob. Still, the recuperation of the piano symbolizes a step toward freedom and a strike against injustice.

Such incidents in Wilson's dramaturgy compel us to ask when breaking the Laws of the "white father" is just. How do we relate this theft to other acts of lawbreaking in Wilson's work and in African American history? As early as the slave revolts of Denmark Vesey and Nat Turner and escapes along the Underground Railroad by Harriet Tubman, lawbreaking within black history has been celebrated as a means to overcome unjust rules and mistreatment. Martin Luther King, Jr., and black freedom fighters in the 1960s broke Jim Crow laws and went to jail for a "higher" principle of justice, an alternative understanding of right and wrong. And yet there are other manifestations of black criminality within the history of black culture as well that have simultaneously liberated and enslaved black men. Iconic black leader Malcolm X found himself in jail early in his life not for higher principles of justice but for "hustling." His early career as a small-time pimp, and petty thief, a time when he was, as he states in his autobiography, an "uncouth, wild young Negro,"[25] led to his eventual repudiation of this lifestyle as well as to what historian Robin D. G. Kelley calls his "brutal exploitation of women, . . . his downward descent and subsequent prison sentence."[26] At the same time, his experiences in the hypermasculine world and illicit economy of hustling, Kelley points out, "'schooled' him to a degree in how capitalism worked" and educated him "in knowing what and how the powerful thought."[27] As such the hustling mentality established an alternative image of black masculinity. For black men past and present like Malcolm X, who feel that the system is stacked again them, hustling, beating the system—or in the more contemporary vernacular, "getting over"—can become significant declarations of manhood, of "bigness." With its denigration of wage labor, its defiance of black subservient stereotypes, its distrust for and clever abuse of white authority as well as its strategic location on the margins of society, hustling offers an explicitly subversive and resistant lifestyle. Consequently, Kelley notes, "Unlike nearly all of his contemporaries during the 1960s, he [Malcolm X] was fond of comparing capitalism with organized crime and refused to characterize looting by black working class people as criminal acts. . . . Indeed Malcolm X insisted that dominant notions of criminality and private property only obscure the real nature of social relations."[28] Malcolm X understood the contradictory and complex nature of black criminality and that it possesses the potential to express or repress black resistance.

Like Malcolm X, Wilson is interested in the paradoxes of black criminality and the "real nature of social relations." Thus, while Sterling's breaking into the white butcher Lutz's shop to steal a ham for Hambone's coffin at the end of *Two Trains* is a crime that can return him to jail, more importantly and conversely, it is a gesture that symbolizes the need for social action and black mutuality. Much as the theft of the piano in *Piano Lesson* functions as means to an end, the theft of the ham serves as a symbolic linkage to a higher cause of black social consciousness and resistance to greater crimes of white oppression. Yet Wilson also cites the potential for black male criminality to devolve into individual opportunism and distrust that overtakes any expression of black revolutionary consciousness. Floyd Barton in *Two Trains* robs the loan offices of Metro finance—a robbery that results in the death of another black man, his coconspirator—and is willing to forsake his girlfriend Vera, his friend Canewell, and any other connections to black kinship for the chance to use this money to get him from Pittsburgh to Chicago, where he can record another song. Kelley warns that "hustling by nature was a predatory act that did not discriminate by color."[29] Mister and King hustle cheap refrigerators to unassuming black buyers in *King Hedley II*, but are outhustled at their own game by the older, hardened Elmore, who tricks them into selling him a refrigerator at a highly discounted price. "You got to look at all the angles and when you see a opening that will get you a little advantage . . . you got to take that," Elmore explains (2.2.71). Mister and King later plan and execute a jewelry store robbery. Imprisoned in these inevitably self-destructive patterns of behavior, neither King or Mister can see a way out or understand when Stool Pigeon tells King he's "got the key to the mountain." Floyd's and King's acts of criminality do not build black collectivity or progressive revolutionary action but rather reproduce systems of imprisonment and white "panoptic" observation in a senseless cycle of black-on-black crime, reaffirming the racist stereotype of black criminal pathology. Wilson raises through them serious questions as to the level of black culpability in the reproduction of this culture of violence and denigration of black worth. *Piano Lesson*'s Berniece bemoans the self-imposed tragedy of black masculinity as she chastises her brother Boy Willie, "You, Papa Boy Charles, Wining Boy, Doaker, Crawley . . . you're all alike. All this thieving and killing and thieving and killing. And what it ever lead to? More killing and more thieving. I ain't never seen it come to nothing" (1.2.52).

Given the tragic potential of black criminality to reinscribe black stereotypes and reinforce patterns of control, Wilson's dramaturgy concerns not the world of prison itself but the aftermath, the return of the ex-con. Wilson's men are not recidivists. Once out of prison, they are determined not to go back. Sterling announces he has just gotten out and is not going back to prison. Canewell tells Louise, "They never get me back in the Cook County Jail" (*Seven Guitars*, 1.3.23). Troy explains that time in prison "cured him" of "that robbing stuff." Boy Willie's friend Lymon escapes to Pittsburgh and decides to remain there in order to avoid the clutches of the law and to prevent his being forced to serve out any additional time at the Parchman Prison Farm. Each of these men expresses a desire to be free and remain free. Even as they are indelibly marked by the experience of prison, they refuse to take on the identity of victim or criminal.

In the same way that negotiating the terrors of slavery required coded black performance skills that enabled survival, Wilson's ex-con black men constantly must perform and reinvent themselves in order to remain outside the prison walls. They leave their incarceration and return to the black community with a renewed ability to improvise on a theme, like the blues musician or the trickster figure. Angered by the lack of black drivers on garbage trucks, Troy protests and surprises both the white management and his fellow black workers by taking his case to the garbage worker's union:

> Told him [the white boss, Mr. Rand], "What's the matter, don't I count? You think only white fellows got sense enough to drive a truck? That ain't no paper job! Hell, anybody can drive a truck. How come you got all whites driving and the colored lifting?" He told me, "take it to the union." Well, hell that's what I done!
>
> (*Fences*, 1.1.106)

Later when he has won his case with the union and is made the first black driver, Troy must deflect his friend Bono's interrogation about his lack of a driver's license:

> *Bono:* Do Mr. Rand know you ain't got no driver's license? That's what I'm taking about. I ain't asked if driving was easy. I asked if Mr. Rand know you ain't got no driver's license.
> *Troy:* He ain't got to know. The man ain't got to know my business. Time he find out, I have two or three driver's licenses.
>
> (*Fences*, 1.4.143)

In each case Troy displays a creative and subversive energy, a willingness to not only improvise but to reinvent himself. Paul Carter Harrison associates Troy with the Yoruba trickster figure Eshu.

> Troy has no respect for the limitations imposed on him by a hostile world and thus avoids engaging in cynical devaluations of self-esteem that might reduce him to a victim. Neither does he repress the immutable hostilities of the world. Instead in the spirit of the Yoruba trickster Eshu—who in addition to being guardian of the crossroads, master of style and stylus, and phallic god of procreativity, is also master of mystical barriers—Troy will erect a fence to set the boundaries of his universe, a barrier that serves the dual function of keeping the profane at bay and containing the divine order within his immediate province where, on the heels of hard labor, he engages in weekly payday drinking rituals to signify his sexual prowess and testify to his personal heroics while straddling the brink of despair.[30]

As Harrison indicates, Troy employs the spirit of the trickster in order not to be victimized, to survive in spite of the odds. He reaffirms his masculinity through his performance of tall tales of valiant struggle and his public display of his sexuality. In the Wilson cycle, other men similarly battle against victimization as they desire to define themselves against a system that does not recognize their value. These are men who are not defeated but continue to proclaim their ability to perform and to improvise. Sterling tells Holloway and others in *Two Trains,* "Hey, I can do anything, I told the judge I could do his job. I got enough sense to sit up there and tell right from wrong" (1.3.52). This refrain is picked up again by King in *King Hedley II:* "I go for a job and they say, 'What I can do.' I say 'I can do anything.' . . . I ain't limited to nothing. I can go down there and do Mellon's job. I know how to count money" (1.3.55). In each case ex-cons, who seemingly are without training, education, or employable job skills, profess profound abilities. The limitations to their achievement, thus, are not within them but externally imposed. The fact that they have endured prison, poverty, and neglect has bolstered their masculine bravado, survival instincts, and improvisatory skills, making anything and everything possible.

Present within these moments of improvisation as well as in the attitudes, gestures, and comradeship of Wilson's black men is a sense of style. Given the externally imposed constraints and limitation on black life, style has come to mean more than substance in signifying and defining black masculinity. Wilson writes,

> They were bad. If only in an abstract of style. A language of aesthetics that created its own rules and knew no limits. They styled because that is who they were. The style was not a comment. It was not how they saw themselves. It was who they were, and it was symphonic in its breadth and complexity.[31]

The idea of style and improvisation becomes a way for black men to determine a place for themselves within an oppressive world. Similarly, Ralph Ellison in *Invisible Man* notes that the young black men the Invisible Man observes on the train have a style that is their own: "I stared as they [the young black men] seemed to move like dancers in some kind of funeral ceremony swaying, going forward, their black faces secret, moving slowly down the subway platform, the heavy heel-plated shoes making a rhythmical tapping as they moved."[32] These men display African American cultural signs and symbols in their self-performance that the Invisible Man comes to recognize as an alternative history. It is this alternative history found in blues music, in the particular, idiosyncratic processes of African American style, struggle, and survival of black men, that Wilson seeks to represent in his history cycle. Lost to these native sons are the possibilities and probabilities common to the American Dream, the conventional measures of masculinity. The marking of prison further indoctrinates Wilson's black men in policies of self-hatred and internalized oppression that they must struggle to overcome.

White Men and the Economics of Masculinity

Not only psychically but materially at issue with Wilson's black men is always "the white man" and his power over black lives; the white man is a "problem" in his ability to stunt black growth. Wilson notes that the power of whiteness in black experiences is often unmarked; it does not have to be seen to be felt. White hegemony is

> pressure—an unseen presence and it's pressure from that outside world that continually and constantly pressures on this world of blacks. I know, for instance, I lived in Pittsburgh. I know blacks that have never seen a white man so to speak. They don't go out of the neighborhood. They don't go downtown. They don't have any contact with them. And yet they are very much a real part—a presence in their life because everything

that affects them is done by the society at large—a lot of the society which is dominantly white. And they certainly feel that and respond and react to it.[33]

As Wilson expresses, the "white father" is a continual absence/presence with real economic and social dominion. His earliest plays chronologically—*Gem of the Ocean* set in 1904, *Joe Turner's Come and Gone* set in 1911, and *Ma Rainey's Black Bottom* set in 1927—are the only three plays that actually feature white characters on stage. In these two plays whites are the minority, outnumbered by the black figures, but they are still the ones in power. With these characters and with other invisible white figures, Wilson not only critiques the unmarked power of whiteness but considers what performative strategies his black men must employ to combat this hegemony.

In Wilson's reading of American history, white economic authority has been built through the exploitation of black labor, and Rutherford B. Selig, the white traveling salesman, who frequents Seth's boardinghouse in *Joe Turner*, embodies this reading; he ingratiates himself within black lives even as he capitalizes on them. Selig, whose surname ironically is German for "holy,"[34] has been nicknamed "the People Finder" for his skill in retrieving souls presumably lost. Yet, Selig's people-finding skills are based in practical material methods, not holiness. Bertha, Seth's wife and co-proprietor of the boardinghouse, reprimands Herald Loomis after he enlists Selig in finding his wife.

> You can call him the People Finder if you want to. I know Rutherford Selig carries people away too. He done carried a whole bunch of them away from here. Folks plan on leaving plan by Selig's timing. They wait till he get ready to go, then they hitch a ride on his wagon. Then he charge folks a dollar to tell them where he took them. Now that's the truth of Rutherford Selig. This old People finding business is for the birds. He ain't never find nobody he ain't took away.
>
> (*Joe Turner*, 1.2.240–241)

Bertha intimates that Selig's skills at people finding are built on his manipulation of black lives and their dependency upon his white privilege. Even after slavery, the unequal system of economics still restricts blacks from controlling their movement and subjects them to the directives of Selig.

Interactions with even a poor white salesman such as a Selig reaffirmed black subservience and white authority. Despite her dislike for Selig and his methods, Bertha still serves him biscuits with hospitality at her table, and Seth, her husband, must forge a working relationship with Selig, because he determines the price for the pots and pans that Seth makes and that Selig will sell. Their forced intimacy speaks to the unequal, fragile balance that existed in black-white working relations in this postslavery era. Such a hierarchy reflects on the history of slavery, a history in which Selig proudly places his lineage, as he explains to Loomis after he procures his finder's fee:

> I can't promise anything but we been finders in my family for along time. Bringers and finders. My great-granddaddy used to bring Nigras across the ocean on ships. That wasn't no easy job either. . . . You're in good hands, mister. Me and my daddy have found plenty of Nigras. My daddy, rest his soul, used to find runaway slaves for the plantation bosses. He was the best there was at it . . . After Abraham Lincoln give you all Nigras your freedom papers and with you all looking all over for each other . . . we started finding Nigras for Nigras.
>
> (*Joe Turner*, 1.2.239–240)

Selig boasts of catching "Nigras" in a room full of black boarders completely oblivious to or at least totally unconcerned with their reaction to his use of this degrading term or to his family's participation in their families' enslavement. Instead, Selig offers his legacy of involvement in the slave trade as a sales pitch and as an assurance to Loomis of his ability to produce results. He proudly points out his parasitic profit from black servitude as he recalls how his forefathers capitalized on the American entrepreneurial ethos. They were businessmen who excelled first at selling then at catching blacks; now, with the change in the law, they have been astute enough to adjust their business strategy in ways to still make money by "finding Nigras for Nigras." Thus, through Selig, Wilson reveals how Selig and his white slave-catching family as well as their black counterparts have been mutually constitutive in the economics of slavery.

Wilson equally uses Selig to explore a different heritage of fathers and sons as Selig, like Wilson's black sons, connects his personal identity to lessons of manhood and responsibility learned from his father. In contrast to Wilson's black men, however, the father's Law serves Selig's interests. Selig celebrates his father's savvy in upholding the laws of slavery by capturing and returning black property to white owners. Selig paints a picture of American capitalism reliant upon the continued manipulation of black bodies and their worth. As with his father and "great-granddaddy," his position within the patriarchy, his masculinity depends on the commodification of blackness. This is his legacy.

With the representation of white manhood in *Ma Rainey*, Wilson again presents an economic system controlled by whites, but dependent upon black labor. The two white characters Irvin, Ma Rainey's manager, and Sturdyvant, the white record studio owner, profit from money made in the Race Recording business. In the 1920s, certain labels and independent white record producers found a lucrative market in producing and distributing black music. Irvin and Sturdyvant have no real interest in the culture or the music of African Americans—just in the potential for making money. The first characters we encounter in the play, these men immediately announce their intentions for the recording session as well as their displeasure with Ma and with the nature of the business. Sturdyvant's commitment is to the bottom line and capitalizing on changes in the marketplace. Ma and her band are merely a commodity: "Times are changing. This is a tricky business now. We've got to jazz it up. . . . You know how many records we made in New York?" (*Ma Rainey*, 1.13). The alignment of the set reinforces the power positions of these white men within the economics of masculinity. Sturdyvant sits above the fray in the sound booth separated by a sheet of glass with the recording studio, which Irvin watches over below, and the band room, the domain of the black men is even one floor lower. In this control booth, Sturdyvant is virtually an absent/presence, a symbolic representative of the white patriarchy. Distanced from the others, he observes the proceedings.

Black men in Wilson's cycle must make appeals to visible and invisible white men such as Sturdyvant for the privilege of economic access. Seth, the owner of the boardinghouse in *Joe Turner*, presents what he perceives as a foolproof, lucrative business plan but finds that the white bankers will not loan him the money, despite his certainty that his skills at making pots and pans would produce a profit. "They can't see that. Neither one of them can see that. Now, how much sense it take to see that? All you got to do is be able to count. One man making ten pots is five men making fifty pots. But they can't see that" (*Joe Turner*,

1.3.242). The inability of these white men to see Seth's profitable potential references his own invisibility within their eyes. Ralph Ellison defines black invisibility as "not a matter of biochemical accident to my epidermis" but rather "because of a peculiar disposition of the eyes of those I come in contact. A matter of the construction of their *inner* eyes, those eyes with which they look through their physical eyes upon reality."[35] Ellison exposes an internalized dominant ideology or perception of blackness that denies its value or even its existence. Wilson twists Ellison's invocation of invisibility here. The white bankers can see Seth only as a commodity that benefits them and that they can put to work. They cannot visualize him through their "inner eye" as someone who has the ability to profit for his own interest. As a consequence Seth must consign himself to working the late shift for another white man, Mr. Olowski. While Seth finds himself subject to the backlash of white repression that marked the early 1900s, Troy in *Fences* benefits from the changing climate and the advent of Civil Rights that provided blacks with increased economic opportunity. When Troy voices his frustration with the lack of visibility of black drivers within the Pittsburgh garbage collection service industry by complaining to his white boss, Mr. Rand, Rand tells him to "take it to the union" with the unexpected result being that Troy becomes a driver. This response to inequity reflects the changing social condition of African Americans in 1957. Yet still within this evolving portrait of black advancement, patriarchal power under capitalism remains in the control of white men. Despite his lifelong service in the mills and the more hospitable racial climate of the 1970s, Becker in *Jitney,* who also has run-ins with Mr. Rand, never is able to earn his union card because of racist practices that lay him off just before he has accrued the necessary hours. Hop, the black contractor that King hopes to work for in *King Hedley II,* must wait as the system holds up his contract to tear down a hotel in East Liberty, despite the fact that he has the lowest bid. Racism remains a problem that informs the economics of masculinity.

Wilson posits black cooperative economics and self-help as necessary correctives to the existent system of white-controlled capitalism. Through Holloway, the wizened, older regular at Memphis's restaurant in *Two Trains Running,* Wilson argues that the inability of black men to achieve economically directly corresponds to the decrease in the need of the white capitalistic system for black labor.

The white man ain't stacking no more niggers. You know what I'm talking about, stacking niggers, don't you? . . . White folks got to stacking . . . and I'm talking about they stacked up some niggers! Stacked up close to fifty million niggers. If you stacked them on top of one another they make six or seven circles around the moon. It's lucky the boat didn't sink with all them niggers they had stacked up there. It take them two extra months to get here cause it ride so low in the water. They couldn't find you enough work back then. Now that they got to pay you they can't find you none.

(*Two Trains Running*, 1.2.35)

Holloway's graphic description of "stacking niggers" conjures images of overcrowded slave ships with black bodies piled up on top of each other herded together like cattle as he describes the devaluation of black labor since slavery. Within this picture of the lack of black worth to the white capitalistic system, Wilson questions what the responsibility of black men is, whether they are complicit in their own oppression by not creating their own economic outlets but in depending on the largesse of whites. Holloway again provides a telling example of the need for black economic empowerment.

That's all you got around here is niggers with somebody else's money in their pocket. And they don't do nothing but trade it off on each other. I got it today and you got it tomorrow. Until sooner or later as sure as the sun shine . . . somebody gonna give it to the white man. The money go from you to me to you, then—bingo, it's gone. From him to you to me, then—bingo, it's gone. You give it to the white man.

(*Two Trains Running*, 1.2.33–34)

Humorously, Holloway bemoans black people's status as consumers. He raises awareness of the lack of business ownership in the black community and thus the dearth of any real power within the system of monetary exchange and capital growth and development. Inherent within Holloway's ironic exchange and Wilson's (w)righting is a nostalgia for a time past, prior to integration, when black communities out of social and economic necessity contained their own doctors, lawyers, and grocers and people frequented black businesses. Lamenting this loss, Wilson says, "It really started in the fifties with the idea of integration. And when you start to lose that—your cultural cohesiveness. And we used to—we used to have a baseball league, believe it or not, that was black only. We don't have nothing now."³⁶ Wilson relates full economic participation and self-help to cultural cohesion and social well-being. Changing economics' function as a measure of black masculinity, *Two Trains Running* implies, requires the development of different systems of economic exchange and black capitalism.

Within the action of *Two Trains Running*, Wilson presents two contrasting examples of black capital acquisition, West and Memphis. West, the undertaker, has established himself as a rich and successful businessman. However, he has made his money by exploiting other black people—he even tries to cheat Memphis out of fair price for his restaurant—and lost his soul in the process. West is both spiritually and culturally bankrupt. Memphis, on the other hand, determines an economic strategy that recognizes his indebtedness to his personal and cultural history. In a seeming contradiction to Wilson's politics of black economic unity, however, Memphis enlists a white lawyer, Joseph Bartaromo, to aid him in suing the city in order to get a proper price for his restaurant, which is to be torn down in the process of urban renewal. Memphis finds this white lawyer after his dissatisfaction with a black lawyer: "Chauncey Ward. Supposed to be a big nigger down there. Chauncey Ward III. His daddy was a judge. You remember Chauncey Ward. The first black judge they had down there. He was death on niggers" (*Two Trains Running,* 1.3.58). Memphis's use of the phrase "big nigger" again raises the question of how size and stature interact with issues of race, masculinity, politics, and privilege. The father, Chauncey Ward, the black judge who was "death on niggers," symbolizes the behavioral patterns bell hooks refers to as "doing it for Daddy," exhibiting more harshness to blacks in order to please "more powerful white males whose approval they need to survive." According to hooks, "To become powerful, then, to occupy that omnipotent location, black males (and white females) must spend their lives striving to emulate white men. This striving is the breeding ground among black males for a politics of envy that reinforces the underlying sense that they lack worth unless they receive the affirmation of white males."³⁷ Chauncey Ward II seeks to please the white patriarchy by selling Memphis short on his request for justice and in the process subordinating himself as well. Memphis, acting as a bluesman at the crossroads, develops an improvisational strategy of resistance and style to beat the system. His hiring of Joseph Bartaromo attests not to his own alignment with the white legal system or his own desire to "do it for Daddy," but his recognition that the dynamics of visibility necessitated a different method of attack. When the case is called, Bartaromo does not even need to talk. His visible presence constructs a different economy.

> They told me, "Well, Mr. Lee . . . we got a clause, and the city is prepared to put into motion"—that's the part I like, "prepared to put into motion"— "the securing of your property at sixteen twenty-one Wylie Avenue"—they had the address right and everything—"for the sum of thirty-five thousand dollars." I liked to fell over. The lawyer [Bartaromo] standing there, he know I'm mad and he ready to fight it. I told him, "Don't you say a word. Don't you open your mouth."
>
> (*Two Trains Running*, 2.4.109)

Memphis takes control saying when and where his lawyer should speak, even as he benefits from Bartaromo's whiteness. Wilson does not suggest that Memphis condones white legal superiority, but given the reality of this hegemonic system, must find a performative strategy that can enable him to prevail. By insisting on being paid a fair price, he asserts his own will. He not only discovers a strategy of self-determination, but uses "the master's tools to dismantle the master house." Bolstered by this victory, Memphis vows to return to Jackson, Mississippi, and fight for the land stolen many years earlier by white men supported by a corrupt southern legal system.

Niggers and Revolution

As evidenced by Memphis's intonation that Chauncey Ward was "death on niggers" or Holloway's tale of "stacking niggers," Wilson in his most overt and excessive use of this word, has black men call each other nigger eighty-seven times in *Two Trains Running*.[38] Wilson acknowledges the word's problematic nature:

> We're all sensitive both Black and white to that word and we're more sensitive if we are sitting next to a white person in the theater. We're doubly sensitive to it because, oh my God, they've heard it too. What's happened is that I've become aware of its use to the point where I can't write it anymore. . . . So probably I won't be using it as much in the future plays as I have in the past. I think *Two Trains Running* was the play in which it was most used, and that was most interesting because it was set in 1969.[39]

Wilson's awareness may have been provoked by the racial composition of his audiences. While on stage, the men apply this term in distinctly black settings, its impact exceeds the stage and assaults the ears and cultural sensibilities of audiences who may be predominantly white. How then does it signify? Randall Kennedy, in his book bearing the sensationalized title *Nigger: The Strange Career of a Troublesome Word,* perceives the word as "a reminder of the ironies and dilemmas, the tragedies and glories of American experience."[40] For Kennedy the meanings, history, force of "nigger" correlate with the shifting constructions of American identity over time. The fact that *Two Trains Running* is set is 1969—a moment when "Negroes" became "blacks" and people gave serious consideration to the cultural and political power of naming—can inform our reading of Wilson's excessive application of the word nigger in this play. While the newly "black" world outside explodes with the urgency of the Black Power movement and celebrates with cries of "Say it loud, 'I'm Black and I'm proud!'" the denizens of Memphis's restaurant, particularly men of the older generation, continue to refer to each other as "nigger." Symbolically, their embrace of "nigger" in changing times—my own grandfather in the 1960s would slip at moments from the appellation "black" and refer to us as "colored"—points to a generational concern with the advent of progress versus the maintenance of tradition and with the hold of the past on the present. Their liberal usage of "nigger" simultaneously evacuates it of meaning and overloads it with new meanings, as this determined usage challenges why and how collective self-worth and cultural identity can be contained within a name.

Wilson's repeated application of the term "nigger" in his theater reinforces its particularized and privatized meanings and foregrounds how this problematic word corresponds to the problematic status of black manhood. At the very opening of *Piano Lesson* an exuberant and locked-out Boy Willie exclaims to Doaker, "open the door, nigger! It's me . . . Boy Willie" (1.1.1). With this moment and elsewhere Wilson employs "nigger" as term of familiarity and even brotherhood. In her article, "Shuckin Off the African American Native Other," Wahneema Lubiano examines how James Alan McPherson has reclaimed "nigger" within a specific African American literary text, *Elbow Room,* as a "sign of affirmation" or even "defiance."[41] In *Two Trains Running,* in addition to its appropriation as term of kinship, Wilson also uses "nigger" as a phrase that denigrates and locates a reactionary politics. As Sterling goads him about not attending a rally for the slain Malcolm X, Memphis assails Sterling with the statement, "Niggers killed Malcolm. Niggers killed Malcolm. When you want to talk about Malcolm, remember that first. Niggers killed Malcolm. . . . and now they want to celebrate his birthday" (*Two Trains Running*, 1.2.41). Memphis's tirade points out not only the contradictions within the meanings of the word, but also complications in the politics of black liberation and positions of black masculinity. On one level, Memphis's vituperation explicates that fellow black men killed Malcolm and thus blacks engaged in the cult of idolatry that has risen around Malcolm must recognize their own complicity in his demise, that assertions of and commitments to "black power" were not only responsible for Malcolm X's ascension but his death. On another level, Memphis separates himself from those "niggers" who killed Malcolm. Those "niggers" who in their brutal action embodied the pejorative connotations of niggerdom and at the same time fulfilled the cultural imperatives of the "great white father" by savagely erasing the dangerous black leader Malcolm X. The same "niggers" now practice the ultimate hypocrisy; "now they want to celebrate his birthday." Wilson emphasizes the complexities inherent in the term, as he brings attention to the need for black men to cultivate a critical historical consciousness.

Throughout his cycle, Wilson calls black men to resistance, to beyond "another nigger" status and realize their own implication within the white patriarchal system that denies black value. In *Ma Rainey's Black Bottom*, Toledo extols his fellow black musicians, "It ain't just me, fool! It's everybody! . . . That's every living colored man in the world got to do his share. Got to do his part. I ain't talking about what I'm gonna do . . . I'm talking about all of us together" (*Ma Rainey*, 1.33–34). Toledo stresses the need for communal action as well as the recognition that black men must act in their own defense. In *Jitney*, Becker comes to a similar realization of his own complicity in his oppression and the power for collective strategies for change. He charges his fellow gypsy cab drivers to join together and fight against the forces of urban renewal that intend to tear down their station. Like Memphis in *Two Trains*, they will hire a lawyer to fight within the legal system for their rights. At the same time Becker realizes the insufficiencies of his past strategies of "doing it for Daddy" and passive accommodation. "Even when it didn't look like they was playing fair I told myself they would come around. Time it look like you got a little something going for you they would change the rules" (*Jitney*, 2.2.85). Not insignificantly, such calls for radicalism occur free of the vernacular use of "nigger." Self-determination and collective resistance requires a different designation that corresponds with an emerging self-awareness and alternative vision of black masculinity.

Self-Defining Acts: The Master-Slave Dialectic

For Wilson the key to defining a new liberatory vision of black masculinity is in the steps his men take toward self-determination. Often this is represented by ritualized acts of self-definition and resistance. Critical here are both Boy Willie's struggle at the climax of *Piano Lesson* with the ghost of Sutter and the originating struggle of his father, Papa Boy Charles, to liberate the piano from Sutter's possession. Both of these acts of opposition correspond to how Paul Gilroy in *Black Atlantic* argues African American slave narratives and historical discourse revise Hegel's master/slave dialectic.[42] Hegel and critics of Hegel, such as Alexander Kojève,[43] theorize that the master-slave dialectic is critical to an understanding of modernity. Hegel imagines the struggle between master and slave as an elemental, primal "trial by death" in which the "bondsman" eventually accepts and prefers the reality of the master to death and, as a consequence, submits to his "Lord."[44] Thus, the bondsman in slavery through work and labor becomes a new man for his master. Gilroy, however, analyzes the slave narratives of Frederick Douglass and the Margaret Garner story to critique, rework, and transform the Hegelian allegory.[45] In each of his three slave narratives, Douglass recounts his "Hegelian" life or death struggle with Edward Covey, his brutal, cruel master. Unwilling to submit to Covey's treatment any longer, Douglass confronts Covey and battles him for two hours. This epic struggle signals a transformation in Douglass and increases his determination to be a man. Margaret Garner escaped from slavery along with her husband, their four children, and nine other slaves. When she found her family separated from the other slaves and surrounded by slave catchers, Margaret killed her youngest daughter and attempted to kill her other children, rather than allow them to be sold back into slavery.[46] Thus, in both Douglass's and Garner's narra-

"I want to see you. You didn't come home last night." Jitney, *Center The-atre Group, Mark Taper Forum, 2000, with Michole Briana White (Rena), Stephen McKinley Henderson (Turnbo), Barry Shabaka Henley (Doub), and Russell Hornsby (Youngblood). (Photograph by Craig Schwartz.)*

tives, the slave is willing to risk death rather than continue to endure slavery. The narratives refigure the slave subject as an agent who will not submit. According to Gilroy,

> The repeated choice of death rather than bondage articulates a principle of negativity that is opposed to the formal logic and rational calculation characteristic of modern western thinking and expressed in the Hegelian slave's preference for bondage rather than death.[47]

This "principle of negativity," as Gilroy terms it, is the understanding by the enslaved that nothing, not even death, is worse than slavery. Analyzing this principle, Gilroy repositions the "primal history of modernity" from the slave's point of view[48] and re-formulates the position of the slave in the Hegelian allegory. From this perspective, the choice of death does not represent an act of Western rationality, nor acceptance of the present social reality, but rather a revolutionary action aimed at what Gilroy terms the "eschatological apocalypse—the Jubilee,"[49] a utopian vision of a liberated future in the hereafter.

Rather than submit to the hegemony of Sutter and the painful legacy of slavery, Papa Boy Charles liberates the piano and is willing to face death as the price for his actions. Through his defiant, revolutionary, and redemptive actions Papa Boy Charles both acknowledges and transforms the original narrative, the peculiarly American grammatical text that equated his black body with the inanimate, nonhuman piano. Metaphorically, the wooden "body" of the piano now becomes the casket for his body as he dies for the trouble of stealing it. Thus, the piano continues to house "Miss Ophelia's niggers"; however, the spirit, the bodies of those "niggers" have been freed, reclaimed, and re-membered by the Charles family through the liberatory action of Papa Boy Charles. Now the body of the piano has been reimagined as a powerful affirmation of the family's history.

The even more significant representation of the "revised" Hegelian master-slave allegory in *Piano Lesson* occurs in the final climactic scene of the play when Boy Willie decides to confront Sutter's ghost. At this moment, Boy Willie does not fear death or the supernatural presence of Sutter; rather he is willing, able, and psychologically prepared for battle. Boy Willie, consistent with the master-slave exegesis outlined by Gilroy, envisions his ability to wield the "power" of death, the power to die or even to kill, as a critical strategy of black resistance in the struggle against white oppression. Rather than submit to the continued threat embodied in the haunting presence of Sutter, Boy Willie charges up the stairs to challenge his ghost. As Wilson notes, "He's not running out the door, he's not relying on Jesus, he's not relying on anything outside of himself."[50] Wilson believes that this encounter is the most pivotal moment in the play: "It's really unimportant what happens to the piano, the important thing is that Boy Willie engages the ghost in battle."[51] For Wilson, the piano is ultimately a conduit that facilitates this articulation of Boy Willie's subjectivity and African American political agency. Symbolically, Boy Willie battles the vestiges of the slave past that still haunt the African American present. Rather than submit to the white father, the absent/presence that "ghosts" his existence, he fights back.

Through Boy Willie's willingness to combat white hegemony, Becker's decision to fight urban renewal in *Jitney,* and Memphis's demand for his fair price in *Two Trains Running,* Wilson re-presents and re-organizes the problematic and problematized nature of black masculinity in acts of responsibility to self and the surrounding community. In each of these moments, the male figure comes to a new understanding of himself in relationship to structures of power and systems of privilege. Wilson presents this dynamic of black male empowerment through divergent images of black men, of different ages and of different historical circumstance. As Keith Clark argues, by depicting black men in a community of black men, "Wilson's plays foreground multiple conceptions of gender that are often contradictory or conflicting."[52] Consequently, his portrait of black masculinity is not a static one. Yet, his representations of masculinity hold no reference outside the heterosexual paradigm; there seems to be no place for a queer black masculinity. Wilson's construction of the black male in history contrasts sharply with the historical projects of Robert O'Hara in *Insurrection: Holding History,* who returns to slavery in order to write a black queer presence into the legacy of slavery where it had previously been erased, or Brian Freeman in *Civil Sex,* whose portrait of Civil Rights leader Bayard Rustin imagines blackness and queerness not as ambiguous or mutually exclusive categories but as potentially collaborative and complementary discourses of resistance. Consequently, even as we understand that Wilson's complex critique of the problem of black masculinity addresses the politics of collective representation, we must not accept Wilson's project simply as representative, but note the ways in which it is predicated on a system of heteronormativity. Nonetheless, this does not negate the ways in which his work meditates on the historical continuum that is black manhood. In his plays, black men, marked by institutionalization, devalued by society, negotiate with each other and with the world around them as they attempt to reclaim their legacy.

Chapter 5
Ogun in Pittsburgh:
Resurrecting the Spirit

I think it was Amiri Baraka who said that when you look in the mirror
you should see your God. All over the world, nobody has a God who
doesn't resemble them. Except Black Americans. They can't even see
they're worshipping someone else's God, because they want so badly to
assimilate, to get the fruits of society. The message of America is "Leave
your Africanness outside the door." My message is "Claim what is
yours."

—August Wilson to Samuel Freedman, "A Playwright
Talks about the Blues" (1984)

Father, Son, and Holy Ghost,
So I make an idle boast;
Jesus of the twice-turned cheek,
Lamb of God, although I speak
With my mouth thus, in my heart
Do I play a double part.
Ever at Thy glowing altar
Must my heart grow sick and falter,
Wishing He I served were black,
Thinking then it would not lack
Precedent of pain to guide it,
Let who would or might deride it;
Surely then this flesh would know
Yours had borne a kindred woe.
Lord, I fashion dark gods, too,
Daring even to give You
Dark despairing features where,
Crowned with dark rebellious hair.

—Countee Cullen, "Heritage" (1925)

Berniece exorcises Sutter's ghost through summoning her ancestors
from the piano as Boy Willie engages the ghost in battle. Gabriel's
atavistic dance opens the gates of heaven for his brother Troy. Stool

Pigeon's ritual incantations and King's blood affect the rebirth of Aunt Ester's spirit. In Wilson's twentieth-century cycle, the spiritual has evolved as a significant force enabling the resurrection of the African in African American experiences. Wilson himself notes that "the metaphysical presence of the spirit world has become increasingly important in my work. It is the world that the characters turn to when they are most in need."[1] The plays' crises create a context for spiritual acts that conjoin politics and culture, past and present, history and memory, individual and community. The embrace of the spiritual, the engagement in what one could call "faith-based" cultural practices—in that they foreground spiritual commitment—serve Wilson's Africans in America as critical survival strategies.

But just what is this spirituality that Wilson expounds? How does he evoke "the spirit of a people"? The expression of "spirit" within his works defies simple codification. Certainly it is not just Christian. Dissatisfied with the relationship African Americans have historically shared with Christianity, as he indicates in his remarks to Samuel Freedman, Wilson seeks a spirituality that more truly than Christianity represents African Americans, and a God that, unlike the conventional Western representations of Jesus, "looks like" them. The Cullen quote from "Heritage" ponders whether a black God with the "precedent of pain to guide it," more than the westernized images of Jesus on the cross, would better understand and serve black needs. Cullen steps with trepidation into the imagining of a dark, woolly-haired god, for Christianity paints it as sacrilege to imagine or represent God in one's own image. Wilson, however, circumvents this problem by having his characters discover the god-force that is within them. The high death rate and palpable presence of violence that was endemic to the slaves' existence still finds manifestation in the lives of blacks in the urban enclaves of America today. Wilson therefore constructs a responsive African American spirituality that negotiates the living presence of the dead in African American experiences. Wilson's African-influenced spirituality fundamentally concerns processes of healing as it connects the everyday trials and tribulations of black life to the forces of the divine.

Wilson envisions an embodied spirituality that connects the practices of "getting the spirit" in African American religious experience with the act of spirit possession in African religious observances. As expressed by Barbara Browning in *Infectious Rhythm*, spirit possession is "an

"You sprinkle some blood on there and she comin' back in seven days if she ain't used up her nine lives." King Hedley II, *Seattle Repertory Theatre, 2000, with Tony Todd (King Hedley), Mel Winkler (Stool Pigeon), and Russell Andrews (Mister). (Photograph by Chris Bennion.)*

opening of the body to divine principles that surpass the power or understanding of any individual."[2] In the cataclysmic scene that ends the first act of *Joe Turner*, Loomis undergoes such a possession. His body becomes a vehicle for transcendent experience. Psychologically and spiritually crippled by his past incarceration, symbolically unable to stand, Loomis needs to understand the power of spirit within him. To extend Browning's point, I find in Wilson's evocation of spirit a connection to the Yoruban concept of *àshe* (or *àse*) that Robert Farris Thompson in his important work *Flash of the Spirit* defines as "spiritual command" and J. Lorand Matory in *Sex and the Empire that is No More* characterizes as a combination of religious and political power.[3] At pivotal moments in the works, characters from Bynum to Aunt Ester and Stool Pigeon evoke the spirit of *àshe*, "the power" as Farris Thompson says, "to-make-things-happen."[4] Assertions of *àshe* in Wilson involve embodied action in which the spirit of God is not outside but within the body of the characters. Thus, Wilson's spirituality overcomes the conventional Christian divide between the spirit and the flesh, between God and individual, between body and soul, through enactments that bring greater psychological awareness, spiritual empowerment, and re-evolutionary determination for both the individual ritual actor and the gathered community.

Critical to Wilson's evocation of spirituality are ritualized cultural practices that negotiate the dynamics of power to create new liberatory possibilities. The action of the plays creates contexts in which ritual is not only possible but necessary. And the enactment of these rituals provides re-evolutionary redress for the crises. Joseph M. Murphy, discussing what he terms "working the spirit," notes that within each of these religious practices the "spiritual state of mind shared by the initiate and the congregation is a prefiguration of the ultimate deliverance promised to God's people. In their different ways each tradition offers ceremonies of freedom."[5] My contention is that the ritual moments in the Wilson cycle are equally ceremonies of freedom. They speak through the spiritual to the possibilities of social, cultural, and psychological liberation in this life. Returning to the idea of the eschatological Jubilee that I considered in the last chapter, the horrors of slavery led the slaves to eschatological beliefs, in which heaven functioned as a practical site of liberation away from the oppression that they endured. James Cone points out in *Black Spirituality* that "many Africans [slaves] believed that death would be the gateway for their reincarnation in Africa."[6] Spiritual faith in the afterlife beyond became a way of infusing Christianity with African rites as well as a methodology for surviving the overwhelming conditions of their existence. Wilson critiques and (w)rights this tradition not through political instrumentalism in this world, but through ritual practices that connect the spiritual with the political, advocating not for liberation in the afterlife but in the here and now. His rituals grounded in a history of survival push toward a future of new potentiality. These rituals, as Catherine Bell suggests, in *Ritual: Perspectives and Dimensions,* drive simultaneously toward "transformation and self-determination."[7] The space of the symbolic within the play, within the liminality of the theater, becomes the seminal site for transcendence and change.

Soyinka's Fourth Stage

The ritual practices and spirituality found in Wilson's dramaturgy have, I believe, a profound connection to Yoruba cosmology, which through the "contagion" of the African diaspora has spread to religious practices of African peoples in Haiti, Cuba, Brazil, as well as the United States. Scholars such as Kim Pereira and Paul Carter Harrison do suggest such correlations in their critiques of Wilson.[8] And yet too often in contemporary cultural and critical practices Yoruba has become the prototypical African faith, the default African religion, and so an invocation of Yoruban theory has the potential for homogenizing Wilson's view of the African in America. Nonetheless, I want to show that reading Wilson in relation to Yoruban cosmology and theory can inform our understanding of his evocation of spirit in productive ways. Yoruban religion thus becomes not a definitive but an exemplary mode of analysis.[9]

Critical for me here is Nobel Prize winner Wole Soyinka's articulation of Yoruban tragedy, "The Fourth Stage," which remains one of the most important theoretical works not only on Yoruba theater but on Yoruban philosophy. Biodun Jeyifou points out in the introduction to Soyinka's *Art, Dialogue, and Outrage* that Soyinka proposes Yoruban tragedy "not in exclusionist, racial-chauvinist terms, but all the same as a distinctive presence in the world on its own terms."[10] Soyinka's project within "The Fourth Stage" has much in common with Wilson's mission in his theatrical cycle. Soyinka seeks to define a theatrical experience that is particularly African, particularly Yoruban. At the same time he is wary of essentializing Africa and continually refutes the romantic notions of Negritude proposed by others on the African continent. Wilson seeks also to define a space that is particularly African American. Yet through his reaching for the particular, Wilson reaches cross-cultural commonalties. He writes that theater "enables us to discover within ourselves an indomitable spirit that recognizes sometimes across wide social barriers, those common concerns that make possible genuine cultural fusion."[11] Jeyifou notes that Soyinka's concept of tragic art is "a ritualistic paradigm which seeks to give affective power and mystical symbolic depth to the tragic performance."[12] A similar argument could be made for Wilson. Within the ritual action of his cycle, Wilson unearths African retentions that dwell beneath black American experiences. He refigures African American spirituality, fusing the African with the American in a distinct form that celebrates a sense of spiritual self-definition and inner self-determination, a secular, sacred, and visual expression of "song."

According to Soyinka, Yoruban tragedy replicates the initiating act of Ogun, one of the central spirits within the Orisha Yoruban pantheon. Soyinka envisions Ogun as the patron god of Yoruban theater, and Ogun's original entrance into and transcendence of the "fourth stage" through the agency of will marks the initiating act in Yoruban tragedy. Within Yoruban culture the world of the living, the dead, and the unborn represent the first three stages. The transitional space between these areas is thus the fourth stage. Soyinka refers to this as the "chthonic realm," the transitional yet "inchoate matrix" of death and becoming.[13] Ogun as the first actor entered into this abyss and was disintegrated but escaped complete annihilation and was able to reassemble through the power and determination of his own will. Will, according to Soyinka, is the "truth of destructiveness and creativity in acting man." Ogun performed a symbolic act that reaffirmed the power of the human will to overcome. Correspondingly, in Yoruban tragedy, the protagonist enters the chthonic realm, and "within the mystic summons of the chasm, the protagonist actor . . . resists, like Ogun before him, the final step toward complete annihilation."[14]

Later in this chapter, I will return to this notion of the fourth stage and the Yoruban tragic actor, but first let me suggest here that the spirit of Ogun, the god of iron, suffuses and infuses the world of August Wilson's dramatic cycle. The title of the play, *Seven Guitars*, in fact, recalls the significance that the number seven holds in diasporic new world versions of Ogun worship. Robert Farris Thompson explains in *Flash of the Spirit* that

> In the *candomblés* of Bahia the deity is praised as "Seven Ogun" (Ogun Meje), which alludes to the multiplication of his *àshe* in tools of iron, and this reflects the influence of Nigerian Yoruban praise poetry and lore, as in the Oyo ballad of the hunters where the deity of war and smithing is saluted with the phrase "seven iron signs of the god of iron."[15]

Correspondingly, the power of Ogun's *àshe* is multiplied through the appearance of the seven black angels in black hats that Vera sights, at the outset of *Seven Guitars,* carrying Floyd to Heaven. These "Seven Ogun" insure his safe passage and the forgiveness of his spirit. In Yoruban as well as in Wilson's dramaturgy faith in Ogun is manifest in the exaltation of metal and metalurgy. With the advent of industrialization Ogun became the god of roads, automobiles, and all metal by-products. J. Lorand Matory points out, "In Oyo [land of Yorubans in Nigeria] territory, his contemporary priests are hunters and blacksmiths. Drivers [of automobiles] as well sacrifice to him. Historically and mythically, he is far more closely associated with warriors and itinerant entrepreneurs than with kings."[16] The warrior spirit found in such Wilsonian protagonists as King in *King Hedley II,* Boy Willie in *Piano Lesson,* or the itinerant Loomis in *Joe Turner* marks them all as children of Ogun. The display of weaponry throughout the Wilson cycle also connects these characters to Ogun. Robert Farris Thompson notes that Ogun "lives in the piercing or slashing action of all iron. Lord of the cutting edge, he is present even in the speeding bullet or the railway locomotive."[17] In a humorous scene from the first act of *Seven Guitars* that simultaneously satirizes the glorification of guns within contemporary expressions of black masculinity while at the same time signifying the presence of Ogun, Floyd, posturing with machismo, produces his thirty-eight. In response, Red Carter takes out his snub-nose thirty-two. Finally, Canewell pulls out "an average but thoroughly professional pocketknife" (1.4.43). Implicitly seeking the protection of the metal god Ogun, Ruby in *King Hedley II* asks for a gold horseshoe to hang over her door to bring her good luck. She receives one from Mister, Red Carter's son, that he has spray-painted himself. Yet, the potentially destructive rather than constructive forces of Ogun still enter, brought by Ruby's own hands. She accidentally kills her son with the derringer, another emblem of Ogun, which she also receives as a gift from Mister. Like Ogun, who "addresses the forest with a sharpened machete,"[18] the West Indian Hedley in *Seven Guitars* wields a machete and uses it to kill Floyd Barton. When this machete is passed on by Stool Pigeon to King Hedley II some forty years later in *King Hedley II*, this "son" of Hedley and Ogun must decide what to do with his father's legacy. As Thompson suggests, Ogun in Wilson "lives in the piercing or slashing action of all iron." In fact, the site of all Wilson's plays save *Ma Rainey*, Pittsburgh, the steel city, seems the logical place for Ogun to resurface on the shores of America.

In his introduction to his most ritualistic and Africanistic play, *Joe Turner's Come and Gone*, Wilson underscores the significance of metal within the industrialization of Pittsburgh and within the desire of southern blacks to migrate toward this city in search of a better life.

> The fires of the steel mill rage with a combined sense of industry and progress. Barges loaded with coal and iron ore trudge up the river to the mill towns that dot the Monongahela and return with fresh, hard gleaming steel. . . . From the deep and the near South the sons and daughters of newly freed African slaves wander into the city. Isolated, cut off from memory, having forgotten the names of their gods and only guessing at their faces, they arrive dazed and stunned, their hearts kicking in their chest with a song worth singing. (203)

Wilson's introduction purposefully collapses time. Despite the end of the slave trade in 1807 and the existence of generations of African Americans before the 1911 setting for *Joe Turner,* Wilson nonetheless refers to blacks of this period as "the sons and daughters of newly freed *African* slaves," underscoring their proximity to Africa in a way that is historically problematic but dramaturgically vital to his (w)righting of history. The African descendants that Wilson describes are the descendants of Ogun, and it is his powerful presence that they must rediscover. Romare Bearden's collage painting *Mill Hand's Lunch Bucket* (1978), a critical inspiration for *Joe Turner,* like Wilson's introduction connects the African migrant world to the world of Pittsburgh industry. Within the foreground of the picture is a dinner table around which two black men sit—including at the center a brooding, haunting figure in black coat and black hat with head bowed whose image propelled Wilson to create the troubled and troubling character of Herald Loomis.[19] In the background, through a window in the right-hand corner of the picture, the spires of the steel mills loom with smoke rising upward toward the sky. The distance of the black figures within the house from the industrialized steel outside reflects their alienation from these New World manifestations of their gods. The world of steel, of Ogun, has been co-opted and commercialized and now is inaccessible to these sons and daughters of Ogun. Similarly, Wilson's introduction makes explicit the dislocation and isolation of these new black migrants and their need for reconnection to Africa and their forgotten gods.

Even as the migration of African Americans from the South to the North uprooted them from intolerable oppression, Wilson's introduction to *Joe Turner* argues, it further distanced them from their ancestral, cultural, and spiritual foundations. Consequently, in his cycle Wilson questions whether northern migration was the best option for African Americans. Seth, the freeborn northerner in *Joe Turner*, denigrates the naïveté of these migratory blacks entering the city in droves:

> Word get out they need men to work in the mill and put in these roads . . . and niggers drop everything and head North looking for freedom. . . . Niggers coming up here from the backwoods . . . coming up here from the country carrying Bibles and guitars looking for freedom. They got a rude awakening.
>
> (1.1.209)

The rude awakening was that the North did not constitute a panacea, but rather was rife with contradictions. Paradoxically, like Ogun, the god of movement, these backwoods black folks took to the road, but in so doing they moved away from their knowledge of him and from an understanding of how the spirit of the past figures in their present search for freedom.

Seth Holly, the owner of the boardinghouse in *Joe Turner*, is perhaps one of the more interesting sons of Ogun in this regard. While his primary income comes from working the late shift in the mills, he earns an additional income by molding sheet metal into pots and pans that he sells to a white traveling salesman, Rutherford Selig. His creativity with metal manifests an implicit connection to the god, Ogun. Seth explains, "I go out there . . . take these hands and make something out of nothing. Take that metal and bend and twist it whatever way I want. My daddy taught me that. He used to make pots and pans. That's how I learned" (*Joe Turner*, 2.1.260). Seth's expression of artistry and metallurgy affirms his kinship to Ogun but also to lessons learned from his father. This tie to the father replays the legacy of fathers and sons found throughout Wilson's cycle and also informs our understanding of what Wilson represents as an inherent link to Africa, a "blood memory," as he calls it.[20] Notably, Seth works with the refuse, the scraps from the factory. African Americans have metaphorically constituted America's refuse, or as Toledo remarks in *Ma Rainey*, "We's leftovers from history." Seth determines that this status is not necessarily a limitation, but in keeping with Ogun, the "essence of creativity,"[21] he imaginatively constructs pots and pans from the leftover sheet metal. Like Bearden, who pulls scraps and found objects together to construct his collage that is *Mill Hand's Lunch Bucket*, Seth understands improvisation and pastiche.

Ironically, Seth does not consciously acknowledge his relationship to his African ancestors but distances himself genealogically, geographically, and economically from other blacks. Seth takes considerable pride in the fact that he is not of southern roots, that his father was never a southern slave but a free, northern property owner: "I ain't never picked no cotton. I was born up here in the North. My daddy was a freed man. I ain't never even seen no cotton!" (*Joe Turner*, 2.2.267). Seth sets his experience as distinct from the other black characters of the play. Wilson writes of Seth in his stage directions, "Born of northern free parents, a skilled craftsman, and owner of the boarding house, he has a stability that none of the other characters have" (*Joe Turner*, 1.1.205). His position is not unlike that established by the black bourgeoisie after slavery and into the twentieth century that E. Franklin Frazier critiques in his classic text, *The Black Bourgeoisie*. The black bourgeoisie structured boundaries of exclusivity to separate themselves from the black masses. They predicated these boundaries on illusionary standards and issues of appearance. Seth similarly focuses on issues of propriety and appearance. He worries about what others will think or say of him and his house. "I ain't gonna have folks talking" (*Joe Turner*, 1.1.216). Yet while Seth fights to maintain the illusion of difference, the realities of racism reconnect him with his black boarders. Seth, like the others, needs to reconnect and to rediscover his African-ness.

Herald Loomis in *Joe Turner* is the figure in the most apparent need of reconnection to his African-ness and to the spirit of Ogun. Because of Loomis's wandering nature, his time on the road in search of his wife as well as the symbolic status he achieves in the play, critics Paul Carter Harrison and Kim Pereira have associated him with the Yoruba deity Eshu, or Esu Elegba.[22] Eshu is the messenger and guide of the Orisha, a companion on the road and the guardian of the crossroads. Loomis's act of self-sacrifice—his slashing his chest with his knife and cleansing himself with his own blood—that ends the play and symbolically creates a path for others to follow can be associated with the spirit of Eshu. For Loomis finds life through this act, and Eshu, as Thompson notes, is "the principle of life and individuality."[23] Eshu, however, is also a trickster figure, a mischievous spirit that plays jokes on both gods and humans. The sense of the trickster is clearly not present in the dispossessed and desperate figure of Loomis. Thus, the associations with Eshu seem incomplete and of service neither to Yoruban connections nor to Wilson's play. Rather than representing an African American descendant of Eshu, I would argue that Loomis is another son of Ogun, the god of the roads and the first tragic practitioner. As such, Loomis represents a direct linkage to the world of Yoruba tragedy as theorized by Soyinka in "The Fourth Stage." He is the tragic protagonist replicating the path of Ogun, desiring spiritual transcendence and facing the great chasm, the gulf of transition:

> On the arena of the living, when man is stripped of excrescencies, when disasters and conflicts (the material of drama) have crushed and robbed him of self-consciousness and pretensions, he stands in present reality at the spiritual edge of this gulf.[24]

Herald Loomis stands in such a position. Through his seven-year incarceration and his subsequent trauma of dislocation, Loomis has experienced "the mystic summons of the chasm," and due to his psychological alienation, he is now threatened with "complete annihilation." Separated from his identity and in danger of dissolution, Loomis enters Seth's Pittsburgh boardinghouse with the need of re-membrance, in need of a spiritual and cultural foundation that he can call his own.

According to Soyinka, "Only one who has himself undergone the experience of disintegration, whose *spirit* has been tested and whose psychic resources laid under stress by the forces inimical to individual assertion, only he can understand and be the force of fusion between the two contradictions."²⁵ Spirit can fuse the contradictions between cultural disintegration and integration, life and death, enabling new processes of becoming. In Soyinka's "Fourth Stage," this particular understanding of spirit, this engagement of will is an act of rememory, a reaffirmation of cultural history: "For the hammering of the Yoruba was done at Ogun's forge, and any threat of disjunction is, as with the gods, a memory code for the resurrection of the tragic myth."²⁶ Correspondingly, evocations of spirit within Wilson purposefully summon memory. Such is the journey that Herald Loomis and other Wilsonian characters negotiate. In times of social and spiritual need, enactments of spirit within the plays act as "memory codes" resurrecting and reconnecting the African and African American past with the present, forging a way, for the future.

Bending Christianity

Needing the power of spirit, Wilson's characters repeatedly find that conventional faith in Christianity proves insufficient in addressing their social ills and racial injustices. Eternally bruised and bitter over Christ's lack of action in protecting his mother from being gang-raped by a group of white men, Levee, the brash young trumpeter in *Ma Rainey*, has determined that the Christian God has no interest in black people.

> God don't pay niggers no mind. In fact . . . God hate niggers! Hate them with all the fury in his heart. Jesus don't love you, nigger! Jesus hate your black ass!
>
> (2.81)

Through Levee and his vehement irreverence, Wilson provocatively questions whether Christianity is inherently racialized. Levee concludes that Jesus is not simply indifferent to the suffering and injustices of black life, but in his vehement hatred of blacks actively causes this suffering. In his famous essay "Everybody's Protest Novel," James Baldwin perceives the initial adoption of Christianity by Africans in America as inherently paradoxical: "Thus, the African, exile, pagan, hurried off the auction block and into the fields, fell on his knees before that

God in Whom he must now believe; Who had made him, but not in His image. This tableau, this impossibility, is the heritage of the Negro in America."[27] As represented by Baldwin, the African created not in God's image is eternally damned, unable no matter how hard she or he tries to be "washed clean." His doom is "written on his forehead, it is carried in his heart."[28] Baldwin like Levee argues that Christianity is racialized and even the source of racism. Despite this perspective, Baldwin still maintains that faith even with its contradictions can be liberatory, and that blacks remain desirous of the same freedoms and possibilities experienced by whites. Wilson too recognizes the compelling desire for spiritual foundation and the hold it has had on blacks' search for freedom. For a people so defined by suffering, where is the meaning of God? How is God made manifest in their struggle for change?

Levee seeks to find any evidence of God's presence in the day-to-day practices of black people. Just before Levee explodes and attacks both God and Cutler with his knife, he listens as Cutler tells a story of black minister, Reverend Gates, who is set upon at a train station by a group of white men and forced to dance. That these white men compel the Reverend Gates to dance denies his humanity and reduces him to a stereotype: the singing, dancing black minstrel. At the same time it also conjures the recurrent Wilson trope: white hegemony in America has sought not simply to suppress but to possess and control black expressivity. As disturbingly, Cutler's story reaffirms in the words of Slow Drag, the bass player: "White folks ain't never had no respect for the colored minister" (*Ma Rainey*, 2.81). Whites emasculate this "man of God," allowing no representation of black patriarchal authority. Yet, from Levee's perspective, colored by his mother's rape and his father's murder at the hands of whites, this humiliation of Reverend Gates, a symbol of religious authority, is not an indictment of white godlessness but of God and his apparent disregard for black needs: "if he's a man a God, then where the hell was God when all this was going on?" (*Ma Rainey*, 2.80). Demanding tangible evidence of God's ability to come to the aid of his black believers, Levee, with knife directed at Cutler, calls God out: "I'm calling Cutler's God. Come on and save this nigger! Strike me down before I cut his throat!" (*Ma Rainey*, 2.82). When God fails to materialize, Levee lords his victory over Cutler, "Your God ain't shit, Cutler" (2.83). He has challenged God man to man, and God has been too afraid to show himself. His triumph is all show, however, all male bravado and posturing. Like any such masculinist display, Levee's is ultimately an empty facade. More than proof of God's indifference, this scene reveals Levee's inadequacy, his own dearth of spiritual foundation. His call for God is not only filled with venom but desire. He lashes out in attempt to hide but instead unleashes his own fears, his own psychic pain, "Where is you? . . . Turn your back on me! Come on! Coward motherfucker" (*Ma Rainey*, 2.83). In the face of a world that denies his access and acceptance, Levee wants salvation but does not know how to tap the god-force within. Instead he turns to the devil because he cannot see evidence of God's action in the world. Levee is quite literally willing to sell his soul to the devil. Interestingly, the notions of the "devil" within *Ma Rainey* implicitly resurrect the Black Nationalist rhetoric of the 1960s and 1970s, which referred to members of the dominant culture as "white devils." Troy in *Fences* tells a story of buying furniture on credit from the Devil, whom he personifies as a "White fellow . . . got on good clothes and everything. Standing there with a clipboard in his hand" (1.1.117). In *Ma Rainey*, the "white devil" to whom Levee is willing to sell his soul is Sturdyvant. Levee's deal with this devil signals his demise.

With Herald Loomis in *Joe Turner*, Wilson further develops this representation of character in spiritual need besieged by the paradoxes of black faith in Christianity. Ironically, Joe Turner captured Herald Loomis while he attempted to spread the Christian gospel on the streets of Memphis as a deacon in the aptly named Abundant Life Church. His years of bondage have turned him away from Christianity. When confronted upon entering the boardinghouse with the other characters engaged in praising the lord and dancing the Juba, Loomis responds with irreverence and questions the rationale for their faith: "You singing for the Holy Ghost to come? What he gonna do, huh? He gonna come with tongues of fire to burn up your woolly heads?" (*Joe Turner*, 1.4.250). Like Levee, Loomis ponders his own relation to God in phallicisms, positioning his virility in relation to that of God: "Why God got to be so big? Why he got to be bigger than me? How much big is there? How much big do you want? *(Loomis starts to unzip his pants)*" (1.4.250). Loomis is prepared to measure his size and potency against that of God. Implicitly his comments racialize the Christian God as they reflect back on what Baldwin called "the impossibility" of Christianity that is the heritage of the "Negro in America": How can he as a black man know God? How can he know God's power and what is God's will? Why must he suffer? With the return of his wife Martha in the play's final scene and their subsequent conversation, Loomis takes the relationship of the Christian God to race a step further: He is not only, as Levee suggests, a white man's God that hates niggers, God himself is a white man. He tells Martha. "Great big old white man . . . your Mr. Jesus Christ. Standing there with a whip in one hand and tote board in another, and them niggers swimming in a sea of cotton" (*Joe Turner*, 2.5.287–288). Loomis paints a picture of black impotence before the power of the white overseer and the plantation system. Such a system kept him prisoner for seven years. Rather than reflecting on the absence of God within this representation, Loomis imagines God as the biggest plantation owner of them all, with blacks desirous of salvation, simply subservient to his will. "And Jeremiah go back and lay up there on his half rations and talk about what a nice man Mr. Jesus Christ is cause he give him some salvation after he die. Something wrong here. Something don't fit right!" (*Joe Turner*, 2.5.288). Loomis wants to reconcile the teachings of the Christian God with his own life experience. Salvation in the afterlife seems insufficient reward for the degradation and despair of the here and now.

While Loomis challenges her and rails against the futility of her Christianity, Martha Pentecost still functions as a catalyst that, even as she goads him to rediscover Christ, facilitates his eventual spiritual epiphany. Wilson endows this character who enters in the play's final scene with anagogic connections to notions of revival and regeneration. Renamed Martha Pentecost, the former Martha Loomis calls on Loomis to return to the church and give his soul to the Lord. "You got to look to Jesus. Even if you done fell away from the church you can be saved again" (*Joe Turner*, 2.5.287). Martha, as indicated by her change of names, has been saved and reborn in her faith in the Christian Lord. After her husband's capture, unable to endure the separation, she migrated with Reverend Tolliver and his congregation to the North and found a new life in the work of the church. Pentecost is the seventh Sunday after Easter, the day in which the Holy Ghost descended upon the disciples, possessing them and causing them to speak in tongues: "And they were all filled with the Holy Ghost, and began to speak with other tongues, as the spirit gave them utterance" (Acts 2:4). Pentecost represented for the disciples a new beginning in faith, a new life marked by their celebration of the Holy Spirit. In addition to the symbolism of "Pentecost," Martha's first name explicitly invokes biblical images of Martha, who greeted Jesus at the sepulcher after he was resurrected on the third day. Wilson reinforces the Christian symbolism by suggesting in the stage directions that Martha be dressed totally in white. Her "virtuous" white contrasts with the looming black figure of Herald; the two images together reflect on Western associations of white with purity and black with evil. James Baldwin satirically critiques this religious iconography: "For black is the color of evil; only the robes of the saved are white."[29]

Wilson in this scene works to disrupt this binary and to refigure the meanings of blackness. In the powerful and passionately ritualistic scene, Martha and Loomis engage in a call-and-response interchange that repeats and revises Christian prayer practices found in black churches. While the antiphony of call-and-response within the black church ultimately leads to union of voices and communal acknowledgment of shared faith, the voices of Martha and Loomis remain disjunctive and discordant. Martha spouts rhetoric from the Bible and calls to reclaim God, as Loomis rejects the validity of Christian salvation and the inherent racism he has felt within the dogma of Christianity. Loomis hears her words but refutes them. Yet and still, her words, reformulated, enable him to develop in the moment a new critical awareness of spirit. "I don't need anyone to bleed for me! I can bleed for myself!" (*Joe Turner*, 2.5.288), he finally responds to her. Their call-and-response ritual initiates Loomis's final act of bloodletting. Through this cataclysmic encounter Wilson creates the social and psychological context necessary for Loomis to be reborn.

Yet the new spirituality that Wilson marks with Loomis and articulates through his cycle is inflected with Christianity even as it critiques Christianity. After all, Loomis's blood sacrifice functions as a syncretic blending and signifying revision of African and Christian religious practices (as I will discuss in much greater depth later in this chapter). Correspondingly, Bynum's story of conversion in *Joe Turner* contains allusions that conjoin the Christian and African. Kim Pereira relates Bynum's spiritual reformation to that of Paul (Acts 9:10–19): "Both took place on a road, both were accompanied by a shining light . . . and both resulted in missions of healing."[30] Pereira also notes that Christ gave St. Peter the binding power, just as Bynum receives the binding power from his father.[31] Yet this reference to St. Peter is equally African, for within Haitian Vodun, a New World descendant of Yoruban observances, Christianity is adapted and St. Peter becomes associated with Eshu, the spirit of the crossroads, the messenger of the gods in worship practices. "In the course of supposed Westernization," Farris Thompson writes, "Haitians actually transformed the meaning of the Catholic icons by observing their similarities to African spirits."[32] Bynum's spiritual acts throughout the play link him to both St. Peter and Eshu, "the ultimate master of potentiality."[33]

Wilson represents the African American resourcefulness within Christianity but also its limitations. He argues that African Americans "have taken Christianity and bent it to serve their African-ness. In Africa there's ancestor worship, among kinds of religious practices. That's given blacks, particularly southern blacks, the idea of ghosts, magic and superstition. . . . Relating to the spirit world is very much part of the African and Afro-American culture."[34]Avery, Berniece's unsuccessful suitor and part-time preacher, explains in *Piano Lesson* how he determined to become a Christian preacher after a spiritual dream. The images in Avery's dream are not "traditionally" Christian. They represent a syncretic mélange of references, from the stories that appear more African in nature, to those that appear merely ridiculous. Avery's mystical dream involves an encounter with sheep people: "They looked like anybody else except they all had sheep heads and was making noise like sheep" (*Piano Lesson*, 1.1.25). The fact that Avery discovers a Christian typology within this seemingly "bizarre" dream or that he cites this dream as the primary justification for his becoming a preacher underscores the irrational rationality of his calling to the priesthood. Despite the desperate images and symbolisms, he situates his fantastical dream within a Christian orthodoxy. Later, when Berniece asks Avery to perform a Christian exorcism to rid her house of the white landowner Sutter's ghost, he suffers a loss of faith and resolve when confronted by the powerful spiritual forces present in the house. "Berniece I can't do it" (*Piano Lesson*, 2.5.106). Avery's inability to remove the ghost not only testifies to his own problems with faith but to the inflexibility of the Christian text that he reads. It has not been sufficiently bent.

African scholar and philosopher Kwame Anthony Appiah argues that Christianity is a religion that depends on written doctrine and the *literacy* of Christianity necessitates a universality and abstraction in the language of its written dogma. The demands of trying to "rephrase speech into writing is . . . bound to move you toward the abstract and universal, and away from the concrete and particular. . . . Write, then, and the demands imposed by the distant, unknown reader require more universality, more abstraction."[35] Accordingly, the lines of exorcism that Avery reads from the Bible are general, applicable to any case or incident of exorcism, and purposefully ambiguous in nature. In fact, the exorcism that Avery reads is designed to exorcise spirits from human bodies, not from pianos. Appiah contrasts this literacy with oral exchange that allows language to be indexical, metaphorical, and context-dependent.[36] In contradistinction to Avery and his vial of holy water, Boy Willie picks up a whole pot of water off of the stove and splashes it all around the house and the piano, calling out, "Get your ass out this house Sutter!" (*Piano Lesson*, 2.5.105). Yet the power of his call fails to exorcise Sutter; rather, it produces him, and Boy Willie dashes up the stairs to take on the ghost "man-to-man."

Wilson himself in his process of revision with *Piano Lesson* continued to bend Christianity. In the version that played at the Huntington Theater in Boston in 1988, Berniece crossed to the piano and played a Christian hymn as Boy Willie went to confront Sutter's ghost and the curtain fell. The fates of Boy Willie and the piano were left unresolved. The ambiguity of this ending recalls the deliberately irresolute ending of Ibsen's *Ghosts*, in which Mrs. Alving vacillates over whether to fulfill her son's suicidal desire. As with that famous final scene of *Ghosts*, the original ending of *The Piano Lesson* relies on the audience to provide the synthesis and resolution. Wilson at first resisted, but ultimately changed the ending:

> For a while I was persistent in my opinion that it didn't matter. I didn't want to make a choice between Boy Willie and Berniece because I thought there was validity in both their arguments. And then I came to understand in the process of writing the play, I had already made a choice. So I decided to keep the lights on for another 60 seconds so the audience can see what happens after Boy Willie comes down from his fight with the ghost.[37]

Wilson in the Broadway version provides resolution but, equally important, he replaces Berniece's intonation of a Christian hymn with a spontaneous, "atavistic," ritualistic chant that underscores the retention of the African in African American experiences. Here, then, Wilson finds conventional Christianity insufficient to his own dramaturgical needs.

Aunt Ester and the Power of Àshe

A critical figure mediating between the African past and the African American present, between the practice of Christianity and an Africanist-based spirituality, is the character of Aunt Ester. Wilson first mentions Aunt Ester, a character as old as the African American presence in America, in *Two Trains Running* and then references her death in *King Hedley II*. In *Gem of the Ocean*, set in 1904, Wilson brings her onto the stage. Aunt Ester, who is 349 years old in *Two Trains*, who dies at 366 years of age in *King Hedley II*, is about 285 in *Gem of the Ocean*. According to Wilson, "Aunt Ester has emerged for me as the most significant person of the cycle. The characters after all, are her children."[38] Wilson literalizes Aunt Ester in *Gem of the Ocean* with the effect of humanizing her. She is now not only an offstage icon but also a flesh and blood woman. Now in her material presence, Aunt Ester becomes subject to human needs, passions, and longings. Most particularly, she has loved and lost. In *Gem* the subject of her love is the wizened, Solly Two Kings, an older representative of Wilson's warrior spirit. Unfortunately, Solly is killed for his revolutionary energies and their love must remain unrequited. Aunt Ester in this play does become a powerful force in the life of Citizen Barlow, who comes to her, early in the play, in search of spiritual sustenance. He wants to have his soul washed; he needs forgiveness for past sins. With the embodiment of Aunt Ester, Wilson is able to make tangible the symbolic. He stages the scene of Barlow's salvation as Aunt Ester leads him to the City of Bones, the graveyard for all the Africans lost during the Middle Passage. Clearly Wilson bestows incredible import on this character in her first onstage appearance. Yet I would argue that it is her *invisibility* in the earlier plays that provides a productive space of creative liminality for Aunt Ester. Like Ogun, the first Yoruban actor, the first to enter and survive the transitional gulf, Aunt Ester mediates between the worlds of the living and the dead through the force of her will and in a manner that is unique. The unseen Aunt Ester might be Wilson's most feminist construction. In *Invisibility Blues*, Michele Wallace bemoans the correlation in contemporary American culture between black women's "high *visibility*" and "their almost total lack of *voice*."[39] Conversely, Aunt Ester finds in her invisibility, in her lack of presence and even of speaking, both voice and power. Ntozake Shange in *for colored girls who have considered suicide / when the rainbow is enuf* (1975), discusses men—such as the infamous Beau Willie Brown—but constructs no male characters. Their absence provides space for the stories of women to move from positions of marginality to the center, for women's voices to be heard, for her female figures to develop greater self-awareness and to progress toward self-determination. Aunt Ester, through her behind-the-scenes presence, empowers the characters to find, paraphrasing Shange, the force of God within themselves.

Aunt Ester exists in the symbolic between the world of the spirit and the flesh. Born with the arrival of Africans in America, Aunt Ester is the actual site of African American legacy, a living *lieu de mémoire*. History and memory congeal in her body. In fact her name, in a riff of aural signifyin', sounds quite similar to "ancestor."[40] "Aunt Ester" is in fact the "ancestor," the connection to the African American past, that is both personal and collective, both material and metaphysical. Rather than abstract signifier, she is blood, she is family, the aunt of her people. And yet prior to *Gem of the Ocean* her body is unseen, a spirit, refiguring Ralph Ellison's trope of black invisibility, in which blacks function as a present absence in white American society. Going to *see* Aunt Ester, for those to whom she is rendered visible, requires faith and the engagement of their inner eye. They then come to reconstruct their physical reality and to see the world anew. Like TJ, the 189-year-old grandfather in Robert O'Hara's *Insurrection: Holding History*—a mere child to the 369-year-old Ester—who has been in a wheelchair for the last 100 years unable to move anything but his left eye and middle toe on his right foot, until he travels back from contemporary times into slavery with his gay grandson Ron—Aunt Ester signifies living, embodied history. The history is at once personal and idiosyncratic, a response to the grand narratives that structure history in conventional linearity. O'Hara's play and his representation of TJ interrogate how we "hold history," how we structure absences and presences in historical narratives.[41] Its fragmented structure and storyline fundamentally critique the notion of a singular authoritative truth. The representation of Aunt Ester similarly confronts conventional notions of truth. How can a 349-

year-old woman be true? Her (w)righting by Wilson rubs history against the grain by demanding a different understanding of the past's interaction with the present.

Aunt Ester as a figure of symbolic import references other "aunts" of consequence in African American history and cultural production. She signifies on the seminal figure of slavery and its abuse, Frederick Douglass's Aunt Hester, whom he introduces at the end of his first chapter in *The Narrative of the Life of Frederick Douglass an American Slave*. In graphic detail, Douglass describes his Aunt's brutal beatings at the hands of his master: "The louder she screamed, the harder he whipped; and where the blood ran fastest, there he whipped the longest."[42] Douglass's recounting sensationalizes for his readers the violence tinged with lust and desire that constituted his Aunt's whippings in order to stimulate abolitionist outrage at the injustices of the peculiar institution. Witnessing his Aunt's suffering defined slavery for him: "It was the blood-stained gate, the entrance to the hell of slavery, through which I was about to pass. It was a terrible spectacle."[43] Through the visceral experience of his Aunt's abuse, Douglass was initiated into the social death of slavery. His Aunt's body as surrogate endured the unwarranted horrors that constituted slavery for so many. His memory of her is both personal and collective, fixing the incident of her torture as *lieu de mémoire*. For Wilson, Aunt Ester has evolved into an equally significant metonymic figure. Refiguring Douglass's Hester, calling on Aunt Ester opens up, for Wilson's characters, an alternative worldview. Significantly, those who visit her enter through a red door—the bloody gate reimagined—at 1839 Wylie Avenue. The date 1839 witnessed a bloody backlash of white resentment toward the growth of free black populations in the North and most particularly an outbreak of racial violence in Pittsburgh in which "whites did considerable damage to the black section of the city by burning and tearing down houses."[44]

Aunt Ester is far from a static site of remembrance, but rather a living force, actively mediating for spiritual and cultural change, evoking the power of *àshe*. She is a conjure woman with spiritual power and otherworldly authority recalling the conjurer figure Aunt Peggy in Charles Chesnutt's famous story "The Goophered Grapevine."[45] When the white "Mars Dugal" finds his grapevine overrun with black folk, he hires Aunt Peggy to put a spell on his vineyard, to "goopher the grapes." The master understands that they all knew Aunt Peggy as "a witch 'sides being a conjuh 'oman" and would fear her power and authority.[46] Similarly, Aunt Ester possesses a spiritual power, and a wisdom of age and experience that others must respect. According to Holloway, "Aunt Ester got a power cause she got an understanding. Anybody live as long as she has is bound to have an understanding" (*Two Trains Running*, 1.1.22). Aunt Ester's healing wisdom is a creolized expression of *àshe*, a divine incarnate force of spirit. Her power of *àshe* emanates from her embodiment of historical memory.

Africanist allusions abound with Aunt Ester. Entrance to Aunt Ester's home is, as mentioned earlier and as evident in the stage design for *Gem of the Ocean*, which transpires in Aunt Ester's house, through a red door. The color red for many Yoruba represents "the supreme presence of color."[47] Her "faith-based practice," her laying on of hands, has a direct relationship to the Yoruba goddess Oshun (or Osun), one of the wives of the powerful thunder god Shango, who when she died fell to the bottom of the river and became the divinity of the rivers. Robert Harris quotes a Yoruban verse of praise to Oshun that emphasizes her healing authority and possession of *àshe*.

> Witness of a person's ecstasy renewed
> She says; bad head—become good!
> Mistress of àshe, of full predictive power
> She greets the most important matter in the water.[48]

At the festival for the river goddess Oshun at Oshogbo in Nigeria, the celebrants praise her by throwing "flowers into her stream."[49] In keeping with the water goddess's realm of authority, Aunt Ester asks all those who come to her for counsel to throw their offering into the river so that she will receive it—her city, Pittsburgh, is known for its three rivers, the Allegheny, the Monongahela, and the Ohio. Interestingly, Sharon Holland credits Oshun as being the figure on whom Toni Morrison modeled Beloved, the spirit who rises out of the water.[50] Oshun is a generous spirit of wisdom and generosity. Known occasionally as the Yoruban "love goddess," she controls all that makes life worth living, such as marriage, children, money, and pleasure.[51] In the earlier plays, Wilson's characters come to Aunt Ester when they trouble over such issues. Ruby reveals to Tonya, now pregnant with King's baby and determined to abort in *King Hedley II*, that thirty-six years earlier, when she was considering aborting King, she visited Aunt Ester.

Aunt Ester laid her hands on Ruby's head and told her, "God has three hands: two for that baby and one for the rest of us" (King Hedley II, 1.3.41–42). Aunt Ester's comment not only assures King's birth, it confirms his spiritual linkages to God as well as to Aunt Ester. In *Two Trains Running*, Sterling goes to visit Aunt Ester about love and life, West about his deceased wife, and Memphis about the money he intends to exact from the city government as payment for its acquisition of his restaurant. Each of these men, save for West, the undertaker, finds spiritual sustenance through communing with their Ancestor. Reconnecting with the past has both practical and spiritual significance for them. West, however, refuses to throw his twenty dollars into the river. He perceives this as a waste of good money, and as a result he remains materially wealthy but spiritually and culturally impoverished.

Aunt Ester's powers as conjurer and as embodiment of *àshe* also link her to other figures within the Wilson cycle such as Bynum in *Joe Turner* and Stool Pigeon in *King Hedley II*, whose ritual practice provides social and psychological healing. Wilson maintains that Stool Pigeon "has a connection to the spirit world of Aunt Ester through Mister Eli [her attendant, whom he also brings on stage in *Gem* in 1904]."[52] In addition it is Stool Pigeon who conducts the burial of Aunt Ester and whose ritual incantations over her grave signal her rebirth. Bynum, the roots worker, the conjure man, functions as a potent visible and invisible presence behind the action of *Joe Turner*, forging a connection between the African and the African American. Early in the first act, Bynum relates the story of his own conversion and the discovery of his own song. Bynum describes being led by a "shiny man" to a mystical place where he encounters his father, whose hands (signifying on the man with an enormous hand who is crossing down the stairs in Romare Bearden's collage, *Mill Hand's Lunch Bucket*) "were as big as hams" (*Joe Turner*, 1.1.212). His father led him to the edge of an ocean, where he showed Bynum "something I ain't got words to tell you" (1.1.213). Bynum's words foreshadow Loomis's later revelation that "Herald Loomis done seen some things he ain't got words to tell you" (1.4.250). Their parallel expression suggests that they have seen a similar vision of the Middle Passage. It foregrounds this vision as an African American "blood memory" as well as a bond that these two men share. Accordingly, when Bynum helps Loomis to give voice to his vision, he is also finding the words to express his own. With Loomis, Bynum sees the reincarnation of his Shiny Man: a man whom he can help as well as a man who has the power and ability to help him. For Bynum his spirit of *àshe* emerges on that day. At the place on the side of the ocean, "my daddy taught me the meaning of this thing that I had seen and showed me how to find my song" (*Joe Turner*, 1.4.213). Here again Wilson repeats the theme of the father, now steeped in mysticism, passing on lessons learned to the son. Bynum's vision of the father engenders a symbolic trinity of sorts. For the image encompasses not only Bynum's immediate, deceased father, but in his father's leading him on the path to *àshe* reveals Bynum as another son of Ogun, the father. Like Aunt Ester, Bynum's spiritual abilities result from linkages to, and embodiment of, African American history.

The presence of water in Bynum's vision symbolically binds him to Aunt Ester, the Pittsburgh river goddess, as well as to Loomis and to the importance of water as a regenerative force within African and African American rituals of conversion. The experience of baptism was and continues to be performed in the black church at the water's edge and to involve the total submersion in water. As a result of this ritual ceremony, the baptismal subject is "born again" within the Christian faith. Deliberately infusing Christianity with an African sensibility, baptism confirms the presence of the spirit within the body of the African American initiate. As Joseph M. Murphy argues, "In . . . baptism . . . the biblical word is both juxtaposed and given expression in the incarnation of the African spirit."[53] At the water's edge Bynum is born again, filled with the spirit, and endowed with the power of his song. The song Bynum receives is the "Binding Song," the ability to bind people's souls, that "takes the power of his song and binds them together." He must locate another "shiny man" like the one who showed him the way to this song. Bynum relates the prophecy to his father: "I asked him [his father] about the shiny man and he told me he was the One Who Goes Before and Shows the Way. Said there was lots of shiny men and if I ever saw one again before I died then I would know that my song had been accepted and worked its full power and I could lay down and die a happy man" (*Joe Turner*, 1.1.213). Loomis is the shiny man he seeks. Later, when Loomis reveals his apocalyptic vision of the "bones people," he again repeats the trope of baptism and of being born again. He tells of the "bones people" being sunk into the water and then emerging with flesh on them and starting to walk. They are reborn on the new land. Water, thus, represents not only the site of initiating rupture and catastrophic loss, but also dichotomously a space of potential healing, a place where the spirit can be re-membered and renewed.

The power of the *àshe* not only bonds Bynum with the African past and regenerates him, it enables him to know and influence events in the play before they transpire. By "binding" Zonia to her mother and in seeking to bind Herald Loomis to his song, Bynum affects Loomis's and Zonia's first appearance at the doors of Seth's boardinghouse. Just after their arrival and following Bynum's distracted pass through the kitchen, Bertha informs Seth that Bynum was out in the yard all morning: "I don't know what he's doing. He had three of them pigeons lined up out there. He dance around till he get tired. He sit down awhile then get up and dance some more" (*Joe Turner*, 1.2.234). Bynum knows of Loomis's coming and must prepare. Significantly, Bynum dances. Embodiment is critical as he rhythmically "works the spirit"; his body becomes a vessel of spiritual power. His "un-scene" individualized rituals mediate between the world of the gods and the world of the living and produce effects that transform the whole community. Later in the play, on the night directly preceding the day that Herald and Zonia are scheduled to move on, Bynum engages in unseen ceremonies that prefigure Martha's return. Reuben, the young next-door neighbor and Zonia's playmate, informs her, "Something spooky going on around here. Last night Mr. Bynum was out in the yard singing and talking to the wind . . . and the wind it just be talking back to him" (*Joe Turner*, 2.4.275). Bynum repeatedly summons the spirits to support him. In fact, Bynum's spiritual powers can be seen as affecting the final climactic confrontation between Martha and Loomis. His "behind the seen" machinations produce her appearance. At the opening of the second scene of act 1, Seth informs Bertha that he knows that Martha, whose name is now appropriately Pentecost, has moved with her church to Rankin into a building that used to be a shoe store. He, however, refuses to tell Loomis her whereabouts: "I ain't gonna tell this old wild-eyed mean-looking nigger nothing!" (1.2.236). Although he is not present at this moment, Bynum appears to deduce her location from Seth. For later, just before Selig leaves on his traveling salesman rounds and in search of Martha, Bynum delivers him a subliminal message:

You going upriver, huh? You going up around my way. . . . Used to go up into *Rankin* and take that *first right-hand road.* I wore many a pair of *shoes* **out** walking around that way. You'd have thought I was a *missionary out spreading the gospel* the way I wandered all around them parts.

(1.2.240; emphasis added)

Bynum loads Selig with clues that direct him to find Martha. When Selig does return with Martha, he explains, "She was right out there in Rankin. You take that first right-hand road . . . right there at that church on Wooster Street. I started to go right past and something told me to stop at the church and see if they needed any dustpans" (*Joe Turner,* 2.5.284). One could ask why he didn't simply tell Selig where Martha was living. However, Bynum's methodology is indirect, enabling the characters to come to decision on their own.

Similarly, Aunt Ester does not dictate a course of action; she asks that her parishioners be proactive in their own lives. Holloway scolds West, "That's what your problem is. You don't want to do nothing for yourself. You want somebody else to do it for you. Aunt Ester don't work that way. She say you got to pull your part of the load" (*Two Trains Running,* 2.1.76). Aunt Ester does not act for the souls who seek her counsel, but rather enables them to determine their way. Aunt Ester dispenses advice in parables that compel her supplicants to interpret them, to think and then act.[54] The spiritual and practical healing that Aunt Ester initiates is internal and psychological: "She make you right with yourself" (*Two Trains Running,* 1.1.22). She does not provide salve for the external wounds of oppression and racism. Her inwardly focused theology is re-evolutionary and distinctly creolized. Only by touching the past, by re-membering the lessons of the ancestor, can the characters move forward. The African spiritualism conjoins with the practical American reality.

On Death and Dying

Aunt Ester's death in *King Hedley II* reverberates loudly. It creates fissures within the community, and constitutes a loss of history that requires its own healing. She dies of grief over the desperate conditions of African American life in the 1980s. More than a testimony to the benign neglect of the Reagan-Bush administration or the power of external forces corrupting African American existence, her death marks the continued drift of blacks away from their "songs." What happens when the spirit of a people passes away, when Aunt Ester, the living symbol of the past, the "ancestor" or Aunt Ester of all African America, dies? Her death should, necessarily, be of major consequence and concern to all those still living, but in the earliest versions of *King Hedley II*, Wilson painted a picture of black disconnection and collective apathy. Ruby mourns Aunt Ester's passing by asking to borrow twenty dollars for some flowers. The younger members of the group, Tonya, King, and Mister, more separated from any personal memory of Aunt Ester, ponder her death only for a moment, and they do not reflect on its particular meaning to their own lives.

In his revision for Broadway, Wilson foregrounds Aunt Ester's death visually and aurally. Her death causes all the lights to go out in the Hill district of Pittsburgh. A voice-over news flash tells of her passing. Stool Pigeon reports that crowds are lined up inside of Aunt Ester's house and outside on the streets below. Following the African tradition, they will remain with the body until she is buried and crosses over to the world of the ancestors. King is scheduled to be one of her pallbearers. Stool Pigeon in both versions senses the magnitude of the loss, celebrates her passing, and enacts rituals that reaffirm her significance and enable her eventual resurrection. The meanings of Aunt Ester's death demand a similar historical literacy on the part of *King Hedley II*'s audiences. To understand the full weight of her death the reader/spectator should be familiar with *Two Trains Running* or know of the import that Wilson now bestows on her. The death of Aunt Ester means the evacuation of spirit, and Stool Pigeon's rituals are intended to revive and renew this spirit.

Death and its aftermath in Wilson, then, are not merely a site for remembering the deceased but re-membering the living; death comes to benefit the gathered community. After Becker's funeral in *Jitney*, all the gypsy cab drivers determine to struggle together against the urban renewal that threatens to shut them down. Hambone's death in *Two Trains Running* galvanizes both Sterling and Memphis to take definitive action in their own lives. Hambone dies alone in his home, another anonymous black death to be easily forgotten. With the scars of slavery that line his back, Hambone represents the corporate black body, the black nation as a whole, a surrogate for all those black souls who have passed on without receiving their just due. Wilson never reveals Hambone's scarred body as spectacle on the stage. During the presentation of abolitionist oratory by escaped slaves, white spectators expected the speaker at some point to display his scarred body before them. The heightened, sensationalized moment of exposition became a drawing card for these events. Frederick Douglass among others decried this exhibitionism—the exploitation of the marked black body as a shocking site of deformity and difference, the diminution of the abolitionist meeting into a carnival sideshow—positing that the speaking black body should be sufficient in remembering and repeating the horrors of slavery. In *Two Trains Running*, Hambone's absent dead body speaks. Rather than an embodied presence on display, his spirit is present and the power of the spirit conveyed in the absence of the material body. When Sterling breaks into Lutz's butcher shop and returns with hands bloodied, holding a ham to be buried in Hambone's coffin, he not only fulfills Hambone's life mission, he finds meaning for his own.

Wilson draws a decided contrast between Hambone's impoverished pauper's casket and humble wake and the excessive services for the deceased Prophet Samuel, and through this contrast he further meditates on the significance of death in black lives. Although Prophet Samuel dies before the action of *Two Trains Running*, his funeral is a process that plays out over the duration of the play. Hambone's body has a paltry sequence of visitors that includes his seeming nemesis, the white butcher, Lutz. Prophet Samuel, on the other hand, has so many mourners that lines wrap around West's Funeral Home, so that "it take you an hour to get in there to see him" (*Two Trains Running*, 1.1.6) Like Aunt Ester, Prophet Samuel never appears in *Two Trains Running*, but his impact is felt as we learn of his life and his death from the onstage characters. As reported by Holloway and Wolf, the people attempt to return Prophet Samuel in death into what he was in life, a theatricalized spectacle and a locus for dreams of financial prosperity. Some industrious souls even transform the "decorous" viewing proceedings into a marketing opportunity: "They had a little basket they put over there right by the casket. They was charging people a dollar to see him before West put a stop to it" (1.1.6).

Joseph Roach notes that "performances in general and funerals in particular are so rich in revealing contradictions: because they make publicly visible through symbolic action both the tangible existence of

social boundaries and at the same time, the contingency of those boundaries on fictions of identity, their shoddy construction out of inchoate
otherness, and consequently, their anxiety producing instability."[55] The
events that comprise the memorializing of Prophet Samuel are replete
with revealing contradictions. Acting to protect the sanctity of his
funeral establishment and the social boundaries around services for the
dead, West stops the money-making activities but, in this process
reaffirms the inessential nature of these boundaries. West, the undertaker, is in the business of death. Even as he chastises those opportunis-
tic denizens for taking up a collection basket, he too profits directly
from Prophet Samuel and from other tragedies of black loss. With its
farcical excess, its emotionalism, pomp, and pretense, its crowds and its
hyperbolic status, the performance of Prophet Samuel's wake and subsequent funeral is a site of constant instability. "They had the boulevard
backed up two miles. . . . They had helicopters flying all over the place"
(*Two Trains Running*, 2.2.80). The characters remark not on the reverence and spirituality of the proceedings but compare the size, spectacle,
and chaos of the funeral rites for a notorious gambler and hustler,
Patchneck Red, a real historical figure in Pittsburgh. The theatricaliza-
tion of Prophet Samuel's passing further points out the import of Wilson's decision not to sensationalize the death of Hambone and the scars
that lined his back, as the exuberance of the Prophet's rites lack the spiritual power present in the observances for Hambone. Risa, a true
believer in the power of Prophet Samuel, refuses to take part in his
funeral, citing its hypocrisy.

Wilson uses the absent Prophet Samuel to trouble the relationship
between wealth and spirit. In a productive play on words, Wilson establishes that the people believe that they can "profit" financially through
their contact with the "Prophet" Samuel. Wilson molds Prophet Samuel
after real black charismatic, apostolic figures such as Daddy Grace and
Prophet Jones. Charles M. "Sweet Daddy" Grace founded his church—
the House of Prayer for All People—in Charlotte, North Carolina, in
1926. Giving to Daddy was seen as his congregation's highest obliga-
tion, and when he died in 1960 he left behind an estimated fortune of
more than $6 million and boasted over three million members and
churches in 110 cities. Prophet Jones left Birmingham in 1934 with $1.47
in his pocket; by 1950 he had a fifty-four-room castle in Detroit and an
international organization worth $2 million with 362 Thankful Centers

in forty-five states and sixteen countries. He, like Wilson's Prophet Samuel, dressed in robes but covered them with a thirteen-thousand-dollar white mink coat. While Wilson's Aunt Ester promises to receive the financial offerings that her believers throw into the river at her request, Prophet Jones—showered in gifts by his 6 million parishioners for supposedly answering the prayers and letters that they sent him—never, in fact, read most of the letters but dumped *them* into a nearby river.[56]

Prophet Samuel, like Prophet Jones and Daddy Grace, promised his black patrons reward for their faith in this lifetime instead of blessings found in the afterlife. They all bent Christianity to suit them and to proselytize strategies for current earthly prosperity as a sign of godliness. Risa latches on to Prophet Samuel because "God sent him to help the colored people get justice" (*Two Trains Running*, 2.2.87). She believes that he is not focused on eternal salvation of souls and sinners, but rather desires through faith to produce some earthly salve for the wounds and sufferings of black people. Memphis, her boss, chastises her for her gullibility: "God ain't paid Prophet Samuel's way. The people paid Prophet Samuel's way hoping they get a financial blessing" (2.2.87). Wilson does not propose monetary acquisitions as antithetical to spiritual power. Holloway tells a story of how Prophet Samuel, under arrest (not unlike Daddy Grace) for tax evasion, caught the attention of the richest man in Pittsburgh, Andrew Mellon:

> Say if they arrested him they had to arrest Mellon too. Say God was gonna send a sign. The next day the stock market fell so fast they had to close it early. Mellon called the mayor and told him to drop the charges. The next day the stockmarket went right on back up there. Except for Gulf Oil, which Mellon owned. That went higher then it ever went before. Mellon was tickled pink. He sent Prophet Samuel a five-hundred dollar donation and a brochure advertising his banking services.
>
> (*Two Trains Running*, 1.1.26)

Whether the rise and fall of the stock market and Mellon's stock was coincidental is inconsequential. Mellon responded. Prophet Samuel utilizes the threat of prophecy to intervene on his behalf in the face of white political and financial authority. His is a "revolutionary theology" of sorts in which he orchestrates his own liberation by linking his fate with that of Mellon and by proclaiming his personal connection with God. After Prophet Samuel's interaction with Mellon, "Prophet Samuel went big. The police didn't bother him no more" (*Two Trains Running*, 1.1.26). Wilson provides no evidence within the play, however, that Prophet Samuel's self-interested actions to prevent his imprisonment are followed by other oppositional, spiritual intercessions that affect the daily lives and impoverished circumstances of his black parishioners.

What Wilson does suggest is that any real expression of spirit in Prophet Samuel results from visiting with the true source of power, Aunt Ester. According to Holloway, "Most people don't know Prophet Samuel went to see Aunt Ester. He wasn't always a prophet. He started out he was a reverend" (*Two Trains Running*, 1.1.25). Thus, Aunt Ester is the enabling force behind Prophet Samuel's miracles. Calling upon her, communing with the ancestor(s), is integral to African American progression, even that of Prophet Samuel. He, however, moves away, keeps her import unremarked ("most people don't know Prophet Samuel went to see Aunt Ester") as he transforms himself from little-known reverend to prophet of profit, distancing himself from the past. Similarly, the characters and community in *King Hedley II* have forgotten their connection to history, and this anticipates Aunt Ester's death. But, as Wilson suggests through the ceremonies performed by Stool Pigeon at her gravesite, hers is a soul we cannot afford to let die in vain. If death benefits the living, then Aunt Ester's death urgently signals the need for an immediate infusion of social activism; it is a call for African American rebirth and reconnection. Her voice—eventually heard in her cat's meow at the play's conclusion—cries out loudly from the grave.

The dead speak in Wilson's plays, the ancestral voices are present and inevitably the action reveals death as a part of life. Sharon Holland argues in *Raising the Dead* that African American experience has an inherent proximity to death. "If black subjects are held in such isolation—first by a system of slavery and second by its imaginative replacement—then is not their relationship to the dead, those lodged in terms like *ancestor* and *heritage,* more intimate than historians and critics have articulated"?[57] The isolation that Holland speaks of is genealogical, the separation of blacks in slavery from their African ancestors. This denial of the living presence of the ancestors in the lives of the slaves contributes to the condition that Orlando Patterson enunciates as "social death."[58] The experience of social death represented a liminal state neither enfranchised nor totally alien, rather institutionally marginalized, stripped of identity, honor, and power.[59] The social death and alienation of slavery separate the slave from knowledge of, or association with, his or her history. Patterson writes:

> Slaves differed from other human beings in that they were not allowed freely to integrate the experience of their ancestors into their lives, to inform their understanding of social reality with the inherited meanings of their natural forebears, or to anchor the living present in any conscious community of memory.[60]

While no longer physically bound to the slave master, Wilson's dramaturgy reveals African Americans, such as Herald Loomis, who are socially dead, who remain spiritually and psychologically imprisoned by the dominant culture. How do you recover from this historical and symbolic condition? How do you anchor the living present of African Americans "in any conscious community of memory?" Through ritual enactments that "integrate the experience" of the ancestors into the lives of his characters, Wilson's theater gestures toward an answer to these questions. As in the simultaneity of the African worldview, the ancestors can and do commune with the living and the unborn in the theater. The live performance, paraphrasing Herbert Blau, is where we as audience, in the immediacy of theatrical space, witness the performer dying each night. The figure of death as unmarked presence lurks in the background, exists in the memory of the spectator, in the space of the theater. Theater, then, is an ideal venue for Wilson's meditations on death and resurrection.

Ghosts and Haunts

Wilson's concern with the embodiment of spirit and the resurrection of African spirituality within the African American inexorably leads him to explore the potentiality of ghosts. Wilson maintains that the belief in ghosts is an African American manifestation of African spirituality: "It's the same people practicing—exercising their spirituality, but it's got a different cover to it. But it's the same people. The same people that believe in tree spirits in Africa. I don't know anyone here believe in tree spirits, but they believe in ghosts."[61] Yet, for African Americans within his plays, the point is not just that ghosts exist and they believe in them, but that ghosts have certain expectations of the living. As Gurleen Grewal points out, "the ancestors can communicate with their descendants especially if certain rites for the dead have not been performed."[62] Miss Mabel returns from the grave and beats young Reuben with a cane in *Joe Turner.* She demands that he fulfill his promise to his deceased friend Eugene. In Wilson's plays, ghosts from the past, both white and black, haunt the world of the living, seeking restitution, and only the enactment of certain ceremonies grants their release or enables their exorcism. His use of this trope correlates with Suzan-Lori Parks's musing on the undead in *Death of the Last Black Man in the Whole Entire World,* in which the "last black man," the Black Man with Watermelon, has died but cannot cross over to the land of the dead until he has passed on his history and is re-membered by the one living character in the play, the Black Woman with Fried Chicken. Until this is accomplished, the Black Man with Watermelon keeps coming back from the dead and keeps dying in a variety of ways, from lynching to electrocution—an ode to all the historical brutality enacted on the bodies of anonymous black souls. The Black Man with Watermelon's death is unfinished and must be replayed until it is effectively re-membered.[63] In Toni Morrison's "ghost story," *Beloved,* Sethe expresses a sentiment reflective not only of her own circumstance in the novel, but of Parks's Black Woman with Fried Chicken, of Wilson's "spooked up" figures, and even of black America in general: "Not a house in the country ain't packed to its rafters with some dead Negro's grief."[64] Haunted by the ghosts of the past, how does the African American house confront these dead Negroes and their grief?

While in Western cultural traditions, faith in otherworldly spirits or ghosts appears unreasonable and irrational and can be dismissed as mere folk superstition, Wilson posits this faith as a critical African retention in African American social and cultural processes. Through Wilson's invocation of ghosts, dead Negroes speak. Critical to Wilson's project of African recuperation in *Piano Lesson* are the mysteries surrounding the Ghosts of the Yellow Dog, the ghosts of Papa Boy Charles and four hobos burned to death aboard a boxcar on the train known as the Yellow Dog. Papa Boy and the others were killed after Sutter discovered the piano missing from his home. Since their deaths, the Ghosts of the Yellow Dog have engaged in a policy of racial redemption. They have not only avenged their deaths but the deaths of other black men who were wrongly killed by white vigilantes. As reported by Boy Willie, "nine or ten, eleven or twelve" white men, all residents of Sunflower County, Mississippi, all guilty of violence against black men, have all fallen down their own wells to their deaths. The latest in this line is Sutter. After the first and then with the succession of these strange "coincidental" deaths, the African American residents of Sunflower County began to attribute these well "accidents" to the Ghosts of the Yellow Dog.

> It was about two months after that [the burning of Papa Boy Charles and the hobos in the boxcar] that Ed Saunders fell down his well. Just upped and fell down his well for no reason. People say it was the ghost of them men who burned up in the boxcar that pushed him in his well. They started calling them the Ghosts of the Yellow Dog.
>
> (*Piano Lesson,* 1.2.45–46)

Appiah points out that traditional African religions, as well as contemporary Africans, share the belief in "an ontology of invisible beings."[65] This belief in invisible spirits constitutes what he terms "explanatory theories."[66] They function in a manner similar to Western scientific theory or Western religious doctrine to explain, predict, and control both the known and the unknown forces operative in the practitioner's world. Accordingly, belief in the Ghosts of the Yellow Dog offers an explanatory theory for the inconceivable coincidence of nine or even twelve men falling down their wells. Appiah maintains that African traditional religions reject the notion that "unfortunate events" can just "happen." Precolonial African cultures believed that everything has a reason, that no event is meaningless or contingent. He effectively argues that this philosophy is consistent with Christian theodicy and "the attitude that the cosmos works a plan."[67] Within the narrative of *Piano Lesson*, the Ghosts of Yellow Dog represent a cosmic plan of correctitude. The actions of the ghosts, unbalancing white men at the well's edge, serve to balance the unequal system of southern justice. While there is the suggestion that Boy Willie may have helped the ghosts in their mission, Wilson presents the Ghosts of the Yellow Dog as a real, tangible retort to lynchings and unequal justice. To justify further his faith in the Ghosts of the Yellow Dog, Wining Boy asserts, "You go ask them white folks in Sunflower County if they believe [in the Ghosts of the Yellow Dog]. You go asks Sutter if he believe" (*Piano Lesson,*

1.2.34). While the white residents of Sunflower County do not subscribe to the principles of ancestral worship connected to the Ghosts of the Yellow Dog, they do acknowledge the palpable threat represented by the unexplained deaths of nine or more white men.

Faith in the Ghosts of the Yellow Dog constitutes a form of ancestral worship that bestows protection and spiritual well-being on the believers. Wining Boy reports:

> It didn't look like nothing was going right in my life. I said everything can't go wrong all the time . . . let me go down there and call on the Ghosts of the Yellow Dog, see if they can help me. I went down there and right there where them two railroads cross each other. . . . I stood right there on that spot and called out their names. They talk back to you, too. . . . I walked away from there feeling like a king. Went on and had a stroke of luck that run on for three years.
>
> (*Piano Lesson*, 1.2.34–35)

Wining Boy's account of meeting the Ghosts of the Yellow Dog has a direct relationship to W. C. Handy's account of "discovering" the blues at a railroad crossing in Tutwiler, Mississippi, in 1903. W. C. Handy, the "Father of the Blues," jolted awake as he awaited his much-delayed train, to the sound of a guitar and a black man singing:

> Goin' where the Southern cross the Dog
> Goin' where the Southern cross the Dog
> Goin' where the Southern cross the Dog[68]

As Houston Baker reports, "This haunting invocation of railroad crossings in bottleneck tones left Handy stupefied and inspired."[69] Then in 1914, Handy published his own "Yellow Dog Blues." Virtually from their inception, the blues have been intertwined with the railways, articulating the triumphs, trials, and tribulations of movement and migration.

Wilson's signifying on the W. C. Handy narrative within *Piano Lesson* evidences the significance of the blues in Wilson's dramaturgy. Wining Boy, the musician, talks to the Ghosts and, in the tradition of blues call-and-response, antiphonally, the Ghosts talk back. When the Charles family exorcises Sutter's ghost at the end of the *Piano Lesson*, "the sound of a train approaching is heard" (*Piano Lesson*, 2.5.107). The presence of the train signifies the presence of the blues spirit, the Ghosts of the Yellow Dog.

Early in the play Berniece vehemently voices her disagreement with this faith in the Ghosts of the Yellow Dog. "I don't care who preached what. Somebody down there pushing them people in their wells" (*Piano Lesson*, 2.2.69). At the same time, Berniece does believe in the Holy Ghost and actually sees Sutter's ghost. She even asks Avery to remove Sutter's ghost through a ritual of Christian exorcism. Why does she acknowledge these other ghosts and not the Ghosts of the Yellow Dog? By rejecting the Ghosts of the Yellow Dog, Berniece is, in effect, denying her heritage, her connection to history. This denial of "ghosts" of the past correlates with her refusal to play the piano. As earlier noted, Berniece's neglect of the piano ruptures her connection to her ancestral spirits. Berniece is fractured, unwilling to accept the import of the past for the present. And yet, she, more than any other character, on some conscious level recognizes the presence, the coexistence, of the ancestors. She confesses to Avery, "I used to think them pictures [on the piano] came alive and walked through the house" (2.2.70). Her decision not to play the piano is a deliberate attempt to avoid waking these spirits. During the final climactic scene, however, when Berniece returns to the piano and plays, she acknowledges the importance of the ancestral spirits and the power of these "ghosts."

Rituals of Blood, Rituals of Life

In critical moments of crises, such as that which ensues when Sutter's ghost attempts to reclaim the piano, Wilson employs embodied ritual acts that symbolically reinforce the past impact on the present as his mode of redress. Berniece's playing of the piano is such a ritual summons that links her to the spirits of the ancestors beyond. Unlike the aborted Christian exorcism of Avery, her action is unmediated: Berniece does not work through a priest or established Christian doctrine but rather determines for herself a methodology for ridding the family of the ghosts of Sutter. Wilson's stage directions are particularly telling here:

> Berniece realizes what she must do. She crosses to the piano. She begins to play. The song is found piece by piece. It is an old urge to song that is both a commandment and a plea. With each repetition it gains strength. It is intended as an exorcism and a dressing for battle. A rustle of wind blowing across two continents.
>
> (*Piano Lesson*, 2.5.106)

Wilson's words paint for the reader the complexity of the ritual act that Berniece performs. The idea that the song is "found piece by piece" affirms that it is a context-specific enactment that speaks to the specific circumstances. Yet and still, it is an "Old urge to song" and a "rustle of wind blowing across two continents." Berniece constructs the song from her memory and yet also constructs memory through the song, for memory is never simply about what happened but what one wants to happen as well. Drawing back on her ancestors whom she knew as well as those she never knew, her construction of memory galvanizes her as it releases the power of the past. Her playing on the piano's keys calls forth the ghosts of her ancestors housed within the carvings on the piano's legs and enables the dead Negroes to speak. Her ritualistic call represents what Toledo in *Ma Rainey* calls "an African conceptualization. That's when you name the gods or call on the ancestors to achieve whatever your desires are" (1.24). But it is also a ritual that bends Christianity. The vehicle for its transmission is a piano, a decidedly Western instrument that has become a key component of black Christian church services. And Berniece is a churchgoing woman. Catherine Bell notes the ritual is "part of a historical process in which past patterns are reproduced but also reinterpreted or transformed."[70] Here, the cultural practice, the black church tradition of piano playing, through Berniece's urgent ritual, is both reproduced and transformed.

Berniece's ritual plea is not only particularly gendered, couched in the remembrance of her mother Mama Ola, but a blood memory of earlier blood sacrifice. Mama Ola polished the piano with her blood, signifying her symbolic offering of herself to the spirits of the dead Negroes within. "For seventeen years she rubbed on it till her hands bled. Then she rubbed the blood in . . . mixed it up with the rest of the blood on it. Everyday that God breathed life into her body she rubbed and cleaned and polished and prayed over it. 'Play something for me, Berniece. Play something for me, Berniece'" (*Piano Lesson*, 1.2.52). Mama Ola's blood, mixed into the piano, united her in a blood bond with her ancestors. Writing in *Rituals of Blood,* Orlando Patterson notes that blood sacrifice "propitiates and atones, but it also performs vital social and psychological functions for the participants."[71] Mama Ola's blood sacrifice protects the shrine that is the family's piano. In an unmediated Africanized revision of the Christian concept of transubstantiation—the doctrine that the eucharistic bread and wine becomes the body and blood of Christ in the ritual of Communion—Berniece ingests the blood and body of her ancestors. With her impassioned cries, "Mama Ola, I want you to help me," she channels that ancestral spirit that liberates her brother from the clutches of Sutter's ghost and frees her from the psychological burdens she has carried since the death of her husband, Crawley. Through Berniece's liberatory action, blood sacrifice becomes blood memory, not as ontology but as (w)righting metaphor.

Wilson engages the metaphor of blood memory through ritualized, collective, cultural embodiment in the final scene of the first act of *Joe Turner,* where the boardinghouse members, save for Herald Loomis, participate in a possessed Juba dance, reminiscent of the slave ring-shout. The sense of possession is, I believe, critical to situating this scene within the ritualized context of *Joe Turner* and its transmutation of the metaphor of blood memory. Lynne Fauley Emery points out in *Black Dance* that "Under the guise of Protestantism, the Ring-Shout retained the characteristics of African sacred dance. The purpose of the Shout was possession, as it was in Voodoo, Shango, and Nanigo. Possession in the Shout, however, was by the spirit of the Lord, not Damballa or Shango."[72] Possession in the African American ring shout, as Fauley Emery relates, established a relationship with the divine that was experiential and personal. The embodied act of dancing connected the celebrant with spiritual forces beyond. Similarly, in Yoruba ritual observances, the act of drumming and dancing materializes the supernatural potential within the phenomenal world and institutes conditions necessary for spiritual possession. The Yoruban possession dance is one in which the priestess of the god, for possession generally is the domain of women, transforms into the medium of the god. Describing the events that led from spirited dance to spiritual possession of an agent of Ogun in the Egbado town of Igbogila, Nigeria, in 1978, Margaret Thompson Drewal writes,

> There was a transformation of her attitude: from outgoing and playful to concentrated, serious and inwardly focused. As if bound to the spot, she stopped moving her feet; her upper torso veered to the side; her head dropped; and her left knee quivered, causing the entire body to tremble. A priest in this state is called the "horse of the god."[73]

As observed by Drewal the moment of possession itself is part of a performance tradition in which the agent, the person possessed, shares his/her spiritual consciousness with the gathered community. Transfigured and transformed, the priest becomes "the horse of the god." When spiritually possessed, your connection with the spirit world is unmediated, for the god is within. Accordingly, to a certain degree each of the characters within the Juba scene from *Joe Turner* is possessed. However, they are not simply possessed by the "Holy Spirit" but rather by the spirit past, by African tradition, by the power of the ancestors, by the "blood memory."

Yet the African diasporic experience of possession is not simply about harnessing the spirit of the god, it is about expressing a subversive freedom, a *jouissance* away from social, cultural, and especially gendered constraints. The black slave, a "being possessed" in real life, found in the experience of spiritual possession a liberation from the normal constraints of his or her everyday plantation existence. And within the malecentric hegemony of the early African American church the act of "getting happy" has been a method for female parishioners to escape the patriarchal dictates of the worship service, to take part in or even lead the services. Telia U. Anderson in her article "'Calling the Spirit': The Performativity of Black Women's Faith in the Baptist Church Spiritual Tradition and Its Radical Possibilities of Resistance," tells us that Jarena Lee, who had previously been excluded from preaching because of her gender, by moving with the spirit in church, became the first female preacher of the African Methodist Episcopal Church, sometime between 1803 and 1810.[74] Catching the spirit, she intervened within the conventional service and began delivering her own sermon. Her spiritual possession disrupted conventional gender performances. It enabled and in ways sanctioned her interjection and her subsequent preaching. Jarena Lee's revolutionary act suggests how the practice of possession within the African diaspora can serve as a subversive space for spontaneous, liberated enactments, expressions of political and social as well as spiritual agency.

Wilson implicitly and explicitly connects the Juba moment in *Joe Turner* to such African traditions of spiritual and social empowerment by granting the actors the license to improvise. Thus, for actors undertaking Wilson's Juba scene, it is often more than simply an acting experience. The performance of possession requires a real commitment to the context, circumstances, and meanings of the enactment. Wilson in his stage directions allows considerable freedom: "It should be as African as possible, with the performers working themselves up into a near frenzy. The words can be improvised" (1.4.249). In this improvisation, the performer concentrates not simply on being his or her particular character, but on doing the dance, experiencing and expressing the free flow of energy and spirit between fellow performers. It is not simply blocked by the director, but becomes real and immediate in its execution. Drewal comments on the potential power of improvisation within the Yoruba ritual:

> It is indeed the play, the improvising, that engages people, drawing them into the action, constructing their relationship, thereby generating multiple and simultaneous discourses always swinging between harmony/disharmony, order/disorder, integration/opposition and so on.[75]

Because of the nature of improvisation, the fervor of the Juba scene within *Joe Turner* is different and new with each performance. If it generates the frenetic ecstatic energy that Wilson requests, then it will verge on the pendulum between the harmony/disharmony that Drewal describes. This is both a captivating and dangerous stage moment capable of sweeping the audience up in its energy.[76] Equally significant, the Juba is performed with musical accompaniment in a call-and-response pattern in which Wilson asks that Bynum serve as caller and that the others in their responses should "include some mention of the Holy Ghost" (1.4.249). Harkening back to African cultural practices, the tradition of call-and-response is purposefully participatory. It is a communal activity that in its production critiques itself, instituting new codes of understanding, energizing its participants in the process.

Herald Loomis's spontaneous intervention, when he comes in and discovers this frenetic, spiritual, atavistic encounter of bodies, I would argue, is not an intolerable disruption, but is itself an accepted part of the ritual processes. Mary L. Bogumil interprets Loomis's interruption and irreverence as antithetical to the African nature of this moment. She writes that "in the play when Herald Loomis attempts to stop the Juba, he disrupts this call-and-response pattern, this cultural tradition—something which is not tolerated in African societies."[77] On the contrary, I believe his actions serve as another improvisation, and within

Yoruba ritual traditions improvisation is not only tolerated, but expected. Correspondingly, within African American church traditions the experience of parishioners "getting happy" or becoming overcome with the Holy Spirit are not disruptive events, but rather spontaneous, spiritual interventions allowed and even encouraged within the dynamics of exchange and participation within the black church. The next morning, when Seth apologizes to his boarder, Molly Cunningham, for Loomis's behavior, Molly responds, "It don't bother me none. I done seen that kind of stuff before" (*Joe Turner,* 2.1.256).

In keeping with the denotation of the word *trope* associated with medieval liturgical performances, Loomis's entrance acts as a "trope" or an interpolation into the ritualistic ceremony. Within this tropic performance, Loomis recounts his vision of seeing "bones walking on water." He envisions and relates in this moment—now using our contemporary understanding of the term—one of the more powerful "tropes" of "blood memory," the trope of Middle Passage. In Suzan-Lori Parks's Obie Award–winning play *Imperceptible Mutabilities of the Third Kingdom,* the notion of the "third kingdom" refers to those people who exist in the transitional zone between Africa and America. The National Book Awards prize–winning novel *Middle Passage* by Charles Johnson cuts across time even as it describes the harrowing experiences of one journey aboard a slave ship. Within each of these works, the author fuses history and memory, constructing alternative visions of the past through processes of recovery. The reiteration of this trope of Middle Passage in contemporary African American cultural production reflects on the significance that this initiating rupture holds within African American collective memory. Through the entrance of Loomis into the Juba scene and Loomis's possessed rememory of the Middle Passage, Wilson tropes a trope.

Under the weight of this powerful vision, Loomis is in all senses of the phrase "a being possessed." In accordance with these African and African American experiences of possession, Wilson notes that just prior to his vision, "Loomis begins to speak in tongues and dance around the kitchen" (*Joe Turner,* 1.4.250). Observing Loomis, Bertha warns her husband Seth, "Leave him alone Seth. He ain't in his right mind" (1.4.250). Loomis certainly is not in his right mind. He is possessed. His possession is particularly masculinized, and yet like the spiritual possession of Yoruba priestesses or the "getting happy" evangelicalism of black women in Baptist church pews, Loomis's possession is liberating. It frees him from the conventional constraints of realism in a moment that is decidedly metaphoric. Loomis's possessed rememory of the Middle Passage reveals not only struggle and death but also transcendence and survival. He visualizes the "bones top of walking on water" until they reach land where they "got flesh on them" and start "standing up at the same time" and begin "walking every whichaway down the road" (1.4.251–252). Despite the losses at sea, the trials and tribulations of the past, these bones people, these "third kingdom" people, are able to make their way in the New World. Obsessed with and possessed by this image, Loomis desires to stand and walk with these people; however, he is unable to do so. Even as he is encouraged by Bynum to stand and walk, his "legs wont stand up" (1.4.252). Herald Loomis is a victim of spiritual and psychological inertia. Through his stated inability to stand and walk, Wilson metaphorically manifests Loomis's complex and contradictory situation, his immobile mobility, his social death. Liberated in the moment of possession, he needs to find a tangible freedom in his actual life.

Gabriel's spirited dance at the end of *Fences* provides a retort to social death as it mediates between the world of the past and the present. Gabriel, the seemingly mentally retarded and now institutionalized brother returns and summons his special faith to open Heaven's gates on the day of Troy his brother's funeral. Gabriel attempts to open the gates by thrice blowing his dysfunctional horn, but the conventional doctrine and mythology of Christianity fails. Thwarted, he begins to dance a "slow strange dance, eerie and life-giving" (*Fences,* 2.5.192). Through this dance, Gabriel "works the spirit" and negotiates between the world of the living and the dead. His connection with the spirit world is embodied, unmediated. Prior to opening Heaven's gates, Wilson writes that Gabriel endures "a trauma that a sane and normal mind would be unable to withstand" (2.5.192). At this moment, placed within a Yoruban context, Gabriel's experience parallels the "tragic terror" that Soyinka theorizes one must undergo when one enters the "fourth stage of transition."[78] Gabriel enters this metaphysical abyss in order to transfer Troy from the world of the living to the world of the ancestors. Soyinka argues that a "titanic resolution of will" is necessary to rescue any person within this abyss. Gabriel survives his entrance into this transitional gulf *because* his mental capacity is not "normal." Because

Gabriel wholeheartedly believes he is the archangel Gabriel, his will is resolute. Wilson goes on to describe Gabriel's dance as being of "atavistic signature and ritual." The dance as ritual enactment remembers the traditions of the African spirituality and even the African America ring shout in which dance enables spiritual transmission. His dance and inaudible horn sounds, his attempt at song, or what Wilson calls "a song turning back into itself," are the embodiment of his "ritual summons," and the expression of his "titanic resolution" of will. Gabriel's transcendent moment unites Yoruba ritual and Christian doctrine. The "Christian" archangel opens the gates of Heaven by engaging in a Yoruban ceremony connecting himself and his family to African traditions.

Within the given context of his brother Troy's death, the first appearance of Raynell, the return of the institutionalized Maxson men Gabriel, Lyons, and Cory, and the familial tensions over Troy's life and his legacy, Gabriel's act serves a social and cosmological redress. He creates a space for Troy's redemption that reconnects the family and empowers their future. Gabriel's "life giving" dance brings symbolic systems and cultural traditions to bear on these real events. His ritual is a strategic "reshuffling [of] cultural categories in order to meet the needs" of a real situation.[79] In his stage directions, Wilson states that as a result of Gabriel's performance, "the gates of heaven stand open as wide as God's closet" (*Fences*, 2.5.192) and then Wilson relies on the director and lighting designer to produce real stage magic.

The character, as well as the performer, as Gabe become empowered through this enactment. For even as Wilson's stage directions reveal to the reader the dynamics of this ritual enactment, they also open up practical challenges for the director and performer: How does an actor as Gabriel "howl in what is an attempt at song, or perhaps a song turning back into itself in an attempt at speech" (*Fences*, 2.5.192)? My sense is that the performer as Gabe, in order to be effective, must commit to the embodied action of possession. The music, the rhythmic song and dance, produce possession, enable this transformation, and then Gabriel must share this new spiritual consciousness with those around him. Notably, the symbolic community for this ritual is not only the extended Maxson family that witnesses the event onstage, but the audience that experiences Gabriel's ceremony as well as its spectacular and theatricalized results, the opening of the heavens as constructed by the lighting designer. "That's the way that go!" Gabriel exclaims upon viewing the fruits of his labors. And as with any ritual the real meaning depends on the ability of the spectators to interpret the ritual symbols. The audience needs to recognize the conflation of the real and symbolic, the personal and communal within this event.

Correspondingly, the climactic ritualized events that end *Joe Turner* present to the spectator personal and collective dynamics of blood sacrifice and blood memory. Loomis, a son of Ogun in a parallel to his Wilsonian "brother" Gabriel, enters into the chthonic real and must summon his will. Mark Rocha argues that like Gabriel, Loomis too is mad, outside the conventions of normalcy.[80] Certainly, he is psychologically and spiritually bereft, driven to the point of desperation and overwhelmed by the haunting forces of his past, his righteous, runaway wife Martha, his faith in Christianity's God, his seven-year imprisonment by Joe Turner. The circumstances create a context of crisis and social drama demanding ritual redress. Brandishing a knife, the emblem of Ogun, "the divine metonym for creativity, new technology, and self definition,"[81] Loomis slashes his chest and bleeds for himself. This act is one that expresses self-determination and agency. It is a resolute act of will. As he cuts and marks himself physically, he liberates himself from his previous debilitating psychological marking as one of Joe Turner's niggers.

Wilson precedes this ritual enactment with another in which Bertha blesses her kitchen and surroundings, preparing the way and creating an atmosphere conducive to Loomis's subsequent ritual transformations. In the presence of her boarders including Zonia and Bynum, just prior to Martha's return with Selig and after Seth has told Loomis that he must leave his house, Bertha, as Wilson states:

> moves about the kitchen as though blessing it and chasing away the huge sadness that seems to envelope it. It is a dance and demonstration of her own magic, her own remedy that is centuries old and to which she is connected by the muscles of her heart and the blood's memory . . . She begins to laugh. It is a near-hysterical laughter that is a celebration of life, both its pain and its blessing.
>
> (*Joe Turner*, 2.5.283).

Wilson's words recall how within African diasporic religion, ritualized enactments, dances, songs can serve for the initiates as a way of transcending the particulars of time and place. Bertha performs an embodied, dichotomous rite of celebration. In this time of liminal uncertainty, she laughs to keep from crying. Her physical engagement in cultural practices, moving around, blessing the house, is a form of "bodily knowing" that enables her to connect "by the muscles of her heart and blood's memory."[82] Drewal relates that, through the manipulation of ritual symbols, the Yoruban ritual practitioner can transpose the social order, and even reconstitute the conventional.[83] Such ritual practices construct meaning and convey values in very specific ways. Bertha's laughing rite is contextual, for ritual is a matter of invention within particular circumstances. Within the ever-changing same of performance, it is reinvented, not only in the diverse interpretations of different actresses as Bertha, but in the non-reproducible, ephemeral moment of "near hysterical laughter" each night. Bertha's laughter is infectious, and it becomes a participatory ritual. Those around her—Mattie, Zonia, and even Seth—become involved in this embodied spirited laughter. Present is the condition of *communitas,* a spiritual effervescence. Bertha transforms not only the practical mood, but the metaphysics, of the kitchen, creating a productive site for Loomis's ceremony of freedom that follows.

As Christ-like agent in his own image, Loomis through his ritualized act of bloodletting signals the need for African American self-determination. Like Berniece's piano playing and Gabriel's dance, Loomis's act of knife-wielding, self-penetration is a syncretic ritual that bends and joins the Christian with the African. Just prior to his slashing, Martha asks Loomis to accept Christ, to understand that Jesus bled for him and to prepare himself to "be washed clean with the blood of the lamb" (*Joe Turner,* 2.5.288). In Christian doctrine, those metaphorically washed clean in the blood of Christ could be born anew, could enter Heaven and receive eternal life. Yet, in *Joe Turner,* just as the ritual action of Gabriel presents an alternative methodology for entrance into Heaven, Wilson's protagonist seeks practical not eternal salvation but inner peace within his here and now. Accordingly, Loomis rejects Martha's pleas: "I don't need no body to bleed for me! I can bleed for myself." His act is unmediated, self-initiated, and self-defining. His bleeding makes literal what is metaphorical in the Christian Communion service. And yet his "real" act is both figurative in its theatrical manifestation and symbolic in its meaning. "I'm standing now!" he exclaims to

"You got to be clean, Herald. You got to be washed with the blood of the lamb." Joe Turner's Come and Gone, *Downstairs Theater, 1989, with Michael Rogers (Herald), Lawrence James (Seth), Tamyah Ward (Zonia), Viola Davis (Mattie), Lorey Hayes (Martha), David Kennet (Rutherford), and Ed Hall (Bynum). (Note that, unlike as requested in Wilson's stage directions, Martha is dressed in black rather than in white.) (Photograph by Mark Morelli.)*

Bynum. Through this act he is born anew, "Heralding" a new day for himself and for African Americans.

Loomis's self-sacrifice equally functions to symbolically reconstruct blackness. Immediately after, Loomis rubs the blood over his face, ritualistically cleansing himself, reimagining other blood rituals within the African Diaspora and within the Wilson cycle. Orlando Patterson in *Rituals of Blood* theorizes that lynching, in all its inhumanity, constituted an act of ritualized human blood sacrifice, a rite of segregation that served to redress the crisis of postslavery transition and uncertainty for white America. By figuratively and actually removing the threatening "black beast," these acts affirmed the baseness of blackness and valorized the privileges and sanctity of whiteness.[84] Loomis's blood sacrifice inverts such processes and notions of black inferiority by structuring the black subject as agent in his own salvation. Rather than defining blackness in relationship to whiteness, he defines it simply in relationship to itself. Through this ritual fragmentation he is made whole, his personal crisis ritualistically redressed.

Just as in the blood ritual that ends Wole Soyinka's adaptation of *The Bacchae of Euripides,* Loomis's individual actions not only serve his liberation but, as ritual, benefit the greater community around him, offering regeneration. In Soyinka's *Bacchae,* the head of Pentheus, torn from its body by his possessed mother Agave and the other bacchants, is placed on a stake above the city's gate. The blood dripping from the severed head transmutes into wine, and the community as a whole partakes, drinking in this transformed spirit that offers new life of forgiveness and change. Loomis, transformed by his blood, now shines "like new money" (*Joe Turner,* 2.5.289). His act makes manifest for himself and others a radical new beginning. In the Yoruban worship rites for Shango, the thunder god, initiations require "bathing in blood." The initiate soaked in blood becomes a "mighty kinsman of the royal house, particularly through the 'blood' extracted and transferred from S[h]ango's emblematic animal—the ram."[85] Loomis is correspondingly empowered with *àshe* through his blood bath. He is made a metaphorical African "blood brother."

Thus, Loomis steps out of the boardinghouse and into a new beginning, but in so doing he looks back to Africa. This Africa is a metaphoric site, "always and already a site of cultural crossing." As Sandra Richards notes, "The Africa that Wilson would have black Americans embrace is first an internal site of self-possession and agency."[86] By finding the god within, Loomis journeys to Africa. He leaves with new knowledge that is gained by his re-evolutionary action, which sends him back to the spot of initiating rupture. Paradoxically, the process brings him "*forward* to a return to Africa."[87] The ending becomes a beginning. He is re-membered and renewed.

A promise of new beginnings catalyzed in ceremonies of freedom marks *King Hedley II* as well. The play opens in a coda with Stool Pigeon alone on the stage. As he takes the lids off of the trash cans so that the dogs can eat, he talks with God. In a metatheatrical moment, he reminds God that "the story's been written. All that's left now is the playing out" (prologue, 1). These meta-theatrics reflexively comment on Wilson's own dramaturgical process. Wilson's *King Hedley II* has been written and rewritten through the course of the actors' playing it out in cities from Pittsburgh, to Seattle, to Los Angeles to Chicago to New York. Furthermore, Stool Pigeon's statement, as oral doctrine, prophecy, and prediction, informs us that this is, in fact, the final stage for these characters and the world around them. "The story has already been written." We soon discover in *King Hedley II* a black community in decay and disarray in which Aunt Ester subsequently dies of grief. What Stool Pigeon establishes is that this play is an endgame—the final moments of a chess game after most of the pieces are removed. As in a chess endgame, from the very beginning of the play, a King is in trouble, and in the "playing out" the characters intensely struggle for survival, to keep the game alive. In Samuel Beckett's classic *Endgame,* the character Hamm adamantly fights to remain alive through orally retelling history and constructing memory. And so it is with the children of Ham within Wilson's endgame, *King Hedley II.* They struggle to construct meaning for themselves without the recognition of what Stool Pigeon calls "the keys to the Kingdom," without awareness of their need for spiritual connection to those that have gone on before. With this loss of history, they are lost, and as predicted by Stool Pigeon, God brings down divine, destructive retribution, paving the way for rituals of new beginning. Wilson's Ruby—like Soyinka's Agave, who unknowingly decapitates her own son Pentheus—accidentally kills her son King, symbolically signaling an end to a cycle of violence and destruction. This end is also a beginning as his blood blesses the shrine that Stool Pigeon has constructed for Aunt Ester. King's blood is the blood of a King, the purifying, sanctified blood of Shango's ram, the blood of human sacrifice that can bring about social, spiritual, and cultural resurrection.

Stool Pigeon's final prayers over this grave of the black cat—the metonymic resting place of Aunt Ester, the cultural repository for African American history—are like Berniece's piano playing, "both a commandment and a plea" to a God with whom he shares a personal connection. He tells his God: "Say I want your best! The fatted calf," the ultimate human sacrifice that is King (*King Hedley II,* 2.5.103). He pleads with God to bring down his blessings, to return Aunt Ester and in the process to redeem the black community. For Stool Pigeon his God is "a bad motherfucker," and as Wilson points out, this affectation is not a blasphemy, but the highest of praise. Says Wilson, "He's not calling God a name—Levee was calling him a name. Levee was cussing him out. Levee was mad. But it's a praise."[88] My sense is that Stool Pigeon not only differs from Levee in his desire to praise God, but in his imagining of this God. The God that Stool Pigeon fears and reveres, as in the lines from Countee Cullen quoted at the outset of this chapter, is fashioned with "Dark despairing features . . . Crowned with dark rebellious hair." The trajectory of Wilson dramaturgy refigures not only the characters' relationship to the spirit and spirit to flesh, but it reconfigures God him- or herself. The God that Stool Pigeon converses with is one who "looks like him" and who gravitates to the particular needs of black people. Unlike the God who does not answer Levee's challenge in *Ma Rainey*, this God hears and answers Stool Pigeon's summons, as evidenced by the audible cat's "meow" that ends the play.

Throughout Wilson's cycle, spirit is both called upon and repositioned. Crises within the practical world are resolved in the realm of the symbolic. Ritualized acts bring together spirit and body. As Catherine Bell writes, these rituals operate as "a central arena for cultural mediation, the means by which various combinations of structure and history, past and present, meanings and needs, are brought together in terms of each other."[89] In these rituals of re-membrance, Wilson posits an Africa that is both spirit and flesh, figurative and actual, past and future. His Africa in America is "a site of cultural becoming."[90] This vision of Africa is ritualized and placed within a decidedly African American context making for an African American re-evolutionary theology, forged in the music, the culture, and the spirit of black lives.

Chapter 6
The Rhetoric of Resistance
by Way of Conclusion

People kept asking for a "black" play. I kept asking, "What's a 'black' play. Four walls, a couch and a mama?" I can't live within those old definitions.

—George C. Wolfe

August Wilson can create moments of magic through his ability to give Negro American nuances aesthetic form. Yet I find his TCG speech out of step with his own accomplishments. . . . In Wilson's keynote address . . . we get Black Power clichés so familiar and so lacking in the bitterly ironic wit of his works that the speech writer could hardly have been August Wilson. The ideas, if we are willing to call them such, are at odds with his plays.

—Stanley Crouch, "Who's Zooming Who?"

Because of his prominence as an African American playwright, August Wilson often has found the weight of the whole race, the need to "keep it real" for the people, thrust upon him. Perhaps his sense of that responsibility led to Wilson's provocative keynote address to the Theatre Communications Group Conference in June 1996. The speech incited national discussions, op-ed pieces, journal articles, conference papers, and a much-ballyhooed public debate between Wilson and Robert Brustein, artistic director of the American Repertory Theater moderated by Anna Deavere Smith in January 1997. It also provided the impetus for a National Black Theatre Summit, convened in March 1998, in which black theater scholars, artists, and practitioners from around the country joined together to consider the state of black theater in contemporary America. As the spark for this explosion of dialogue, Wilson's TCG address resurrects passions centered around the import and impact of black theater that supposedly had died out after the Black Theater movement of the 1960s and 1970s. In fact, Wilson's oration, one could argue, should be placed alongside W. E. B. Du Bois's declaration "Four Principles of Negro Theater" (1926) and LeRoi Jones's (Amiri Baraka's) incendiary treatise "The Revolutionary Theatre" (1966) as a critical black theater manifesto. In a manner related to these earlier documents, Wilson's speech seeks to answer the question asked by George C. Wolfe, a question repeatedly revisited since the inception of African American playwriting; "What is a black play?" Wilson's remarks not only address the aesthetic implications of this query but also challenge the material conditions that govern black theatrical production.

Because Wilson is one of the most decorated and lauded playwrights operating on the American stage today, achieving critical and cross-cultural success, his speech also provokes questions of his own aesthetic practice: How do Wilson's theories on black theater work within his own dramas? Does he practice the black theatrical prescriptions that he preaches? Stanley Crouch argues that Wilson does not: his TCG speech is "out of step with his own accomplishments."[1] Crouch accuses Wilson of an antiquated logic and of lacking irony in his TCG presentation. And yet I believe that Crouch and others overlook how within this speech Wilson situates himself in history by imaginatively employing strategies of the past in conjunction with a distinct perspective on the present. The speech provides leverage for reconsidering the content and context of black theater practice. Taken comparatively, Wilson's (w)righting history through his plays and his radical claims in this historic manifesto present a prescription for decentering American normative whiteness and reflect a politics of difference that offers not separatism, but a recognition of diversity. Nevertheless, Wilson's declaration of social activism in art is paradoxical. The paradox in Wilson, however, is not, as Crouch and others have claimed, between outmoded black power rhetoric and the politics of the current moment, but in the ways in which Wilson as that singular black voice is both complicit with and oppositional to the existent white hegemony in American theater.

If Crouch condemns the 1960s for essentialist black power clichés, Wilson historically locates black power as a crucial moment in a race's coming of age in real time and space. Wilson's title for his TCG address, "The Ground on Which I Stand," "grounds" this speech in a particular rhetoric of black cultural nationalism that implicitly and explicitly recalls the black revolutionary platforms of the 1960s and 1970s. After all, central to any affirmation of national identity is the ground, the land, the nation. In the absence of a land base, black cultural nationalism in the 1960s and 1970s claimed cultural territory and used the space of cultural practice to celebrate and define the "black nation." Wilson's discussion of land, the ground on which he stands, is both material and figurative. The land he wants to claim for black theatrical production is a geographic as well as a symbolic space within the American theater system. He points out that at the time of his TCG address only one of the sixty-seven League of Regional Theaters (LORT) in America was devoted to black theater. In making his demand and breaking new ground for black theater, he positions himself within histories and traditions that give him the right and reason to seek such participatory ownership: "I have come here today to make a testimony, to talk about the ground on which I stand and all the many grounds on which I and my ancestors have toiled, and the ground of theatre on which my fellow artists and I have labored to bring forth its fruits, its daring and its sometimes liberating and healing truths."[2] Reimagining the paradigms of cultural nationalism, Wilson links the ground of the American theater with the ancestral ground of African American labor. It is these past, unreparated efforts of his black forebears that foster his current claims and shape his rhetoric. For Wilson, black power politics of the 1960s and 1970s represented a methodology for restitution, for reclaiming the legacy of uncompensated and under-appreciated black toil as well as for realizing his own self-worth: "That is the ground of the affirmation of one's being, an affirmation of his worth in the face of society's urgent and sometimes profound denial. It was this ground as a young man coming into manhood searching for something with which to dedicate my life that I discovered the Black Power movement of the 60s" ("Ground," 14). The Black Power movement enabled him not only to honor the past, but also to craft his social and aesthetic commitment.

Wilson historicizes black power in his speech and thus particularizes it. He constantly positions it in time and space. Fusing aesthetics and ethics, Wilson roots himself in a tradition of functional black art that rises out of the particular social conditions and struggles of African American life: "I stand myself on the self-defining ground of the slave quarters and find the ground to be hallowed and made fertile by the blood and bones of men and women who can be described as warriors on the cultural battlefield that affirmed self worth" ("Ground," 16). This grounding directly correlates with his own (w)righting of history. Through his plays Wilson re-visits and remakes history, questioning specific choices blacks have made in the past, while underscoring how they have maintained the will to survive. He imaginatively resurrects collective memories and individual histories, reconstructs cultural practices and enables previously silent and silenced voices to speak. His TCG speech, in fact, revisits his own history, as ideas presented in the speech have appeared in earlier Wilson writings, including the September 1990 *Spin* magazine article "I Don't Want Nobody Just 'Cause They're Black," the December 1992 *Life* magazine article "The Legacy of Malcolm X," and the preface to *August Wilson: Three Plays,* published by the University of Pittsburgh Press in 1991.[3] In each of these essays, Wilson reflects on the personal and collective power of African American history. With his TCG speech, Wilson asks other African American playwrights to utilize history as impulse for their art. Noting the attempts by the dominant culture to deny black history, Wilson calls on black artists to serve as cultural purveyors and protectors: "We must defend and protect our spiritual fruits. . . . To give expression to the spirit that has been shaped and fashioned by our history is of necessity to give voice and vent to the history itself" ("Ground," 72). The role that Wilson defines for black playwrights is an activist one. It is functional through its engagement with and demands on history. Recalling the urgency and idealism of the Black Arts movement, Wilson proclaims that "we can be the spearhead of a movement to reignite and reunite our people's positive energy for a political and social change that is reflective of our spiritual truth rather than our economic fallacies. . . . What we do now becomes history by which our grandchildren will judge us" ("Ground," 73). Wilson perceives that the historic responsibility for black theater artists rests not simply in the reckoning with the past, but in preparing a way for the future.

Still, we must ask, is Wilson's proclamation for black artists overly prescriptive? Reading Wilson's TCG speech and his subsequent response to critic Robert Brustein provides a somewhat contradictory perspective. Wilson writes to Brustein, "I would never be so arrogant as to tell any artist what kind of work they should be doing."[4] And yet in his TCG address, Wilson argues that black artists must not escape their collective history: "We all share a common past, and despite what some of us might think and how it might look, we all share a common present and will share a common future" ("Ground," 73). This shared legacy and destiny, Wilson maintains, compels the direction and directives of African American theatrical practice. He exhorts black playwrights, "It is time to embrace the political dictates of our history and answer the challenge of our duties" ("Ground," 73). Within such a call, there appears little room for deviation or space for African American artists to envision an alternative theatrical mission. Yet unlike the seminal manifestos of the Black Arts movement, Amiri Baraka's "Revolutionary Theater" or Larry Neal's "Black Arts Movement," Wilson's exhortation does not outline specific dynamics of form or content to which black theater must adhere. Rather, Wilson allows that the past, as Toni Morrison suggests, is "infinite,"[5] and that this history is fertile ground for the exploration of cross-cultural commonalties.

According to Wilson, "there is no idea that cannot be contained by black life" ("Ground," 16). How can we reconcile this assertion with Wilson's division of black arts into two binary and oppositional camps?

> There have always been two distinct and parallel traditions in black arts: that is, art that is conceived and designed to entertain white society, and art that feeds the spirit and celebrates the life of black America by designing its strategies for survival and prosperity. ("Ground," 16)

What Wilson loses in this Manichaean division is any accurate reflection of the African American cultural history that he treasures. Black arts that entertain whites and arts that celebrate the black experience are not necessarily antithetical. In slavery, African Americans created art that, simultaneously, could delight the master but also contained coded messages about clandestine meetings, escape strategies, or plans for black resistance. Black arts have historically been polyvocal, able to be translated differently depending on the experience and circumstances of the audience. Wilson's own dramaturgy is a case in point. The cross-cultural popularity of all of his plays challenges his own premise. Structuring this binary division between reactionary and revolutionary black art sets up a potentially dangerous exclusionary/inclusionary dynamic that allows certain black art or black artists to be discounted or demeaned if their work is not seen to sufficiently serve the cause of black advancement.

Consequently, following the TCG speech, critics from Robert Brustein to Stanley Crouch to Henry Louis Gates, Jr., have lined up to chastise Wilson for what seem like his regressive identity politics and his return to outdated constraints placed on black theater. Gates, in particular, critiques Wilson for replicating the proclamations of the Black Arts movement, which he faults for failing to mobilize the black masses. Ignoring the accomplishments of Amiri Baraka's Spirit House in Newark and the meteoric spread of black guerilla theater in America's urban enclaves during the late 1960s and early 1970s, Gates maintains that "by the late sixties, it was clear that the vitality of Black Arts had come to center upon two New York–based theaters: the Negro Ensemble Company (NEC) based uptown . . . and the New Lafayette Theater based in Harlem."[6] Gates's critique focuses on institutions in too limited a fashion, neglecting the smaller arts groups, revolutionary publishing efforts, and alternative educational practices that emerged in this period, all of which benefited from the energy and dynamic engagement of the Black Arts movement with the politics of representation.[7]

Even in the postmodern climate of the 1990s, with its denigration of the exclusionary dynamics of identity, Chicana playwright Cherríe Moraga maintains there is still a "longing for that once uncompromising cultural nationalism of the Sixties and Seventies that birthed a new nation of American Indian, Chicano, and Black artists."[8] As Moraga and Wilson, in contradistinction to Gates, suggest, the Black Arts movement continues to resonate in the radical insurgencies of contemporary artists of color and their desires to create socially minded art. Wilson's own critically acclaimed practice, not unlike that of Lorraine Hansberry or Bertolt Brecht before him, seeks to both delight and instruct. Brustein, in his rejoinder to Wilson, asserts that political ends limit artistic practice. Steeped in the ideals of modernism, Brustein's attack seems both paternal and naive.[9] Wilson counters in their much-publicized debate, by arguing that all arts are inherently political: some reinforce the political status quo, while others attempt to subvert it. Moreover, social truths are not antithetical to human truths but rather are grounded, Wilson argues, within the specifics of their social and cultural conditions.

In his TCG speech, however, Wilson pushes the significance of race as a social and human truth even further than he does in his plays, calling race "the largest category of identification because it is the one that most influences your perception of yourself and it is the one to which others in the world of men respond" ("Ground," 16). The TCG statement on race ignores the fact that sexuality and gender profoundly interact with race and that identity is always about positioning. He does not comment on matters of imposition, the ways that others impose their perceptions, "coloring" one's sense of self. The homogeneity of his statement is offset by the constructions of blackness in his cycle. In Wilson's dramaturgy, blackness is not an ontological or essential category but one of political, cultural, and social construction. He celebrates the vernacular, the music, and the cultural practices of a people that transcend time but are clearly a product of their historic moment. Accordingly, the conditions of blackness that Ma Rainey and Levee encounter in *Ma Rainey's Black Bottom* (1927) are different from those that Memphis and Risa face more than forty years later in *Two Trains Running* (1969). For these characters and the others in Wilson's cycle, the truth of race lies in the intersections of lived experience and the social, cultural, and historical constructions of blackness. The critics of Wilson's TCG statement are right, I would argue, in noting that he privileges race, but for the wrong reason. He does not construct it as an ahistorical category but does overdetermine its significance in relation to issues of sexuality and gender.

Wilson, in his TCG address, seems to suggest that the nature of lived experience has demarcated strict boundaries between black and white culture and experience. These cultural borders, coupled with the dominant culture's paternalism toward black arts, necessitate his call for the separate development of black arts. Wilson demands funding that would make it possible for black theater to evolve and flower on its own. Brustein, as a result, asserts that Wilson calls for "subsidized separatism," and Gates charges Wilson with "sentimental separatism." Yet Wilson explicitly states, "We are not separatists. . . . We are artists who seek to develop our talents and give expression to our personalities. We bring advantage to the common ground that is American theater" ("Ground," 73). Here, then, is a seeming paradox in Wilson's platform that reflects the paradoxical position of people of color in the American theater. Wilson correctly points out that black and other minority theaters have insufficient funding because corporations instead have supported efforts at diversity in mainstream regional theaters. Such arrangements have kept theaters of color on the bottom of the stratified professional theater system and maintain predominantly white regional theaters as the arbitrators of art and culture.

My sense is that Wilson's call for "separatism" is neither subsidized nor sentimental but strategic, an example of what Harold Cruse terms "black particularism." Discussing the continued need for Black Studies programs, Cruse maintains that

> the question of a black studies program is intrinsically a two-way street: a black studies program—even if it expresses black particularism—is a kind of particularism which understands its own limits and social function. Its social function is not to replace one particularism with another particularism but to counterbalance the historical effects and exaggeration of particularism toward a more racially balanced society, a society which would include expectations regarding the democratic creed.[10]

Cruse envisions black particularism as a response to and compensation for the "cultural particularism" of the dominant culture, which denies "the validity of other kinds of cultural values that might compete with its own standards—whether in the social sciences, the arts, literature, or economic activity."[11] As such a strategy, black particularism entails the situational adoption of a separate ideology because of its particular political advantage at a specific historical moment. In line with this strategy, Wilson has refused to let *Fences* become a film without a black director. He outlines his rationale in an essay entitled "I Want a Black Director": "No wonder I had been greeted with incredulous looks when I suggested a black director for *Fences*. I sat in the office of Paramount Pictures suggesting that someone who was affected by an undesirable condition, who was a violator of public regulations, who was sullen, unqualified, and marked by a malignant influence, direct the film."[12] Wilson desires a black director not simply because a black director would have more cultural familiarity with and sensitivity to the material, but because American cultural politics have historically denied black cultural value.[13] As Michael Awkward writes,

> Of preeminent importance to the playwright, I believe is whether, given the preeminence of caucacentric discourse and actions in our nation, Afro-Americans can afford to allow patterns of expressive cultural distribution to continue wherein blacks remain pawns to the whims and racialist will of white entrepreneurial forces interested primarily in economic bottom lines rather than in working to destroy the still-evident barriers to

social, economic and cultural power for a large portion of the black population.[14]

Wilson's black particularism thus asserts black self-determination against the hegemony of the white-controlled culture industry. Notably, Wilson has allowed *Fences* to be produced in Mainland China with a Chinese cast and a white American director. He has also permitted white directors to stage American productions of *Ma Rainey's Black Bottom* and *Joe Turner's Come and Gone*. At the end of his one-man show, *How I Learned What I Learned,* at the Seattle Repertory Theatre in May 2003, Wilson commended the show's white director, Todd Kreidler, and invited him up onto the stage where they shook hands. In each of these cases he felt that the directors understood the cultural sensibilities of the texts and characters. The Chinese production, Wilson argues, also occurred in a distinctly different cultural climate and political context, outside of the American theatrical history of black artistic subjugation. What Wilson's black particularism does, then, is to demand an American space for black artistic achievement and recognition. Wilson wants African American art to be valued as its own unique cultural expression.

Perhaps the most controversial articulation of black particularism in Wilson's speech was his rejection of color-blind casting. Wilson objects to color-blind casting as "an aberrant idea that has never had any validity other than as a tool of the Cultural Imperialists who view American culture, rooted in the icons of European culture as beyond reproach in its perfection. It is inconceivable to them that life could be lived without knowing Shakespeare or Mozart" ("Ground," 72). I think it is important to note Wilson discusses color-blind rather than nontraditional casting and to acknowledge their distinctions. Nontraditional casting does not attempt to obscure or to "e-race" racial or gendered meanings. Rather, nontraditional casting inverts, subverts, or potentially illuminates those meanings by casting across gender, cross-racially, against the traditional norms as implied within the written text. Color-blind casting, on the other hand, implies that race does not matter, that the casting is blind to color. Alan Nadel points out that Wilson's opposition to color blindness challenges the basic tenets of such strategies: "Of course, all things being equal, Wilson is wrong. *But all things are not equal, and that is exactly Wilson's point.*"[15] Color-blind discourse within the theater as well as outside in our contemporary American social context is inherently flawed because, as Cornel West articulated and Wilson reiterates, race does matter.[16] Manning Marable argues that in lieu of color-blind strategies we need color-conscious policies to achieve social equity:

> In the 1950s and early 1960s, liberal educators declared proudly that they were committed to the goal of a "color-blind environment." . . . But how do we get there? How can we "deconstruct" race? We cannot get there by pretending that "race" and "color" no longer matter, that they have magically declined in significance since the 1960s. In a racist society, color symbolizes the inequality of power relations, the ownership of property and resources, between various groups and classes. To end racial prejudice, we must restructure the power relations between people of color and upper- to middle-income whites. This means that we must pursue a "color-conscious" strategy to create the conditions where color is one day irrelevant to determining the positions of power, educational access, health care, and other opportunities of daily life.[17]

Marable's color-conscious philosophy would foreground the disparities of race in order to foment change. Under the notion of color blindness, on the other hand, any articulation of race or assertion of color consciousness becomes suspect. Color-blind devotees from Brustein to Clarence Thomas maintain that racial awareness has outgrown its significance. Consequently, there is no need for identity politics, no reason to institutionalize racial power or policies to achieve racial balance. The goal of a color-blind world is one that precludes race as a system of analysis or identification.

The foundation for such a utopian vision of America or the American theater, as Marable suggests, is seriously flawed. White racism as well as the values of normative whiteness are too firmly entrenched. By normative whiteness I mean the system that structures and associates privilege, wealth, power, social norms, and progress all with whiteness. In American cultural production the powers of normative whiteness are particularly pernicious. During an interview, Oscar-winning black actress Halle Berry naively celebrated landing the leading role in the Hollywood film *The Rich Man's Wife* because it was originally written for a white woman—or as Berry put it, "a normal woman not a black one." Inherent in Berry's remark and other coded language that black stars and white producers engage in as they discuss crossover appeal is the desire to transcend race and the burden of blackness. Yet this transcendence does not e-race but rather reinforces normative whiteness. Due to the present racial climate and the power of normative whiteness, transcendence does not lead to a raceless space. Kimberle Williams Crenshaw in "Color-Blind Dreams and Racial Nightmares," examines how the politics of "race neutrality" correlate with attempts to "neutralize blackness by acquiring the accoutrements of whiteness."[18] Normative whiteness in American social, cultural, and legal practices operates as a virtually invisible but seductive agent figuring achievement, success, and rationality as properties of whiteness.

Color blindness within the theater, as Alan Nadel suggests, "has the assumption of white neutrality built into it."[19] The American realities of race directly impact the theater. While black theater is always marked as black within the dominant culture, white theaters can operate under the privileged illusion of being racially nonspecific. Black theaters do not have the luxury of reversing this strategy; it is not commensurate. Accordingly, color-blind casting—a white theater placing an actor of color in a role conventionally assigned to a white actor—implicitly or even explicitly preserves "the myth of neutral white space."[20] An all-black production of *Death of a Salesman* or *Glass Menagerie*, therefore, might suggest to a white audience, "Look, these black actors can perform this great white play too." I do not mean to infer that cross-racial casting is a bankrupt strategy, but rather that when it is undertaken, the racial politics of this casting need to be fully recognized and interrogated. William Sonnega in his article "Beyond a Liberal Audience," discusses a 1991 production of *Death of a Salesman* at the Guthrie Theater in Minneapolis that featured blacks in the major roles and was directed by Sheldon Epps, a black director. Sonnega reports, "Epps's Loman mirrored and made oddly familiar the racial imbalance explicit in Minneapolis cultural life. Familiarity with such imbalance does not always engender commitment to its rectification, however, and it may be that, for many Guthrie spectators, the theatrical simulations of a black familiarity in their midst simply reinforced their sense of exteriority to actual blacks and their experiences."[21] Sonnega concludes embedded systems of white privilege may be reinforced even by a production like Epps's that calls attention to racial imbalance. He calls for a practice that "exposes, rather than reinvents racism."[22] Wilson similarly argues for a theater of exposure, a color-conscious policy that disrupts the racial status quo:

"You start thinking something's wrong with black. When white people say, 'I don't see color,' what they're saying is 'You're affected by this undesirable condition, but I'll pretend I don't see that.' And I go, 'No *see* my color. Look at me. I'm not ashamed of who I am and what I am.' "[23] Wilson's attention to color visibility rather than blindness grounds it in a history of American race relations, while the ideology of color blindness too often defines a more ahistorical strategy.[24]

I do not hear in Wilson's comments on color-blind casting the denial of black ability to perform Shakespeare or Arthur Miller assumed by Gates and other critics.[25] What I do hear is that directors, actors, and producers need to be extremely sensitive to the racialized meanings that result from such a production. Repeatedly regional theaters across the country reinforce normative whiteness as they maintain a naive paternalism. Artistic directors practice color-blind casting with the classic shows included in their seasons and then, in addition, may do one minority show, most often that of Wilson himself. For actors of color these are the only opportunities to work within the regional theater structure. For black directors, the one black show is the only one for which they will be hired. And unfortunately because of the embedded system of economics, privilege, and normative whiteness, success within the American theater demands working in white-controlled mainstream Broadway or regional theaters, not black ones, which are too often economically challenged. Wilson rails against this system of "Cultural Imperialism" ("Ground," 72) that promotes and maintains standards he finds antithetical to black self-definition and determination. Accordingly, he calls not simply for a reaffirmation of black theater but for a reorganization of the American theater as a whole. His TCG speech asks the American theater to re-examine its critical standards, its economic principles, and its institutionalized separatism. The black voice, as Wilson suggests in *Ma Rainey* and in subsequent works, has been subdued, suppressed, and commodified within this system, and black artists retain little economic control. Voicing a strategy of black particularism, Wilson calls for a restructuring of the American theater that enables the black performer to sing his or her song.

Sitting in the audience in Princeton, New Jersey, on that date in June 1996 when Wilson delivered his "impassioned case for change," was Chicana playwright Cherríe Moraga. Despite their differences of race and gender, Moraga felt a distinct affinity for Wilson's message.

Every time Wilson mentioned "Black," I inserted Chicana. With every generic "he," I added "she." When he named Black artists who insisted on their own self-worth in what he referred to as the "cultural imperialist" world of American theater as "warriors on the cultural battlefield," I knew he wasn't thinking of me guerrera and embattled; but I knew I carried the same weapons (more crudely made than his) and the same armor (mine surely more penetrable in my colored womanhood, in my sexuality), I knew, whether he recognized me or not among the ranks, that I was a "sister" in that struggle against a prescription for American theater that erases the lives of every one I call my "pueblo."[26]

Moraga reads in Wilson's remarks not separatism or essentialism but rather an appeal for artists of color previously limited by the American theater system of normative whiteness. She identifies with his politics of difference, a politics that foregrounds and acknowledges difference while recognizing positions of negotiated consensus or commonality. Within the American theater such a politics protects the heterogeneity of interests while collectively resisting the homogeneity of normative whiteness. Brustein romantically refers to the regional theaters not as "white" but as mixed theaters and terms their standards of assessing aesthetic merit and achievement as universal. However, as suggested by the few playwrights of color produced during Brustein's tenure at the American Repertory Theater in Cambridge, Massachusetts, such purported concepts of universality tend not to recognize the achievements by voices of color and to preserve "the myth of white neutrality." Despite the advancements forged by efforts of diversity, the putatively open regional theater system has virtually remained closed to plays and peoples of color.

While Moraga has remained largely outside of this closed system— her plays are rarely produced by the large regional theaters—Wilson, on the other hand, has been the ultimate insider. His plays remain among the most produced plays on the contemporary regional theater circuit. Thus, by critiquing this system so blatantly in his TCG speech Wilson, bit voraciously the hand that fed him. Perhaps only a voice with the stature of Wilson's, only an insider with the position afforded him, could have generated such resounding drama, discourse, and debate. Director Marion McClinton concurs: "He took a hit for a lot of other people. That's what a champion does—a champion fights."[27] After all, Wilson's stature caused the TCG executive board to invite him as their keynote speaker in the first place and gave him the platform for his manifesto. And yet, how does Wilson, the two-time Pulitzer Prize winner, come to criticize the very theater institution that harbors and celebrates him? Is this a paradox? What of Wilson's two Pulitzer Prizes for *Fences* and *The Piano Lesson*? Should he return and reject them as tokenism from the white "cultural imperialist"? Do the prizes reaffirm a white critical standard, or do they recognize the value of Wilson's work on a scale that transcends race? Do these prizes affirm the jurors' ability to recognize cross-racial commonalties in Wilson work? In 1983 Amiri Baraka wrote a scathing attack on Charles Fuller's *Soldiers Play* for *Black American Literature Forum* that deemed the awarding of the Pulitzer Prize to the play as the ultimate verification of the play's reactionary status.[28] Is it possible for a work to champion black liberation and still win a Pulitzer Prize? Not surprisingly, Wilson's two winning plays are works of American family drama and therefore conform to the conventions of American theater more than any of the other plays in the Wilson cycle.

David Savran in his important essay on Tony Kushner's *Angels in America*, "Ambivalence, Utopia, and a Queer Sort of Materialism: How *Angels in America* Reconstructs the Nation," notes a paradox in Kushner's political position that correlates with the politics of Wilson's location. "As an avowed leftist and intellectual," Savran writes of Kushner, "he is committed (as *Angels* demonstrates) to mounting a critique of hegemonic ideology. Yet as a member of the bourgeoisie and as a recipient of two Tony Awards, he is also committed, if only unconsciously, to the continuation of the system that has granted him no small measure of success."[29] Wilson similarly is complicit in the system that he wishes to critique and in which he imagines himself only "a visitor." Commenting on his experience at the Huntington Theater in Boston during rehearsals for *Jitney,* Wilson said, "I am an invited guest. As such, I'm treated with respect and dignity. But I can't move the furniture around. It's not my furniture. And eventually I will have to leave because it's not my home."[30] As Wilson continues to operate within a regional theater system and to move his plays through this network to Broadway, he inevitably must conform to a hegemonic system that he concurrently decries for its diminution of black art.[31] Savran makes the broader claim that within our capitalist system, not only are the positions of artists such as Kushner or Wilson riddled with dichotomies, but the cultural producer in America today is "placed in an irreducibly contradictory position":

> On the one hand, he or she is licensed to challenge hegemonic values insofar as it is a particularly effective way of accruing capital. On the other hand, the more effective his or her challenge, the less economic capital he or she is likely to amass. Because of the theater's marginality in American culture, it seems to be held hostage to this double bind in a particularly unnerving way: the very disposition of the field guarantees that Broadway and regional theaters (unlike mass culture) are constantly in the process of having to negotiate this impossible position.[32]

As Savran, employing the theories of Pierre Bourdieu, points out, theater operates with relative autonomy in a system of high symbolic capital but with miniscule levels of economic capital. The achievement of economic success means, therefore, proportionally limiting one's accrual of cultural capital and one's ability to apply social critique. Consequently, finding space within the conventional American theater for the advocacy of black theater that Wilson desires is extremely difficult.

Wilson's work on the National Black Theatre Summit in March 1998 and the resultant establishment of the new African Grove Institute of the Arts (AGIA) might be read as strategies to confront this paradox. Anticipating his subsequent activism, Wilson's TCG speech asks for black theater practitioners to convene in March 1998 "so that we may enter the millennium united and prepared for a long future of prosperity." Reflecting on Wilson's valorization of the South as the African American homeland and symbolic site of rupture to which repeatedly in his plays black characters need to return, the speech calls for the meeting to take place, "In a city in our ancestral homeland in the southern part of the United States" ("Ground," 73). In reality, however, the first summit occurred in the upper northeast, near Dartmouth College in Hanover, New Hampshire, and was dubbed the "Summit on Golden Pond." Perhaps the decision to meet at this location need not be read as contradictory, but reflective of a principle that Sandra Richards discusses in relation to *Joe Turner* and one that is present throughout Wilson's dramaturgy: the principle of *both/and*. Richards argues that in *Joe Turner* "the binary of *either/or* is replaced by the principle *both/and*: the ring shout is both Christian and African; Martha recites the twenty-third Psalm of the Christian Bible in the manner of an African conjurer.

Likewise constancy and change are not opposites."[33] Thus, drawing on the Du Boisian notion of double consciousness, the dynamic of *and/but* does not produce debilitating ambivalence but productive contestation through difference. "Constancy and change are not opposites." Translating the principle of *both/and* to the National Black Theatre Summit, the location represented *both* a history of white privilege *and* a legacy of black resistance that were not antithetical. Rather, the summit orchestraters foregrounded the seeming contradictions of their geographics and maintained that the significance of the place could help provide a new direction and energy in black theater. Summit executive director Victor Leo Walker II notes, "This picturesque site for The Summit was the location for the Academy Award–winning film, *On Golden Pond.* Just under one hundred miles off the Dartmouth campus and nearly the same distance from the Canadian border, Ashland, New Hampshire has both historical and symbolic significance as the location of The Summit. The area currently known as Ashland, New Hampshire was one of the final stops on the road to freedom en route to Canada. Hence the choice of this location is precisely in keeping with the struggle for justice and equity not only for Black Artists but ALL artists."[34] Certainly, Walker's response overlooks the practical expedience of the location, that he as an associate professor at Dartmouth at that time had certain access to the facilities. It does, more significantly suggest that just as escaped black slaves passed through this location on their way to freedom, black artists will not remain on Golden Pond but move through the summit on their way to more liberated strategies on black theater practice and self-determination.

The goal of this summit, as well as a strategy within Wilson's TCG speech, was not only the reaffirmation of black theater, but also the reorganization of American theater, particularly in terms of economics. The TCG speech suggests that attracting audience through subscription systems and other mechanisms needs to be rethought. In a bold and innovative move the National Black Theatre Summit not only invited black theater artists, practitioners, and scholars but also business leaders and financial analysts with the intention of creating a black theater that is not only viable but self-sufficient. It has yet to be determined whether these goals can be achieved. Moreover, in its plan for organizing a comprehensive national black theater, the AGIA will need to find ways to maintain inclusiveness and encourage diverse expressions of blackness.

Yet and still, if, as Savran argues, the economic demands of operating within the American theater necessitate compromise and help produce the ambiguities of message and meaning that he finds even in Kushner's radically minded gay fantasia, *Angels,* what then of Wilson's cycle? Should we ultimately conclude that only compromise enabled him to be the most produced American playwright in 1990 and to have found fame and success within a theater system he desires fervently to change? Certainly Wilson's process of (w)righting history provides *both* immediacy *and* distance. Contemporary spectators can watch from a position of self-satisfied separation with the conviction that the racial climate is now much different than it was in the time periods of Wilson's historical plays. While the unmarked presence of white hegemony is always lurking behind Wilson's characters and their fates, he does not paint these black characters simply as victims, nor does his work vehemently attack whites, as playwrights did in the black revolutionary theater of the 1960s and 1970s. Rather, the social change that he outlines is one in which his black characters must turn inward toward personal and collective healing. They must discover their own agency and ability to act for themselves. The battle that his characters face, in fact, parallels the struggle that Wilson perceives for black arts and black artists: to negotiate the madness of race, to find a space despite the overwhelming odds to define yourself and determine your own destiny, to mediate productively the tensions of being *both* African *and* American. We must remember that not only is history a process but that Wilson's dramaturgy is in process, that even as he completes his twentieth-century cycle, the past remains unstable, a place for renegotiated relations, a place for re-evolution. His work holds open the possibility of reworking the past, of redefining what is real, of inciting new beginnings—new beginnings that acknowledge the presence of the past.

The Doing and Undoing of History
An Epilogue

I lived a blessed life. I am ready
—August Wilson, August 2005

On Sunday, October 2, 2005, just two weeks after *Radio Golf,* the tenth and final play of his twentieth-century cycle, ended its run at the Mark Taper Theater in Los Angeles, and some three months before the play opened at the Seattle Repertory Theatre, August Wilson died from complications due to liver cancer. He was only sixty years old, a relatively young age within our contemporary register of longevity. Yet within this brief time, he accomplished something unmatched within the annals of American theater: the completion of a cycle, a play for each decade of the twentieth century. Wilson passed knowing that he had accomplished this remarkable, self-proclaimed goal. While other noted playwrights such as Eugene O'Neill and Ed Bullins have attempted to write dramatic cycles, only Wilson succeeded in finishing one. In August 2005, Wilson made public what he, his family, his close friends, and his doctors already understood: that his liver cancer was inoperable, that he had only months to live. "'I lived a blessed life,' Wilson said. 'I'm ready.'"[1] These words resonate with me and make me reflect again on Wilson's determined central figures who face death with resolve and awareness, men such as Troy Maxson in *Fences* and Boy Willie in *Piano Lesson.* Purposefully, Wilson released the announcement of his terminal illness first in Pittsburgh, the city of his birth; the site for nine of the ten plays in his twentieth-century cycle; and the setting for his funeral and burial on Saturday, October 8, 2005. Through his work and his words, Wilson has changed the face of American theater and of African American theater most particularly. On October 17, 2005, the Virginia Theater at 245 West 52nd Street in New York City was renamed the August Wilson Theater, making Wilson the first African American to have a Broadway theater named in his honor. His plays, his legacy, will endure in the present and will animate the future.

Wilson's next to last play, *Gem of the Ocean,* ends with the benediction and charge of Mr. Eli, Aunt Ester's gatekeeper, over the newly deceased body of his friend Solly, a benediction that might be said to reflect the life and enduring presence of Wilson himself. *"Eli pours a drink and raises it in a toast.* 'So live,'" he says.[2] It is a noble petition of hope for the future of the gathered community and a purposeful plea for African Americans to live a life founded on personal integrity and committed to the collective struggle for social justice. "So live." And so ends the beginning of Wilson's history plays, the first play in the cycle, set in 1904 just at the dawn of the first migration of blacks from the South to the North. Wilson has situated this play at this moment, just as he has positioned every work within the cycle, at a critical historical juncture within the course of the story of Africans in America. Yet, in *Gem of the Ocean* as well as in his other works, Wilson is not simply reviewing this past and reevaluating history. His project is so much more provocative, as he considers how this past now impacts on the African American present. For as I have discussed throughout this book, Wilson engages in a process of (w)righting history through his cycle, making black people not tangential to but central to the motion of history.

Moreover, in his (w)righting Wilson engages actively in the doing and the undoing of history. With each new play Wilson charts a course of renewal and reconstruction. In the cycle history is always in process, constantly being made and remade, refigured with each subsequent work. Thus, history is not simply a linear progression but one that, as Wilson writes in his stage notes on Gabriel's eerie, life-giving dance at the conclusion of *Fences,* is an attempt at song that "turns back on itself" and starts again. By working nonsequentially, visiting different moments in time, Wilson does not just fill the gaps or provide a teleology. Rather his craft suggests that a recuperative history or progressive chronology itself is not the answer. History is an active process that occurs in the now. His reimagining of history as an act of doing and undoing stops it from being simply mythologized or romanticized; instead history has active, material consequence in the present.

Most significantly, in Wilson's project, history, as it is done and undone, is far from agonistic, a question of one historical account over another. Rather, history becomes redemptive. This concern with the redemptive power of history is critical to *Gem of the Ocean* and to the entirety of Wilson's twentieth-century cycle. The idea of going back and confronting the past as Citizen Barlow must do in *Gem of the Ocean;* or as Herald Loomis does through his meeting with his estranged wife, Martha, at the climax of *Joe Turner's Come and Gone;* or as Memphis offers to do at the end of *Two Trains Running* initiates emancipatory processes for each of these figures. Working through their relationship with history transforms them. Accordingly, history is not simply a lesson for these characters: their relationship to history is vertical. History's redemptive dimensions deliver, endow, impart various kinds of salvation for these characters.

The critical figure mediating the redemptive power of history in *Gem of the Ocean* and the cycle as a whole is Aunt Ester, a woman as old as the African presence in America. Early in the action of *King Hedley II,* Aunt Ester dies of grief due to the desperate conditions of African American life in the 1980s. Pointedly, in *Gem of the Ocean,* the next play that Wilson writes after *King Hedley II,* Aunt Ester is quite literally reborn. History is undone and done, through this resurrection, as Wilson brings a 285-year-old woman onto the stage. In chapter 5, I discuss in depth the behind the scenes, unseen force that Aunt Ester—the "ancestor," the repository of black history—represents in the cycle prior to her appearance in *Gem of the Ocean.* How should we, then, read in *Gem of the Ocean* the material presence of the previously invisible Aunt Ester? How should spectators react? For certainly there must be some disjuncture when they see her and hear of her age. In fact, in the earlier draft and at the first production of *Gem* in Chicago 2004, her age was stated by Ester and other characters several more times than it is now in the Broadway script. With each mention, the audience laughed, perhaps out of incredulity, perhaps out of nervousness. Does her embodied presence on stage merely require that the audience realize the power of theater to make possible the impossible and suspend their disbelief? Should the spectators, upon seeing her enacted on Broadway by the beautiful and talented Phylicia Rashad, recognize the so-called ageless quality of black skin and the lore that black folk just don't wrinkle like white folks? Does the Chicago audience's unease and laughter reveal that they just didn't know what to make of this old, old woman? If Aunt Ester exists in the symbolic between the world of the spirit and the flesh, can placing her onstage potentially dissolve this imaginative, metaphysical power? For Wilson, her power does not emanate simply from the fact that she was previously disembodied. Aunt Ester is far from a static site of remembrance, but rather a living force, actively advocating for spiritual and cultural change. She not only embodies the collective history but possesses a personal history, for she is a woman who has loved and lost, who has been married and has given birth. Hers is an embodied knowledge that she shares with others. Her embodiment makes the metaphysical an element of the everyday. For instance, she tells Citizen Barlow upon his arrival at her home, after she has caught him in the act of pilfering bread, "You remind me of my Junebug. He was the only one of my boys that cause me trouble" (*Gem* 1.1.17). She understands and imagines her new child, Citizen, as Junebug, as the child lost and gone. Remembrance becomes the vehicle to remake the present as the past. Aunt Ester is not merely a spirit unseen but a material force: her actions have weight.

Of considerable material presence in *Gem of the Ocean*, and another example of the undoing and doing of history, is the "City of Bones," the site of Citizen Barlow's redemption. The City of Bones is the mystical, spiritual city below the surface of the water where lost black souls have come to rest. It is built from the bones of those who perished on the perilous journey across the ocean that was the Middle Passage. The Middle Passage has traditionally been conceived as a fixed moment in time that marks the difficult transition from free peoples into captive Africans in America. It is not usually represented as a place in and of itself. Wilson constructs the City of Bones, however, in *Gem of the Ocean*, as a locality rather than as transitionality. Aunt Ester explains to Citizen:

> It's only a half mile by a half mile but that's a city. It's made of bones. Pearly white bones. All the buildings and everything is made of bones. I seen it. I been there, Mr. Citizen. My mother live there. I got an aunt there and three uncles live there down there in that city made of bones. . . . That's the center of the world. In time it will all come to light. The people made a kingdom out of nothing. They were the people that didn't make it across the water. (*Gem* 2.1.51)

The City of Bones actively re-members the loss of those that didn't make it across the water. Reconstructing history at the bottom of the sea, those seemingly forgotten black travelers, those who were too infirm for the journey, those who mounted unsuccessful insurgencies, those who jumped into the cold and uncertain water rather than face the cold uncertainties ahead have built a city. Improvising on a section from his long jazz poem *Wise, why's, y's,* Amiri Baraka, one of the most important influences on the playwriting of August Wilson, muses:

> It's my brother, my sister.
> At the bottom of the Atlantic Ocean there's a
> Railroad made of human bones.
> Black ivory
> Black ivory[3]

Baraka's poem notes the loss of black bodies below the sea but, more importantly, suggests through the image of an underground railroad that one can connect to those lost black family members. Tracks of history made out of black ivory. Similarly, Wilson's City of Bones is a site that reunites or re-members the collective black body, those lost old bones, making them into a unified structure, a communal site. It is a city that joins past to present and that overcomes loss by recuperating and dynamically maintaining a living African American history. Recalling Baraka's allusion to his brother and sister below the sea, Aunt Ester reports that she has relatives who live there, not who rest there but who *live*. Thus, the City of Bones functions for Wilson not simply as a memorial to the Middle Passage but as a vibrant place, a destination even, where Citizen Barlow and the other travelers in need of redemption go to visit.

My invocation of "re-membering" harkens back to my discussion of re-memory in the play *Joe Turner's Come and Gone* in the introductory chapter of this book. In fact, the ritualistic journey to the City of Bones functions as a signifying revision of Herald Loomis's re-memory, his vision of the Middle Passage that he confesses to Bynum: a vision of "bones walking on the water." While Loomis's obsessed and possessed re-memory occurs at the end of the first act of *Joe Turner,* Citizen Barlow's journey occurs in the beginning of the second act of *Gem of the Ocean,* the middle passage of the play. Barlow's journey then embodies an idea that it symbolizes, repeating and revising Wilson's earlier play, even as it speaks to the specifics of this play. In addition, the title, *Gem of the Ocean,* is a signifying revision. Aunt Ester tells us that the *Gem of the Ocean* is the name of a slave ship and the craft that will carry Barlow back down to the City of Bones, but the title also remembers the song "Columbia, the Gem of the Ocean" written in 1843 by David T. Shaw. This song was extremely popular during Abraham Lincoln's Civil War administration and later became a staple of the United States Marine Corps marching band. Even earlier, back in 1775, slave Phyllis Wheatley wrote poems about Columbia, celebrating the new nation. Almost two hundred years later, in 1973, Amiri Baraka wrote a play called *Columbia, the Gem of the Ocean* about efforts to free blacks from the psychological tyranny of white hegemony and to build black solidarity. With its discussions of slavery, of nation, and of spiritual healing, Wilson's *Gem of the Ocean* revisits and revises the work of Wheatley and Baraka and even that of Wilson himself. Fittingly, as they travel to the City of Bones, Citizen Barlow and the others hear the people singing, "Remember me" (*Gem* 2.2.67). Wilson asks that the trauma of these bones people be re-membered, in order to address the unfinished business of the past within the circumstances of the now.

Throughout the Wilson cycle, urgent situations within the present dictate the course of remembrance. Aunt Ester shares with Black Mary: "People say you crazy to remember. But I ain't afraid to remember. I try to remember out loud. I keep my memories alive. I feed them" (*Gem* 1.5.43). Memory is not something to be buried but to face. It must be spoken out loud. The trials and tribulations of the black past are not something to be denied, or kept to oneself, but are to be shouted out and shared publicly. Moreover, as expressed here, for Wilson memories must daily be renewed and kept alive. They must be grown and animated. His dramaturgy functions as a devotional and ritual act in which memory is nourished.

Yet, his cycle is also ideologically engaged with the African American present. When Aunt Ester declares that this City of Bones is "the center of the world," she creatively invokes contemporary intellectual discourse on the Black Diaspora. Paul Gilroy's seminal work of the early 1990s, *The Black Atlantic,* powerfully theorizes the intersections between America and Europe. Most significantly, Gilroy inserts black people as critical participants in the creation of the modern world in this movement between the continent and the New World.[4] More recently, Joseph Roach and others have built on Gilroy in their discussion of a "Circum-Atlantic," insisting on the centrality of "the diasporic and genocidal histories of Africa and the Americas North and South," to modernity, not as something past but as something relevant to the construction of our present.[5] Aunt Ester's proclamation on the City of Bones takes this argument even a step further. The City of Bones is not just the cutting edge of future worlds but is crucial to the world as we know it now. By recovering, reclaiming, and reconnecting the bodies discarded there, Wilson refigures not just the black Atlantic but the world. Not merely the core of blackness or seminal just to the collective memory of African Americans, the City of Bones is the heart from where the intellectual and cultural power of humanity emanate. Hence, black history must no longer exist only as a footnote or a chapter at the end of the history book, but rather it must be read as constitutive of all history.

Significantly, the conduit for Citizen Barlow's pilgrimage to the City of Bones is a paper boat that Aunt Ester molds out of her documents of indenture that identify her as a slave. Barlow balks when Aunt Ester hands it to him. "This is a piece of paper." he exclaims. Aunt Ester replies, "Look at that boat, Mr. Citizen. That's a magic boat. There's a lot of power in that boat. Power is something. It's hard to control but it's hard to stand in the way of it" (*Gem* 2.1.52–53). Indeed the papers of indenture were very powerful instruments as they declared that Aunt Ester and other black people constituted property that could be bought and sold. The power these papers once had over her life, Aunt Ester now employs to her own ends. Aunt Ester's documents of indenture are at once material, symbolic, and functional. Now the medium of enslavement becomes the method of transcendence.

Repeatedly in *Gem of the Ocean* and elsewhere in the cycle, Wilson reminds us that the battle to remove the shackles of slavery is not simply an external struggle but an internal one. Later in *Gem,* when the black constable Caesar brings another piece of paper, a warrant for Aunt Ester's arrest, charging her with aiding and abetting the fugitive Solly, Aunt Ester asks him to read the same papers that earlier served as Barlow's magical boat.

> I see you got a piece of paper. I got a piece of paper too. . . . Sit down there Mr. Caesar. I want to show you something. . . .Tell me how much that piece of paper's worth, Mr. Caesar. . . . That piece of paper say I was property. Say anybody could buy or sell me. The law say I need a piece of paper to say I was a free woman. But I didn't need a piece of paper to tell me that. (*Gem* 2.4.82–83)

Aunt Ester differentiates the legal authority of these papers to dictate black freedom from the spiritual and psychological power she already possesses to determine her own identity and self-worth.

The power of the law and the concept of a higher power of justice and judgment are also matters that Wilson revisits in his canon. While the law serves the interest of whites and the white power structure, there is the potential and hope within these works that the power of faith, hope, and struggle can bring justice for African Americans. Notably in *Gem of the Ocean,* the symbol of the white legal system is the black constable, Caesar, who lords his authority over the black mill workers and chastises them for their ignorance.

> People don't understand the law is everything. What is it not? People think the law is supposed to serve them. But anybody can see you serve it. There ain't nothing above the law. You got to respect the law. (*Gem* 1.3.35)

Caesar's claims that nothing functions "above the law" stand in stark contrast to Aunt Ester's belief that there are higher laws and that justice can prevail for African Americans.

In *Radio Golf,* the source of legal and ideological conflict is also black: Roosevelt Hicks, a black developer and banker, is willing to sell out the black community and align himself with a corrupt white industrialist in the name of profit. He is even ready to tear down Aunt Ester's house as part of an urban renewal project. In this play more than any of the previous ones, Wilson explores the intersections of race and class. As in black scholar E. Franklin Frazier's classic *The Black Bourgeoisie* (1962) before him, Wilson questions in *Radio Golf* the allegiance of the black middle class to the black masses. Hicks has lost connection to any sense of the black legacy, to the force of history that is Aunt Ester. For Hicks's partner, the central figure of *Radio Golf,* Harmon Wilks, the play is a journey of self-discovery and reawakening consciousness. Wilks, who originally sides with Hicks and plans to run for mayor of Pittsburgh, finds his fundamental beliefs and principles tested. Elder Barlow, who claims he is the rightful owner of Aunt Ester's house, frequently enters Wilks's real estate office and interrupts Wilks's plans in ways that compel him to reconsider his redevelopment strategy. Barlow is literally the presence of the past: he is the descendant of Citizen Barlow, the troubled traveler in *Gem of the Ocean*. As the play unfolds, Elder is found to be also related to Harmon Wilks, the descendant of Caesar Wilks, as Caesar's sister Black Mary eventually married Citizen Barlow. Thus Wilks is the living consequence of history. Wilks's reinvestment in the past and his association with Barlow function as a form of social and psychological redemption that leads him to take a very different view of the law, social justice, and capitalist expansion than those expressed by Hicks.

As the symbol of the law in *Gem of the Ocean*, Caesar, not unlike Hicks, purposefully separates himself from his black past and present and wields his own form of power. Like West in *Two Trains Running*, Caesar has accepted the rewards of money over the possibilities of collective action and consciousness. He exploits his own people, once selling them supposedly magic bread that supposedly made them twice as full. While West refuses to follow through on Aunt Ester's directives and throw twenty dollars into the river, Caesar takes his alienation from Aunt Ester a step further. He comes to arrest her and removes her from the house, calling the law and penal code his bible. As a consequence he is bereft of the sort of spirit and spiritual justice that Wilson ultimately promotes.

Revealingly, the name "Caesar" references not only Julius Caesar but the blaxploitation film of 1973, *Black Caesar*, written and directed by white filmmaker Larry Cohen and featuring black actor and former football player Fred "the Hammer" Williamson. In the film, Black Caesar, with the help of a corrupt white police officer, rules over Harlem. Caesar in *Gem of the Ocean* equally lords it over his black subjects in Pittsburgh. Yet, although Caesar's sister in *Gem of the Ocean* bears the name Black Mary, Caesar is not "Black" Caesar but only Caesar. His name, or rather the lack of blackness in his name, underscores his distance from the concerns of the black masses who suffer under his reign.

Wilson, who himself grew up as August Frederick Kittle only to become August Wilson—after taking the maiden name of his mother as a statement of his affinity with her and his black roots—is profoundly interested in names and the power of naming. His Caesars, Citizens, Heralds, Kings, Roses all speak to how a name can convey not only a sense of individual identity but of history and of culture. Caesar's name also recalls the legacy of slave naming. Southern masters often gave their slaves ancient Greek and Roman names, such as "Pompey" and

"Caesar," as a means of ridiculing slave pretensions and belittling them, preemptively satirizing black attempts at dignity or pride or history. In the aftermath of slavery, these names were generally rejected by the newly freed blacks as slave designations. Citizen Barlow explains that his mother named him after freedom came. Solly, Aunt Ester's friend and suitor, explains that he rejected his slave name of Uncle Alfred once free.

> I used to be called Uncle Alfred back in slavery. I ran into one fellow called me Uncle Alfred. I told him say "Uncle Alfred dead." He say, "I'm looking at you." I told him, "You looking at Two Kings. That's David and Solomon." . . . But my name is Two Kings. Some people call me Solomon and some people call me David. I answer to either one. I don't know which one God gonna call me. If he call me Uncle Alfred then we got a fight. (*Gem* 1.3.24)

Solly thus subverts or inverts the former process of slave naming, finding in this biblical history of greatness a sense of his own purpose and power in the world, finding the collective spirit of two kings. Moreover, his naming himself Two Kings references the earlier kings of August Wilson's dramaturgical kingdom, King Hedley I and King Hedley II, who, like Solly Two Kings, exemplify an oppositional spirit, a warrior energy out of step with the constraints of white hegemony but also out of step with the social status quo. Near the climactic end to *King Hedley II*, King discovers he is not actually the son of King Hedley I but of Leroy. Leroy loosely translated into the French "le roi" means "the king." Therefore, King Hedley II is the son of two kings, his spiritual father King Hedley I and his biological father Leroy. Repeating and revising this notion of naming and kings in *Gem of the Ocean*, Wilson gives us Solly, who names himself the product of two kings.[6] Solly sees his self-given name as a sign of his identity and his liberation. Caesar, however, purposefully tries to return Solly to his earlier state of captivity and social death by referring to him only by his slave name, Alfred Jackson, not by the name of either Solomon or David, when he comes to arrest him for burning down the mill. Wilson's characters' names signify on personal and collective histories, on the power of naming, and even on the evolution of racial designations—from Negro to colored to Black to Afro American to African American with and without the hyphen.

One name that we encountered earlier in *Joe Turner's Come and Gone*, Rutherford B. Selig, reappears in *Gem of the Ocean*. In *Joe Turner*, the white peddler Rutherford B. Selig—the name Selig in German means holy—proudly and shamelessly announces to a room full of black people that his inherited family business has been trafficking in black bodies: "we been finders in my family for a long time. Bringers and finders. My great-granddaddy used to bring Nigras across the ocean on ships" (*Joe Turner* 1.2.239). And now some seven years earlier in *Gem of the Ocean*, he becomes one of the more complex and even contradictory disciples of Aunt Ester. Upon the request of Aunt Ester and in the face of the law of Caesar, Selig is willing to carry the fugitive Solly back down south, hidden in his wagon. "I ain't never known you to be on the wrong side of anything," Selig tells her. "I ain't scared of Caesar," he proclaims (*Gem* 2.4.78). He's right. As a white man of this time period, certainly Selig need not fear Caesar and his black codes. Selig functions as a participant on a redirected underground railroad. Rather than heading north, he plans to take Solly down south despite the fact that the roads are blocked and passage will be difficult. The plan is to go back and save Solly's sister. So, the path of progress he repeats is the central Wilson trope: that you must go back and connect with your past in order to move forward.

For Citizen Barlow, traveling to the City of Bones equally means reconnecting with his past. Functioning ritualistically, his journey removes his earlier sins and psychological burdens. Citizen takes on this journey to cleanse his soul after another man, Garret Brown, died for his crime of stealing a bucket of nails. Accused of the theft and unwilling to go jail for a crime he did not commit, Garret Brown ran into the river and remained in the cold current until he drowned. In a repetition with revision of Christian theology, Garret Brown died for Citizen's sins. Citizen is free because of Brown's fateful action. With the water as his grave, Brown now resides in the City of Bones, a spiritual place of sacrifice where all the residents have died sacrificial deaths so that others, the Bones People that Herald Loomis describes in *Joe Turner* as rising up out of the water and walking on the land, can survive. Citizen must confront Garret Brown at the City of Bones, for he is the gatekeeper: "The gatekeeper . . . the gatekeeper . . . it's Garret Brown the man who jumped in the river" (*Gem* 2.2.72). Only by telling Brown his story can Citizen cleanse his guilt-ridden soul and enter the redeeming city. "You got to tell him, Mr. Citizen. The truth has to stand in the light" (*Gem* 2.2.72). Citizen must confess. This ritual act of confession is good for his soul. Yet, unlike in Catholicism where confession is followed by acts of contrition, Citizen's confession is linked to the mandate to "live in truth." In this play the notion of living in truth means acknowledging a responsibility to others. When he does admit his crime, the gates of the city open and Citizen Barlow experiences the redemptive power of the collective. Overwhelmed by the spectacle, the glory of the people calling "on God with one voice," as Aunt Ester says, he sits down and cries.

Significantly, this ritual, like other ritualized enactments in the Wilson cycle, brings the African past and African American present into relation. Overcome by the atavistic power, the emotional weight of his spiritual odyssey, Citizen Barlow, following Wilson's stage directions, "*begins to sing to himself an African lullaby*" (*Gem* 2.2.69). Wilson provides no information on where this son of a slave would have learned this African lullaby. It is simply part of his blood memory. Similarly, Wilson provides no detail for the actor or the director staging the play as to exactly what lullaby from what African country should be sung. The production must discover its own Africa. Here and throughout Wilson's work, Africa functions not simply as a "native soil" but as an empirical abstraction and a metaphorical space (w)ritten within the context of the moment or within each different production of a play such as *Gem of the Ocean*.[7]

Africa is made tangibly and symbolically present when Solly gives Citizen a link of chain to carry with him on his travels to the City of Bones. Aunt Ester has told Citizen that he needs to take a piece of iron for protection. More than a mere safeguard or totem of security, this gift of iron conjoins Solly and Citizen as sons of Ogun, the Yoruban warrior god of metallurgy. Fittingly, as I discuss in chapter 5, Pittsburgh, the steel city, becomes in Wilson's dramaturgy the place for Ogun and his worship to be reconstituted on the shores of America. Significantly, the link of iron Citizen receives from Solly is also one of the pieces of the ankle chain that once enslaved him. Solly keeps this remnant of the past as "a good luck piece." As he bestows it on Citizen, its history is done and undone. While it functions as spiritual protection and a conduit linking him to Ogun, it also serves as a link to the collective memory of African American struggle and survival.

Citizen's actions link him to powerful spiritual forces beyond him but also serve to locate the force of God within him. Such embodiments of spirit and spirituality prove crucial to Wilson's dramaturgy and its processes of cultural regeneration. For Wilson, such spiritual salvation is not antithetical to but a necessary component of a progressive historicism and revolutionary politics. Invoking rites that connect the spiritual, the cultural, the social, and the political does and undoes history in ways that impact powerfully on the present. For Citizen Barlow, redemption through history, his spiritual cleansing, is just a step toward self-determination. In its aftermath, he resolves to take revolutionary action. He too will travel down south with Solly, inverting the path of the underground railroad, in an attempt to reach Solly's sister and to aid Solly in escaping Caesar. With a new recognition and appreciation of the need to be spiritually right with oneself, Citizen tells Black Mary:

> Black Mary, is you right with yourself? Cause if you is I believe when I come back from down Alabama, I'd come by and see you. If I was still right with myself. Then maybe we could be right with each other. (*Gem* 2.4.80)

Their budding relationship is to be built not simply on the mutual desire expressed earlier in the play but on an awareness of the power of self-realization. Black Mary takes steps in this direction when she stands up to Aunt Ester for the first time, asserting that after trying to please Aunt Ester for three years, Black Mary will now do things her own way. Aunt Ester responds, "What took you so long?" (*Gem* 2.3.77). Through a demanding form of love, Aunt Ester moves Black Mary too toward self-empowerment.

Perhaps the leading advocate for black self-determination in the play is Solly, the former conductor on the underground railroad, who lives by the principle of Frederick Douglass that with no struggle there is no progress. Solly's life is a constant battle not only to live in truth but to give meaning to the hard-earned freedom that he and other slaves now have. "You got to fight to make it mean something" (*Gem* 1.2.25). Thus, Solly is willing to burn down the mill in the name of justice as a strike against oppression. Ultimately, he is willing to die for his beliefs. For Solly, the willingness to risk death rather than continue to endure oppression is built on his experience in slavery and the understanding that nothing, not even death, is worse than slavery: "Ain't nothing worse than slavery! I know. I was there" (*Gem* 2.2.56). Solly believes that the conditions present in the mill perpetuate a system of psychological and economic enslavement for its black workers. Solly's resistance in the face of death is a revolutionary act and evidence of his warrior spirit. Like Boy Willie's climactic death-defying battle with Sutter's ghost in *Piano Lesson,* it is a symbolic act of black self-determination.

In the Wilson cycle such self-possessed actions are critical because freedom by itself is not enough. Early in *Gem of the Ocean,* Solly asks, "What good is freedom if you can't do nothing with it?" (*Gem* 1.3.25). This question informs Solly's own determination to resist as he recognizes that for African Americans the new condition of freedom poses equally new challenges. The play makes clear that the act of Emancipation by itself did not make black people free. Yet, the matter of freedom is not simply one left in the past. Wilson, in this play and throughout his canon, asks that the question of freedom's utility and viability continually be reconsidered.

Wilson's interrogation of the conditions of African American freedom recognizes the racism that persistently keeps blacks at the bottom of the economic system in America. Accordingly, Holloway, the wizened, older regular at Memphis's restaurant in *Two Trains Running,* cynically explains blacks' lack of economic utility in the white-controlled capitalistic system: "The white man ain't staking no more niggers," he explains. In slavery he reports, "They couldn't find you enough work back then. Now that they got to pay you they can't find you none" (*Two Trains Running* 1.2.35). Similarly recognizing black economic devaluation, Toledo, the piano player in *Ma Rainey's Black Bottom,* suggests to the other band members that in the new economic order, black people are leftovers from history: "See, we's the leftovers. The colored man is the leftovers." Toledo goes on to ask, "Now what's the colored man to do with himself?" (*Ma Rainey* 1.47). This question is in effect a reworking of Solly's question, which, as I mentioned, hovers over the cycle as a whole: "What good is freedom if you can't do nothing with it?" (*Gem* 1.3.25). Repeatedly, Wilson wonders how black people can change this condition. What empowering acts can African Americans take in the present informed by the past that will change the future? How are black people to redefine themselves and determine their own history? What Wilson's dramaturgy reveals is that in each decade this struggle must be taken up again and history perpetually done and undone.

Gem of the Ocean serves as a touchstone for his cycle initiating these processes of contestation and regeneration. As he worked on *Gem* and *Radio Golf* Wilson stated in an interview that with these plays he hoped to build an "umbrella under which the rest of the plays can sit."[8] The metaphor of the umbrella is a significant and telling one. Certainly the cohesive structure of an umbrella functions as a form of protection under which the other plays sit. Equally important, as it is generally configured an umbrella has many different spokes emanating from it. Much like this image of the umbrella, Wilson's cycle is not one seamless linear history but rather a multidirectional one, with diverse stops and starts and different connections along the umbrella spokes. What Wilson has created is not simply a chronicle of the African American past but a spoked genealogy of both personal and collective significance.

This genealogy does not offer linear explanations but rather a re-evolutionary logic that not only excavates the past but also conceives of alternatives. Connections Wilson creates between plays serve as points of coherence as well as departure. Repetition with revision happens not simply through major figures—the recurring image and embodiment of Aunt Ester; characters such as Ruby and Canewell that appear in *Seven Guitars* and then resurface some forty years later in *King Hedley II;* Selig, the white peddler in *Joe Turner* who ironically reemerges in a play written later about an earlier time period, *Gem of the Ocean*—but also in the developmental disparities found in minor unseen figures. The white boss, Mr. Rand, an offstage presence, whom Troy discusses in *Fences* is the unseen landlord who is a source of friction between Becker and his son in *Jitney*. The same Reverend Tolliver with whom Martha Pentecost ventures north to Pittsburgh in *Joe Turner* petitions the mayor of Pittsburgh on behalf of his near riotous black congregation of mill workers in *Gem of the Ocean*. Sterling Brown from *Two Trains Running* returns in *Radio Golf* to paint Aunt Ester's house. These catalytic relationships, like the umbrella spokes, radiate outward. Wilson's re-evolutionary genealogy returns us to the past, to the cycle of time, to the recurring movements and moments within African American history. History is done and undone. And so the cry goes out from *Gem* and from Wilson's cannon to black America past, present, and future: "So live."

Notes

The Overture

1. Suzan-Lori Parks, *The American Play,* in *The American Play and Other Works* (New York: Theatre Communications Group, 1995), 164, 171.

2. Certainly, this artistic attention to the political construction of history in this period correlates with the concurrent theoretical developments in poststructuralism and postmodernism from Roland Barthes to Jacques Derrida, from Hayden White to Frederic Jameson and others that interrogate history as discourse and question how history as narrative operates in relationship to the real. But rather than rehearse those arguments here, I want to turn to the particular interconnections of art, politics, and history in African American experience.

3. W. E. B. Du Bois, quoted by David W. Blight, "W. E. B. DuBois and the Struggle for American Historical Memory," in *History and Memory in African-American Culture,* ed. Geneviève Fabre and Robert O'Meally (Oxford: Oxford University Press, 1994), 69.

4. Blight, "DuBois and the Struggle," 59.

5. Walter Benjamin, "These on the Philosophy of History," in *Illuminations,* ed. Hannah Arendt, trans. Harry Zohn, 1955 (New York: Schocken, 1978), 257.

6. Glen Ligon, "To Disembark," November 11, 1993–February 20, 1994, Hirshorn Museum, Washington, D.C.

7. James Baldwin and Margaret Meade, *A Rap on Race* (New York: Dell, 1971) quoted in Byron Kim, "An Interview with Glen Ligon," in *Glen Ligon Un/Becoming,* ed. Judith Tannenbaum (Philadelphia: Institute of Contemporary Art, University of Pennsylvania, 1998), 54.

8. Brian Philip Harper, "Nationalism and Social Division in Black Arts Poetry of the 1960s," in *African American Literary Theory: A Reader,* ed. Winston Napier (New York: NYU Press, 2000), 461.

9. See Mike Sell, "The Black Arts Movement: Performance, Neo-Orality, and the Destruction of the 'White Thing,'" in *African American Performance and Theater History: A Critical Reader,* ed. Harry J. Elam, Jr., and David Krasner (New York: Oxford University Press, 2001), 56–80.

10. See Harper, "Nationalism and Social Division," 460–74. See David Lionel Smith, "The Black Arts Movement and Its Critics," *American Literary History* 1 (spring 1991): 93–113.

11. Suzan-Lori Parks, "An Equation for Black People Onstage," in *The America Play and Other Works*, 20.

12. Byron Kim, "An Interview with Glen Ligon," in Tannenbaum, *Glen Ligon Un/Becoming*, 54.

13. Giorgio Agamben, "Project for a Review," in *Infancy and History: Essays on the Destruction of Experience*, trans. Liz Heron (London: Verso, 1993), 148.

14. Marion McClinton, quoted by John Lahr, "Been Here and Gone," *New Yorker*, April 16, 2001, 54.

15. Lahr, "Been Here and Gone," 54.

16. August Wilson, quoted by Sandra Shannon, "August Wilson's Autobiography," in *Memory and Cultural Politics*, ed. Amritjit Singh, Joseph T. Skerret, Jr., and Robert E. Hogan (Boston: Northeastern University Press, 1996), 179–180.

17. He wrote his play of the 1970s, *Jitney*, in 1979 and then revised it from 1996 to 2000; *Ma Rainey's Black Bottom*, set in 1927, was his first play to come to Broadway in 1984; *Fences*, which Wilson places in 1957, received the Pulitzer Prize in 1987; the action of *Joe Turner's Come and Gone*, occurs in 1911, but the play won the New York Drama Critics Circle Award for 1987–88; *Piano Lesson*, his play of the 1940s, won the Pulitzer Prize in 1990; while *Two Trains Running* is set in 1969, it premiered on Broadway in April 1992; *Seven Guitars* plays out in 1948 and won the New York Drama Critics Circle Award for 1996; *King Hedley II*, with its events transpiring during the decade of the 1980s, came to New York in April 2001; *Gem of the Ocean*, set in 1904, premiered at the Goodman Theatre in Chicago in April 2003; and *Radio Golf*, set in 1997, premiered at the Yale Repertory Theater in April 2005 and moved to the Mark Taper Forum in July 2005.

18. August Wilson, quoted by Kim Powers, "An Interview with August Wilson," *Theater* 16, no. 1 (1984): 52.

19. Chris Jones, "Homeward Bound: August Wilson," *American Theatre*, November 1999, 16.

20. August Wilson, "American Histories: Chasing Dreams and Nightmares; Sailing the Stream of Black Culture," *New York Times*, April 23, 2000, sec. 2.1.

21. August Wilson, quoted by John Lahr, "Been There and Gone," 54.

22. See Lynn Nottage, *Crumbs from the Table of Joy* (New York: Dramatist Play Service, 1998); Kathleen Collins, *The Brothers*, in *Nine Plays by Black Women*, ed. Margaret Wilkerson (New York: New American Library, 1986), 293–346.

23. Karen D'Souza, "Teaching the Fine Points of 'The Piano Lesson,'" *San Jose Mercury News*, March 25, 2001, sec. E.9.

24. My thanks to Ebony E.A. Coletu for her email conversation and her recommendations for this section.

25. See August Wilson, preface to *August Wilson: Three Plays* (Pittsburgh: University of Pittsburgh Press, 1991), xii.

26. Ralph Ellison, *The Invisible Man* (1947; rpt. New York: Vintage, 1995), 9.

27. August Wilson, "The Ground on Which I Stand," *American Theatre*, September 1996, 16.

28. Sandra Richards, "Yoruba Gods on the American Stage: August Wilson's *Joe Turner's Come and Gone*," *Research in African Literatures* 30, no. 4 (1999): 100.

29. Richards, "Yoruba Gods," 101.

Introduction

1. Dating Wilson's plays can prove difficult because he rewrites them as they move through various permutations on the regional theater circuit toward an eventual premier on Broadway. This process may take two years. Consequently, all of August Wilson's plays considered in this text are dated from their premiere Broadway production.

2. August Wilson, *Joe Turner's Come and Gone*, in *August Wilson: Three Plays* (Pittsburgh: University of Pittsburgh Press, 1991), 249. Subsequent citations are given in the text.

3. "Rememory" as presented by Toni Morrison in her Pulitzer Prize–winning novel *Beloved* (1987) symbolizes the process in which the horrors and lessons of the past materialize in the present. See Gayle Greene, "Feminist Fiction and the Use of Memory," *Signs* 16, no. 2 (1991): 290–321.

4. Walter Benjamin, "Theses on the Philosophy of History," in *Illuminations*, ed. Hannah Arendt, trans. Harry Zohn (1968) (New York: Schocken, 1988), 261.

5. Cathy Caruth, *Unclaimed Experience: Trauma, Narrative, and History* (Baltimore: Johns Hopkins University Press, 1996), 61.

6. See Frantz Fanon, *Black Skins/White Masks*, trans. Charles Lam Markmann (New York: Grove Press, 1968), 11.

7. August Wilson, "American Histories: Chasing Dreams and Nightmares: Sailing the Stream of Black Culture," *New York Times*, April 3, 2000, sec. 2.1.

8. Giorgio Agamben, *Infancy and History: Essays on the Deconstruction of Experience*, trans. Liz Heron (London: Verso, 1993), 91.

9. Bert O. States, *Great Reckonings in Little Rooms: On the Phenomenology of Theater* (Berkeley and Los Angeles: University of California Press, 1985), 50.

10. Saidiya Hartman, *Scenes of Subjection* (Oxford: Oxford University Press, 1997), 67.

11. Hartman, *Scenes of Subjection*, 69.

12. Agamben, *Infancy and History*, 91.

13. Henri Lefebvre, *The Production of Space*, trans. Donald Nicholson-Smith (Oxford: Blackwell, 1991), 95.

14. Gunilla Theander Kester, "Approaches to Africa: The Poetics of Memory and the Body in Two August Wilson Plays," in *August Wilson: A Casebook*, ed. Marilyn Elkins (New York: Garland, 1994), 108.

15. One Saturday morning in September 2000, as I worked on this book, I

was reminded of how critical negotiations of time were to black radicalism in the 1960s and the direct relationship of these strategies to the work of August Wilson. As I was involved in my weekly game of pickup basketball for men over forty still remembering a fictive past when they could run, jump, and shoot, one of the players asked, "What time is it?" Civil Rights historian and basketball regular Clay Carson responded jokingly, "It's Nation Time!" I joked back, "Wasn't Nation Time some thirty years ago?" To which he retorted, "It's always Nation Time." This seemingly playful and innocent interchange captures the complexities and the problems found in any attempt to racialize time. Emerging out of Black Nationalist politics of the 1960s and 1970s, the cries for "Nation Time" embodied the belief that that time was ripe for revolutionary change. The rallying cry "It's Nation Time!" acknowledged the cultural and social efforts to establish black possession and control of time and space, to found a black nation. Present within those times was a condition that I have defined elsewhere as *urgency*. Frustrated by the lack of access, opportunity, and rights, black urban enclaves swelled with a sense of urgency. As evidenced by the civil unrest that ensued, the urgency of the times provoked demands for immediate change and affirmed the collective faith of the disenfranchised that radical change was not only possible but imminent. It was indeed Nation Time. The urgency produced an environment conducive to the emergence of black revolutionary theater. August Wilson claims that his own youth "was fired in the kiln of black cultural nationalism as exemplified by Amiri Baraka in the sixties" (*Three Plays,* ix). In his black revolutionary dramaturgy, Baraka preached cultural nationalism through a denigration of white Western ideals and aesthetics, including the institution of time. "Time, that evil white thing," Baraka bemoans in *Black Mass* (1967), one of his *Four Black Revolutionary Plays.* While the urgency of those times has long passed and the material conditions of black life have changed, the underlying conditions of racism, both internalized and externalized, remain. This continuum of oppression and self-denigration has necessitated continued efforts toward black liberation in art and politics. Moreover, this continuum stretches not only forward but also backward into time. The paradigms for a black activist theater that W. E. B. Du Bois calls for in the 1920s are not unlike those demanded by Amiri Baraka in the 1960s or even those outlined by August Wilson in the 1990s. See W. E. B. Du Bois, "Krigwa Little Theatre Movement," *Crisis* 32 (July 1926): 135; LeRoi Jones, "The Revolutionary Theatre," in *Selected Plays and Prose of Amiri Baraka/LeRoi Jones* (New York: William Morrow, 1979), 131; and August Wilson, "The Ground on Which I Stand," *American Theatre,* September 1996, 16. There is circularity in black politics, black art, and in black time—some would even say a stasis. As Clay Carson notes, "It's always Nation Time." Yet and still, in the absence of urgency, how do you produce theater and art that has immediacy, that responds to the needs of the people and galvanizes them to think and to act? This is the dilemma of August Wilson as he seeks to reinvigorate the legacy of that now mythic time of black power, unity, consciousness, and commitment. Excited by this burst of inspiration as I dribbled the basketball around the top of the key, I explained my thinking to Clay Carson, who responded, "Man, it's 9:00 A.M. on a Saturday morning and I'm just trying to play basketball."

16. Alan Nadel, "Boundaries, Logistics, and Identity," in *May All Your Fences Have Gates: Essays on the Drama of August Wilson*, ed. Alan Nadel (Iowa City: University of Iowa Press, 1994), 103.

17. Suzan Lori-Parks, *Death of the Last Black Man in the Whole Entire World*, in *America Play and Other Works*, 111.

18. Henry Louis Gates, Jr., *The Signifying Monkey: A Theory of Afro-American Literary Criticism* (Oxford: Oxford University Press, 1988).

19. Gates, *The Signifying Monkey*, 102.

20. Judith Williams, production notes, *Joe Turner's Come and Gone*, Stanford University, November 3–6, 9–12, 1994.

21. Nadel, "Boundaries, Logistics, and Identity," 103.

22. Nadel, "Boundaries, Logistics, and Identity," 103.

23. Ariela J. Gross, *Double Character: Slavery and Mastery in the Antebellum Southern Courtroom* (Princeton, N.J.: Princeton University Press, 2000), 3.

24. Eric Hobsbawm and Terence Ranger, *The Invention of Tradition* (New York: Cambridge University Press, 1983).

25. Joseph Roach, *Cities of the Dead: Circum-Atlantic Performance* (New York: Columbia University Press, 1996), 11–12.

26. August Wilson, *Ma Rainey's Black Bottom* in *August Wilson: Three Plays* (Pittsburgh: University of Pittsburgh Press, 1991), 1.46. Subsequent citations are given in the text.

27. John Timpane, "Filling Time: Reading History in the Drama of August Wilson," in Nadel, *All Your Fences*, 78.

28. This history corresponds to the thesis of Friedrich Nietzsche in *On the Advantage and Disadvantage of History for Life*, which rejects old "memorial" history as ridiculed with self-interest and argues that "man" produces his own being and that history is the record of that self-production. Thus "it is the activity of a historical being recovering the past into a present which anticipates the future" (*On the Advantage and Disadvantage of History for Life*, trans. Peter Preuss [Indianapolis: Hackett, 1980], 1). Building on Nietzsche, Michel Foucault asserts that history is a struggle of endlessly repeating dominations and a product of "a will to knowledge" (*Language, Counter-Memory, Practice: Selected Essays and Interviews*, trans. Donald F. Brouchard and Sherry Simon [Ithaca, NY: Cornell University Press, 1977]). Foucault's view allows for both conflict and interpretation and thus space for contestation, in particular the progressive views of history present in Wilson. Wilson's project, like Foucault's, shows that history is not a seamless flow. He depicts the specific life of Herald Loomis, or of Troy Maxson of *Fences*, of Berniece in *Piano Lesson* and explores its historicity. Even in his one play that features a character of legendary historic import, *Ma Rainey's Black Bottom*, blues singer Ma Rainey is not the central figure. Thus, Wilson's is not a traditional history but a particularized one, rife with cultural conflict and individual struggle that seeks to empower the present. Significantly, Nietzsche also argues that only by turning history into art and accentuating the

art in history can one save history and produce a history that can really effect change: "In such effects art is opposed to history: and only if history can bear being transformed into a work of art, that is, to become a pure art form, may it perhaps preserve instincts or even rouse them" (*On the Advantage*, 39).

29. Benjamin, "Theses," 255.

30. August Wilson, *Two Trains Running* (New York: Plume/Dutton, 1993), 1.3.59. Subsequent citations are given in the text.

31. August Wilson, interview by the author, Mark Taper Forum, Los Angeles, September 9, 2000.

32. James Grammar, telephone interview by the author, April 4, 2001.

33. Wilson, interview, September 9, 2000.

34. Sandra Shannon, "The Role of Memory in August Wilson's Four-Hundred Year Autobiography," in *Memory and Cultural Politics*, ed. Amritjit Singh, Joseph T. Skerrett, Robert Egan, and Arjun Appaduria (Boston: Northeastern University Press, 1996), 176–77.

35. Jeanette R. Malkin, *Memory-Theater and Postmodern Drama* (Ann Arbor: University of Michigan Press, 1999), 26.

36. Toni Morrison, *Beloved* (New York: Penguin, 1987), 25.

37. David Palumbo-Liu, "The Politics of Memory: Remembering History in Alice Walker and Joy Kugawa," in Singh et al., *Memory and Cultural Politics*, 215.

38. August Wilson, *Fences* in *August Wilson: Three Plays* (University of Pittsburgh Press, 1991), 103. Subsequent citations are given in the text.

39. Singh et al., introduction to *Memory and Cultural Politics*, 8.

40. Pierre Nora, "Between Memory and History: Les Lieux de Mémoire," in Fabre and O'Meally, *History and Memory*, 295. Reprinted from *Representations* 26 (spring 1989): 7–25.

41. Malkin, *Memory-Theater*, 24.

42. Fabre and O'Meally, *History and Memory*, 9.

43. Fabre and O'Meally, *History and Memory*, 8.

44. Roach, *Cities of the Dead*, 3–4.

45. Morrison, *Beloved*, 273.

46. See discussion of blood memory in the Overture.

47. Catherine Bell, *Ritual: Perspectives and Dimensions* (Oxford: Oxford University Press, 1997), 83.

48. For discussion of ritual, symbolic mediation, and social protest theater see Harry J. Elam, Jr., *Taking It to the Streets: The Social Protest Drama of Luis Valdez and Amiri Baraka* (Ann Arbor: University of Michigan Press, 1996), 12–14.

49. For discussion of ritual and signifying practices and social protest theater see Elam, *Taking It to the Streets*, 12–14.

50. See Bell, *Ritual*, 80–83.

51. Bell, *Ritual*, 83.

52. Bell, *Ritual*, 82.

53. Terry Eagleton, *Marxism and Literature* (Berkeley and Los Angeles: University of California Press, 1973), 23.

54. Hannah Arendt, *On Revolution* (New York: Viking Press, 1963; reprint, New York: Penguin, 1990), 42–43.

Chapter One

1. Robert G. O'Meally, "On Burke and the Vernacular: Ralph Ellison's Boomerang of History," in Fabre and O'Meally, *History and Memory*, 245.

2. Margaret Wilkerson, "Music as Metaphor: New Plays by Black Women," in *Making a Spectacle: Feminist Essays on Contemporary Women's Theatre*, ed. Lynda Hart (Ann Arbor: University of Michigan Press, 1989), 62.

3. James Baldwin, quoted by John Russell Rickford and Russell John Rickford, *Spoken Soul: The Story of Black English* (New York: John Wiley and Sons, 2000), 3.

4. Kimberly Benston, *Performing Blackness: Enactments of African-American Modernism* (New York: Routledge, 2000), 119.

5. Baz Kershaw, *The Politics of Performance: Radical Theatre as Cultural Intervention* (New York: Routledge, 1992), 36.

6. See Addison Gayle, *The Black Aesthetic* (Garden City, N.Y.: Doubleday, 1971).

7. Paul Carter Harrison, "August Wilson's Blues Poetics," in Wilson, *Three Plays*, 299.

8. Wilson, "Ground on Which I Stand," 16.

9. Houston A. Baker, *Blues, Ideology, and Afro-American Literature: A Vernacular Theory* (Chicago: University of Chicago Press, 1984), 14.

10. Wilson, preface to *Three Plays*, ix–x.

11. Baker, *Blues, Ideology*, 63.

12. Ralph Ellison, "Blues People," in *Shadow and Act* (New York: Random House, 1964), 256.

13. Baker, *Blues, Ideology*, 3.

14. Baker, *Blues, Ideology*, 3.

15. Baker, *Blues, Ideology*, 7.

16. Allan Wallach, "Fenced in by a Lifetime of Resentments," *New York Newsday*, March 27, 1987, in *New York Theatre Critics Reviews*, 1987, 319.

17. Wilson, interview, September 9, 2000.

18. Rickford and Rickford, *Spoken Soul*, 29, 28.

19. Charles Dutton originated the role of Levee in *Ma Rainey's Black Bottom*. He also played Herald Loomis in *Joe Turner's Come and Gone*, and Wilson wrote Boy Willie in *Piano Lesson* with Dutton in mind. He was also scheduled to play King in *King Hedley II* on Broadway in 2001, but his schedule would not allow it. L. Scott Caldwell won a Tony award for her portrayal of Bertha in *Joe Turner's Come and Gone* and has played Berniece at different regional theaters around the country.

20. See Alice Rayner and Harry J. Elam, Jr., "Unfinished Business: Reconfiguring History in *The Death of the Last Black Man in the Whole Entire World* by Suzan-Lori Parks," *Theatre Journal* 46 (December 1994): 447–61.

21. See Geneva Smitherman, *Talkin' and Testifyin': The Language of Black America* (Detroit: Wayne State University Press, 1997); and Gates, *The Signifying Monkey.*

22. Baker, *Blues Ideology,* 11.

23. Tzvetan Todorov, *Mikhail Bakhtin: The Dialogic Principle,* trans. Wlad Godzich (Minneapolis: University of Minnesota Press, 1984), 66.

24. Justine Tally, *The Story of Jazz: Toni Morrison's Dialogic Imagination,* Forum for European Contributions to African American Studies, vol. 7 (Hamburg: LIT, 2001), 82.

25. Wilson, interview, September 9, 2000.

26. Wilson, interview, September 9, 2000.

27. Ellison, *Shadow and Act,* 78–79, quoted by Craig Werner, "August Wilson's Burden: The Function of Neoclassical Jazz," in Nadel, *All Your Fences,* 27.

28. August Wilson, interview, in David Savran, *In Their Own Words: Contemporary American Playwrights* (New York: Theatre Communications Group, 1988), 293.

29. Albert Murray, *The Blue Devils of Nada: A Contemporary American Approach to Aesthetic Statement* (New York: Pantheon, 1996), 216.

30. Ben Brantley, "Finding Drama in Life and Vice Versa," *New York Times,* August 26, 2000, sec. E1.

31. Marion McClinton, quoted by Wilborn Hampton, "A Combo of Actors Learns the Joy of Jamming," *New York Times,* June 25, 2000, sec. B4.

32. Barry Shabaka Henley, quoted by Hampton, "Combo of Actors," sec. B4.

33. *King Hedley II* (New York: Theatre Communications Group, 2005), 2.4.92. Subsequent citations are given in the text.

34. Benston, *Performing Blackness,* 139.

35. August Wilson, quoted by Andrea Allen, "Inspired by the Blues," Seattle Repertory Theatre notes to *Seven Guitars,* April 2000.

36. Ellison, "Blues People," 257.

37. Harrison, "August Wilson's Blues Poetics," 307.

38. Wilson, in Savran, *In Their Own Words,* 305.

39. See August Wilson, "I Want a Black Director," in Nadel, *All Your Fences,* 200–204.

40. August Wilson, *Seven Guitars* (New York: Plume/Dutton, 1997), 74–75. Subsequent citations are given in the text.

41. Wilson, in Savran, *In Their Own Words,* 300.

42. Zue Robertson quoted by Donald M. Marquis, *In Search of Buddy Bolden* (Baton Rouge: Louisiana State University Press, 1978), 44.

43. Funky Butt Hall was the nickname given to Union Sons Hall on Presidio

Street in New Orleans. Buddy Bolden became its most famous performer, and the tune "Funky Butt" was his best-known and most requested song.

44. Benston, *Performing Blackness*, 140. Benston cites Fela Sowande, *The Role of Music in African Society* (Washington, D.C.: Howard University Press, 1969).

45. Benston, *Performing Blackness*, 140.

Chapter Two

1. Francois Verges, "Chains of Madness, Chains of Colonialism: Fanon and Freedom," in *The Fact of Blackness: Frantz Fanon and Visual Representation*, ed. Alan Read (Seattle: Bay Press, 1996), 52.

2. W. E. B. Du Bois, *The Souls of Black Folk* (New York: Penguin, 1969), 45.

3. Hortense Spillers, "All the Things You Could Be by Now, If Sigmund Freud's Wife Was Your Mother: Psychoanalysis and Race," *Boundary 2*, 23, no. 3 (1996): 104.

4. Sandra Richards, "Yoruba Gods on the American Stage: August Wilson's *Joe Turner's Come and Gone*," *Research in African Literatures* 30, no. 4 (1999): 92.

5. Shelly Eversley, "The Lunatic Fancy and the Work of Art," *American Literary History* 13, no. 3 (2001): 445.

6. Eversley, "Lunatic Fancy," 460.

7. Paul Gilroy, *The Black Atlantic: Modernity and Double Consciousness* (Cambridge: Harvard University Press, 1993), 161.

8. Ralph Ellison, *Invisible Man* (1947; reprint, New York: Modern Library, 1994), 433, 436.

9. For a discussion of history in *The Invisible Man*, see O'Meally, "Burke and the Vernacular."

10. LeRoi Jones, *Dutchman* (1964), in *Selected Plays and Prose*, 94.

11. Jones, *Dutchman*, 94.

12. Food serves as an important trope in Wilson's dramaturgy. He repeats and revises food metaphors, recognizing that food has certain cultural, historic, social weight. Food can operate as *lieu de mémoire* as it recalls cultural history and collective memories. In slavery times, African Americans denied the food of the master's table creatively survived with meals carved from every part of the pig, even the intestines. Chitterlings have now become a cultural delicacy. Clearly, Wilson is not the first to use food or food products metonymically for processes of social and cultural interaction. Coined by Nathan Glazier and Daniel Patrick Moynihan in the 1950s, the metaphor of the melting pot has come to stand in for the critical process of assimilation then deemed necessary for immigrants and ethnic minority groups in American society. More recently in our postmodern climate of diversity, the concept of a salad bowl with different vegetables that mix but maintain their difference has replaced the melting plot as an analogy of how American society needs to function. Wilson riffs on

the notion of the melting pot, creating and repeating what Jay Plum calls "the metaphor of a cultural stew." Jay Plum, "Blues History and the Dramaturgy of August Wilson," *African American Review* 27, no. 4 (1993): 563. In *Ma Rainey's Black Bottom*, using the image of a stew, the piano player Toledo explains to the other band members that blacks are leftovers from history:

> Now I'm gonna show you how this goes . . . where you just a leftover from history. Everybody come from different places in Africa, right? Come from different tribes and things. Soon-awhile they began to make one big stew. . . . Now you take and eat the stew. You take and make your history with that stew. Alright. Now it's over. You history's over and you done ate the stew. But you look around and you see some carrots over here, some potatoes over there. That's stew's still there. You can't eat it all. So what you got? You got some leftovers . . . and you can't do nothing with it. You already making you another history . . . cooking you another meal, and you don't need them leftovers no more. What to do?
>
> See, we's the leftovers. The colored man is the leftovers. Now, what's the colored man gonna do with himself? That's what we waiting to find out. (1.46–47)

Toledo's stew story humorously conveys the collective memory of the African diaspora and of African American diversity that reaches a pivotal, historical juncture in "the big stew" of slavery. Toledo's imagery cleverly takes hold as he expresses the inability of the black "vegetables" to assimilate within the stew. As a consequence, in the aftermath of the slave economy, blacks have outlived their utility. The question, then, is how black people are to redefine themselves and determine their own history. Wilson repeats and revises the image of a racial stew in *Fences* as he critiques black complicity in subjugation. The protagonist Troy Maxson bemoans to wife Rose the treatment of blacks by black restaurateur, Pope.

> Man bought him that restaurant down there . . . fixed it up real nice . . . and then didn't want nobody to come in it! A Negro go in there and can't get no kind of service. I seen a white fellow come in there and order a bowl of stew. Pope picked all the meat out of the pot for him. Man ain't had nothing but a bowl of meat! Negro come behind him and ain't got nothing but the potatoes and carrots. (1.2.123)

Now in this revision of the cultural stew, black people, rather than being the leftovers in the stew, are resigned to consume only those leftovers, "the potatoes and the carrots." The devaluation of black life is equally inherent in the story, but now another black man facilitates the processes of that dehumanization.

13. William Faulkner, *Absalom, Absalom!* (1936; New York: Vintage, 1990), 27.

14. Gilroy, *Black Atlantic*, 56.

15. Wilson, in Savran, *In Their Own Words,* 295–96.

16. Joni L. Jones, "Performance Ethnography: The Role of Embodiment in Cultural Authenticity," *Theatre Topics* 12, no. 1 (2002): 7, 10.

17. States, *Great Reckonings,* 32.

18. In one production of the play in San Jose, California, 1993 the director, Viera Whye, constructed and staged the Zonia/Reuben scenes as if she were talking to an imaginary playmate and their conversations transpired in the world of her mind. Sandra Shannon informs us that Reuben was based upon the childhood remembrances of artist Romare Bearden. "Reuben . . . is based upon Bearden's life as a boy; the character grew out of Wilson's ideas of how the young Bearden may have responded to this environment." See Sandra Shannon, *The Dramatic Vision of August Wilson* (Washington, D.C.: Howard University Press, 1995), 123.

19. Harrison, "August Wilson's Blues Poetics," 315.

20. Joan Fishman, "Romare Bearden, August Wilson, and the Traditions of African Performance," in Nadel, *All Your Fences,* 134. Fishman also points out in concurrence with Sandra Shannon in *Dramatic Vision,* that Reuben is a representation of Bearden. Bearden, living at his grandmother's boardinghouse in Pittsburgh in the mid-1920s, met Eugene, a sickly child, who taught him to draw. Fishman writes, "Bearden's grandmother immediately moved Eugene into her home, and he brought with him his collection of pigeons and doves, which Eugene made Bearden promise to free when Eugene died. This occurred one year later."

21. Miss Mabel is equally based on Romare Bearden's *Mill hand's Lunch Bucket.* A picture within a picture of an older black woman with large hands hangs in the background of the boardinghouse that Bearden depicts—this is Wilson's Miss Mabel.

22. August Wilson, *King Hedley II,* unpublished manuscript, January 16, 2000, 1.4.81–82.

23. Wilson, interview, September 9, 2000.

Chapter Three

1. bell hooks, "Feminism as a Persistent Critique of History: What's Love Got to Do with It?" in *The Fact of Blackness: Frantz Fanon and Visual Representation* (Seattle: Bay Press, 1996), 84.

2. See Harry J. Elam, Jr., "August Wilson's Women," in Nadel, *All Your Fences,* 165–87.

3. Nathan L. Grant, "Men, Women, and Culture: A Conversation with August Wilson," *American Drama* 5, no. 2 (1996): 110.

4. Jill Dolan, *The Feminist Spectator as Critic* (Ann Arbor: University of Michigan Press, 1988), 108.

5. Angela Y. Davis, *Women, Race, and Class* (New York: Vintage, 1983), 17.

6. hooks, "Feminism as Persistent Critique," 84.

7. Angela Y. Davis, *Blues Legacies and Black Feminism* (New York: Vintage, 1998), 41.

8. Hazel V. Carby, "Women, Migration, and Blues Culture: Policing the Black Woman's Body in an Urban Context," in *Cultures in Babylon: Black Britain and African America* (London: Verso, 1999), 36.

9. Lawrence Levine reminds us that the blues also express the element of self, "the song centered upon the singer's feelings, experiences, fears, dreams, acquaintances, problems, idiosyncrasies" (*The Opening of the American Mind* [Boston: Beacon Press, 1996], 153). And thus within the blueswomen and Wilson's women, there are individual articulations and differences as well as commonalties. Angela Davis critiques Levine, noting that "Levine is certainly accurate in his emphasis on the personal and personalizing dimensions of the blues, but he fails to recognize a more complicated persistence of the call and response form" (*Blues Legacies,* 55).

This antiphonal form allowed for the community to participate in the blues performance and made the performance "one of the only arenas in which working-class black women could become aware of the deeply social character of their personal experiences" (Davis, *Blues Legacies,* 55–56).

10. Hazel V. Carby, "The Sexual Politics of Women's Blues," in *Cultures in Babylon,* 18.

11. Davis, *Blues Legacies,* 11.

12. Davis, *Blues Legacies,* 53.

13. Dolan, *Feminist Spectator as Critic,* 99.

14. Patricia Hill Collins, *Black Feminist Thought* (Boston: Unwin Hyman, 1990), 69.

15. Collins, *Black Feminist Thought,* 83.

16. Sandra G. Shannon, "The Long Wait: August Wilson's *Ma Rainey's Black Bottom,*" *Black American Literature Forum* 25, no. 1 (1991): 138.

17. Hortense Spillers, "Interstices: A Small Drama of Words," in *Pleasure and Danger: Exploring Female Sexuality,* ed. Carol S. Vance (Boston: Routledge and Kegan Paul, 1984), 88–89.

18. The second professional production after the Broadway production at the Studio Theatre in Washington, D.C., featured Alfie Brown, another actress in her sixties, as Ma Rainey.

19. Daphne Duval Harrison, *Black Pearls: Blues Queens of the 1920s* (New Brunswick: Rutgers University Press, 1990), 104.

20. In reading the play in classes, my students have generally been oblivious to the implied lesbian relationship between Ma and Dussie Mae because of its subtlety.

21. Sandra Richards, "Writing the Absent Potential: Drama, Performance, and the Canon of African-American Literature," in *Performativity and Performance,* ed. Andrew Parker and Eve Kosofsky Sedgwick (New York: Routledge, 1995), 64–88.

22. Richards, "Writing the Absent Potential," 83.

23. Shannon, "The Long Wait," 139.

24. Wilson not only conceived of the bifurcated set structure but the play itself was disjointed in its construction. As first imagined in 1976, the play did not include the four band members. In 1981 after listening to male blues singers, he added these four black male musicians.

25. Richards, "Writing the Absent Potential," 80.

26. Shannon, "The Long Wait," 140.

27. Collins, *Black Feminist Thought*, 11. Collins uses the term to describe the position of black women domestic workers "within" the household of their white employers but "outside" white culture. In this article, this term is appropriated to refer to the status of Wilson's female characters within but outside the male-dominated social order in the plays.

28. Collins, *Black Feminist Thought*, 62.

29. For discussion of *communitas* see Elam, *Taking It to the Streets*.

30. Wilson, interview, September 9, 2000.

31. Collins, *Black Feminist Thought*, 55.

32. Hazel Carby, "'It Jus Be's Dat Way Sometime': The Sexual Politics of Women's Blues," in *Unequal Sisters: A Multicultural Reader in United States Women's History*, ed. Elene Carol DuBois and Vicki L. Ruiz (New York: Routledge, 1990), 242–43.

33. Wilson, interview, September 9, 2000.

34. Hazel Carby, "Policing the Black Woman's Body in an Urban Context," in *Cultures in Babylon*, 23.

35. Wilson, in Savran, *In Their Own Words*, 294.

36. Wilson, in Grant, "Men, Women, and Culture," 115.

37. As Wilson points out, his creation of Berniece is always and already relational to men. "Here's a woman who's still largely defined by men. Her function and presence in the world is in relation to them, basically in service to them. But I very pointedly have her uncle Doaker taking care of himself. It's no accident that he irons his clothes and cooks for himself. Someone else with a woman in the house would have her do all the 'woman things.' But it was very important to me that Berniece not do these things and that Doaker be self-sufficient. She still exists in relation to him, although she is trying desperately to define herself." Wilson, in Grant, "Men, Women, and Culture," 111.

38. Richards, "Writing the Absent Potential," 83.

39. Richards, "Writing the Absent Potential," 83.

40. See René Girard, "'Triangular' Desire," in *Deceit, Desire, and the Novel*, trans. Yvonne Freccero (Baltimore: Johns Hopkins University Press, 1965), 1–52.

41. After the relationship between Troy and Rose has eroded, he wants to continue this money exchange that invokes her dependence on him and reaches out to hand her his weekly pay, saying, "Well . . . here go this money." Rose, however, tells him, "Put it in there on the table Troy" (*Fences*, 2.4.175).

42. Wilson, interview, September 9, 2000.

43. Patricia Hill Collins, *Black Feminist Thought: Knowledge, Consciousness, and the Politics of Empowerment,* 2d ed. (New York: Routledge, 2000), 181.

44. Collins, *Black Feminist Thought,* 2d ed., 178.

45. *Rachel* used theater as a means for social ends, to the consternation of some, including black playwright Willis Richardson and scholar Alaine Locke, who believed that building a Negro Theater required plays that celebrated Negro folk traditions. Others accused the play of advocating genocide.

46. Collins, *Black Feminist Thought,* 2d ed., 194.

47. Angelina Grimke answered critics of her play by writing that "the appeal is not primarily to the colored people, but to whites. . . . If anything can make all women sisters underneath their skins, it is motherhood. If, then, I could make the white women of this country see, feel, understand, just what their prejudice and the prejudice of their fathers, brothers, husbands, sons were having on the souls of colored mothers everywhere, and upon the mothers that are to be, a great power to affect public opinion would be set free and the battle would be half won." Quoted in Kathy Perkins, *Black Female Playwrights: An Anthology of Plays before 1950* (Indianapolis: Indiana University Press, 1989), 9.

48. Wilson, interview, September 9, 2000.

49. Kim Marra, "Ma Rainey and the Boyz: Gender Ideology in August Wilson's Broadway Canon," in Elkins, *August Wilson,* 150.

50. Collins, *Black Feminist Thought,* 1st ed., 86.

51. August Wilson, *Jitney* (Woodstock, N.Y.: Overlook Press, 2001), 2.1.74. Subsequent citations are given in the text.

52. Wilson, in Grant, "Men, Women, and Culture," 114.

53. Wilson's note of introduction to *Seven Guitars* is particularly informative in this regard. He writes, "I am not a historian. I happen to think that the content of my mother's life—her myths, her superstitions, her prayers, the contents of her pantry, the smell of her kitchen, the song that escaped from her sometimes parched lips, her thoughtful repose and pregnant laughter—are all worthy of art" (*Seven Guitars,* "A Note from the Playwright"). Wilson, raised by a single black mother, attributes his cultural inheritance to this figure. The memories, the traditions, the artifacts, the cultural practices garnered from life with mother become the foundation for his drama and survives through his (w)righting.

54. Hortense J. Spillers, "Mama's Baby, Papa's Maybe: An American Grammar Book," in *African American Literary Theory: A Reader,* ed. Winston Napier (New York: NYU Press, 2000), 278.

55. Spillers, "Mama's Baby, Papa's Maybe," 278.

Chapter Four

1. Trey Ellis, "How Does It Feel to Be a Problem?" in *Speak My Name: Black Men on Black Masculinity and the American Dream,* ed. Don Belton (Boston: Beacon Press, 1995), 10.

2. Patricia J. Williams, "Mediations on Masculinity," in *Constructing Masculinity*, ed. Maurice Berger, Brian Wallis, and Simon Watson (New York: Routledge, 1995), 241.

3. August Wilson, foreword to Belton, *Speak My Name*, xiii.

4. Wilson, foreword to Belton, *Speak My Name*, xii.

5. Homi Bhabha, "Are You a Man or a Mouse?" in Berger, Wallis, and Watson, *Constructing Masculinity*, 58.

6. David Marriott, *On Black Men* (New York: Columbia University Press, 2000), xv.

7. Marriott, *On Black Men*, 96.

8. Charles R. Lyons, "Shepard's Family Trilogy and the Conventions of Modern Realism," in *Rereading Shepard*, ed. Leonard Chaise (New York: St. Martins Press, 1993), 126.

9. Lyons, "Shepard's Family Trilogy," 129.

10. August Wilson, quoted by Hilary DeVries, "A Song in Search of Itself," *American Theatre*, January 1987, 25.

11. Wilson, quoted in DeVries, "Song in Search of Itself," 25.

12. August Wilson, *The Piano Lesson* (New York: Plume/Dutton, 1990), 46. Subsequent citations are given in the text.

13. Gwen Berger, "Myths of Masculinity: The Oedipus Complex and Douglass's 1845 *Narrative*," in *The Psychoanalysis of Race*, ed. Christopher Lane (New York: Columbia University Press, 1998), 254.

14. Richard Wright, *Native Son* (New York: Harper and Row, 1940), 392.

15. See Rayner and Elam, "Unfinished Business."

16. Wright, *Native Son*, xx.

17. Wright, *Native Son*, xvii–xviii.

18. Wright, *Native Son*, xx.

19. Marriott, *On Black Men*, xv.

20. When I teach this scene, students react to the seeming brutal insensitivity of Troy's words, and they lament that the father demonstrates no love for the son in this needy moment. Yet my sense is that this scene demonstrates a different form of love. For Troy, taking responsibility for his family is an act of love.

21. A case could be made that Wilson's reference to black men in prison in his plays is not unlike the period between 1980 and 2000—the period during which Wilson penned most of his cycle—when the number of black men in prison rapidly increased and far outnumbered the number of black men of similar age attending college.

22. Michel Foucault, *Discipline and Punish: The Birth of the Prison*, trans. Alan Sheridan (New York: Vintage, 1977) 195–230.

23. Foucault, *Discipline and Punish*, 200.

24. Wilson's reading of unequal justice in his dramatic cycle resonates in the contemporary American judicial system, where black men face longer sentences and prison time for crimes comparable to those of their white counterparts.

25. Malcolm X and Alex Haley, *The Autobiography of Malcolm X* (New

York: Grove Press, 1964), 77, quoted by Robin D. G. Kelley, "The Riddle of the Zoot: Malcolm Little and Black Cultural Politics during World War II," in *Race and The Subject of Masculinities,* ed. Harry Stecopoulos and Michal Uebel (Durham, N.C.: Duke University Press, 1997), 246.

26. Kelley, "Riddle of the Zoot," 246.

27. Kelley, "Riddle of the Zoot," 245–46.

28. Kelley, "Riddle of the Zoot," 246.

29. Kelley, "Riddle of the Zoot," 243.

30. Harrison, "August Wilson's Blues Poetics," 303.

31. Wilson, foreword to Belton, *Speak My Name,* xii.

32. Ralph Ellison, *Invisible Man* (1947; New York: Vintage, 1995), 440.

33. Wilson, interview, September 9, 2000.

34. Observation from Margaret Booker, May 2000.

35. Ellison, "Prologue," *Invisible Man,* Modern Library ed., 3.

36. Wilson, interview, September 9, 2000.

37. bell hooks, "Doing It for Daddy," in Berger, Wallis, and Watson, *Constructing Masculinity,* 99.

38. I must admit I did not count this number myself, but the stage manager for the production of *Two Trains* that I directed in 1995—undoubtedly bored by the tedium of following the script and correcting the actors' mistakes on line readings—announced this number after one night's rehearsal.

39. Wilson, in Grant, "Men, Women, and Culture," 119–20.

40. Randall Kennedy, *Nigger: The Strange Career of a Troublesome Word* (New York: Pantheon, 2002), 176.

41. Wahneema Lubiano, "Shuckin Off the African American Native Other: What's 'Po-Mo' Got to Do with It?" *Cultural Critique,* spring 1991, 175–76.

42. Gilroy, *Black Atlantic,* 46–71.

43. See Alexander Kojève, *Introduction to the Reading of Hegel,* assembled by Raymond Queneau, ed. Allan Bloom, trans. James H. Nichols, Jr. (New York: Basic Books, 1969).

44. G. W. F. Hegel, *The Phenomenology of Mind* (London: Allen and Unwin, 1910, 1961), 228–40.

45. Gilroy, *Black Atlantic,* 69.

46. The historical accounts of Margaret Garner's suicide were an important source for the action in Toni Morrison's *Beloved.*

47. Gilroy, *Black Atlantic,* 68.

48. Gilroy, *Black Atlantic,* 55.

49. Gilroy, *Black Atlantic,* 56.

50. August Wilson, quoted in "Theater: Tuning 'The Piano Lesson,'" *New York Times Magazine,* September 10, 1989, 2.60.

51. August Wilson, quoted by Lynn Carey, "Playwright Lets His Characters Do the Work," *Time Out,* October 6, 1991, 9.

52. Keith Clark, "Race, Ritual, Reconnection, Reclamation: August Wilson and the Refiguration of the Male Dramatic Subject," in *Black Manhood in*

James Baldwin, Ernest J. Gains, and August Wilson (Urbana: University of Illinois Press, 2002), 101.

Chapter Five

1. Wilson, "American Histories," 1.
2. Barbara Browning, *Infectious Rhythm: Metaphors of Contagion and the Spread of African Culture* (New York: Routledge, 1998), 117.
3. See Robert Farris Thompson, *Flash of the Spirit* (New York: Vintage Press, 1984), 5–9; and J. Lorand Matory, *Sex and the Empire That Is No More: Gender and the Politics of Metaphor in Oyo Yoruba Religion* (Minneapolis: University of Minnesota Press, 1994), 69, 109.
4. Thompson, *Flash of the Spirit*, 5.
5. Joseph M. Murphy, *Working the Spirit: Ceremonies of the African Diaspora* (Boston: Beacon Press, 1994), 200.
6. James Cone, "Black Worship," in *The Study of Spirituality*, ed. Cheslyn Jones, Geoffrey Wainwright, and Edward Yarnold (Oxford: Oxford University Press, 1992), 483.
7. Bell, *Ritual*, 267.
8. See Kim Pereira, *August Wilson and the African-American Odyssey* (Chicago: University of Illinois Press, 1995); and Harrison, "August Wilson's Blues Poetics," 291–318.
9. Discussion with Professor Sandra Richards of Northwestern University back in 1997 sparked my own interest in Wilson's Yoruban connections. Her article "Yoruba Gods on the American Stage" is an important source for this chapter.
10. Biodun Jeyifou, "Wole Soyinka and the Tropes of Disalienation," in Wole Soyinka, *Art, Dialogue, and Outrage: Essays on Literature and Culture* (New York: Pantheon, 1988), xi.
11. August Wilson, "American Histories," 1.
12. Jeyifou, "Wole Soyinka," xix.
13. Wole Soyinka, "The Fourth Stage," in *Art, Dialogue, and Outrage*, 35.
14. Soyinka, "The Fourth Stage," 28.
15. Thompson, *Flash of the Spirit*, 57.
16. Matory, *Sex and the Empire*, 6.
17. Thompson, *Flash of the Spirit*, 53.
18. Thompson, *Flash of the Spirit*, 52.
19. See Fishman, "Romare Bearden."
20. See Wilson, preface to *Three Plays*, xii.
21. Soyinka, "The Fourth Stage," 28.
22. See Kim Pereira, *"Joe Turner's Come and Gone: Seek and You Shall Find,"* in *August Wilson and the African-American Odyssey* (Champagne: University of Illinois Press, 1995), 66; see Harrison, "August Wilson's Blues Poetics," 312.

23. Thompson, *Flash of the Spirit,* 19.

24. Soyinka, "The Fourth Stage," 32.

25. Soyinka, "The Fourth Stage," 33.

26. Soyinka, "The Fourth Stage," 36.

27. James Baldwin, "Everybody's Protest Novel" (1949), in *Norton Anthology of African American Literature,* ed. Henry Louis Gates, Jr., et al. (New York: Norton, 1997), 1658.

28. Baldwin, "Everybody's Protest Novel," 1658.

29. Baldwin, "Everybody's Protest Novel," 1658.

30. Pereira, "Seek and You Shall Find," 72.

31. Pereira, "Seek and You Shall Find," 72.

32. Thompson, *Flash of the Spirit,* 69, 72.

33. Thompson, *Flash of the Spirit,* 19.

34. Wilson, in Savran, *In Their Own Voices,* 302.

35. Kwame Anthony Appiah, *In My Father's House: Africa in the Philosophy of Culture* (Oxford: Oxford University Press, 1992), 131–32.

36. Appiah, *In My Father's House,* 132.

37. August Wilson, quoted by Mervyn Rothstein, "Round Five for a Theatrical Heavy Weight," *New York Times,* April 15, 1990, sec. 2.8.

38. Wilson, "American Histories," 1.

39. Michelle Wallace, *Invisibility Blues: From Pop to Theory* (New York: Verso, 1990), 5.

40. I thank Margaret Booker for bringing this to the class's attention in our seminar on August Wilson at Stanford University during the spring of 1997.

41. I thank Faedra Chatard Carpenter for her illuminating discussion of Robert O'Hara's *Insurrection,* in an unpublished essay, 1999.

42. Frederick Douglass, *The Narrative of the Life of Frederick Douglass, an American Slave* (1845; New York: Penguin, 1986), 51.

43. Douglass, *Narrative,* 51.

44. John Hope Franklin and Alfred A. Moss, Jr., *From Slavery to Freedom,* 8th ed. (Boston: McGraw-Hill, 2000), 185.

45. Others have noted the influence of Charles Chesnutt's work on Wilson. Sandra Shannon in *Dramatic Vision,* 125, points out the parallels in *Joe Turner*'s plot to another of Chesnutt's stories, "The Wife of His Youth" (1899). Wilson himself draws connections to his use of black vernacular and that of Chesnutt in his "Conjure Woman Tales" (in Grant, "Men, Women, and Culture," 116).

46. Charles W. Chesnutt, "The Goophered Grapevine," in *The Conjure Woman and Other Conjure Tales,* ed. Richard Brodhead (Durham NC: Duke University Press, 1993), 527.

47. Thompson, *Flash of the Spirit,* 6.

48. Thompson, *Flash of the Spirit,* 79.

49. Thompson, *Flash of the Spirit,* 79.

50. See Sharon Holland, *Raising the Dead: Readings of Death and (Black) Subjectivity* (Durham, N.C.: Duke University Press, 2000), 55.

51. Holland, *Raising the Dead,* 55.

52. August Wilson, interview, September 9, 2000.

53. Murphy, *Working the Spirit,* 151.

54. A provocative repetition with revision of Aunt Ester finds expression in the 1999 science fiction adventure film *The Matrix* with the figure of the Oracle, "a guide who helps you find the path." The protagonist (played by Keanu Reeves) and his mentor (Laurence Fishburn) go to visit the Oracle, a figure Fishburn describes as "very old," who has been with them "since the beginning of the resistance." Reeves enters through a door of an inner-city tenement apartment and finds an attendant dressed in white; he walks down a long narrow hallway not unlike that one described by Sterling in *Two Trains Running* at the home of Aunt Ester. When Reeves meets the Oracle, she is an elderly black woman, played by Gloria Foster, in her kitchen cooking biscuits. Like Aunt Ester, the Oracle speaks to Reeves in riddles that he must decipher over the course of the film.

55. Roach, *Cities of the Dead,* 39.

56. The information on Prophet Jones and Daddy Grace comes from Elizabeth Brodersen, "Prophets of Profit," *Stagebill* 5, no. 8 (1999): 19–22; dramaturgical notes for production of *Tartuffe* by Molière, American Conservatory Theater, July 1999.

57. Holland, *Raising the Dead,* 15.

58. Orlando Patterson, *Slavery and Social Death* (Cambridge: Harvard University Press, 1982), 38.

59. Patterson, *Slavery and Social Death,* 46.

60. Patterson, *Slavery and Social Death,* 5.

61. August Wilson, interview, September 9, 2000.

62. Gurleen Grewal, "Memory and the Matrix of History: The Poetics of Loss and Recovery in Joy Kogawa's *Obasan* and Toni Morrison's *Beloved,*" in *Memory and Cultural Politics* (Boston: Northeastern University Press, 1996), 160.

63. For a discussion of this play see Rayner and Elam, "Unfinished Business."

64. Morrison, *Beloved,* 5.

65. Kwame Anthony Appiah, "Old Gods, New Worlds," in *In My Father's House,* 134.

66. Appiah, *In My Father's House,* 115.

67. Appiah, *In My Father's House,* 124.

68. W. C. Handy, *Father of the Blues* (New York: Macmillan, 1941).

69. Baker, *Blues, Ideology,* 4.

70. Bell, *Ritual,* 83.

71. Orlando Patterson, *Rituals of Blood: Consequences of Slavery in Two American Centuries* (New York: Basic Civitas, 1998), 182.

72. Lynne Fauley Emery, *Black Dance in the United States from 1619 to 1970* (New York: National Press Books, 1972), 120.

73. Margaret Thompson Drewal, *Yoruba Ritual: Performers, Play, Agency* (Bloomington: Indiana University Press, 1991), 183.

74. Telia U. Anderson, "'Calling the Spirit:' The Performativity of Black Women's Faith in the Baptist Church Spiritual Tradition and Its Radical Possibilities of Resistance," in *African American Performance and Theater History: A Critical Reader*, ed. Harry J. Elam, Jr., and David Krasner (Oxford: Oxford University Press, 2001), 118.

75. Drewal, *Yoruba Ritual*, 7.

76. At one performance at the Penumbra Theater in St. Louis, described to me by Robert Baum, a group of black women from a local Pentecostal church, during the Juba scene and subsequent entrance and possession of Herald Loomis, pulled their Bibles from their purses, rose from their seats, and walked down to the front of the stage and participated with the actors in antiphonal call-and-response prayer for the soul of Herald Loomis.

77. Mary L. Bogumil, "'Tomorrow Never Comes': Songs of Cultural Identity in August Wilson's *Joe Turner's Come and Gone*," *Theatre Journal* 46 (December 1994): 468–69.

78. Soyinka, "The Fourth Stage," 145.

79. Bell, *Ritual*, 78.

80. Mark Rocha, "Black Madness in August Wilson's 'Down the Line' Cycle," in *Madness in Drama*, ed. James Redmond (Cambridge: Cambridge University Press, 1993), 191–201.

81. Richards, "Yoruba Gods," 100.

82. Jones, "Performance Ethnography," 7–8.

83. See Drewal, *Yoruba Ritual*, 10.

84. Patterson, *Rituals of Blood*, 184–223.

85. Matory, *Sex and the Empire*, 191.

86. Richards, "Yoruba Gods," 101.

87. Richards, "Yoruba Gods," 98.

88. Wilson, interview, September 9, 2000.

89. Bell, *Ritual*, 83.

90. Richards "Yoruba Gods," 101.

Chapter Six

1. Stanley Crouch, "Who's Zooming Who? Beyond the Wilson-Brustein Debate," *Theater* 27, nos. 2–3 (1997): 21.

2. Wilson, "Ground on Which I Stand," 14. Subsequent citations are given in the text, abbreviated "Ground."

3. See August Wilson, "I Don't Want Nobody Just 'Cause They're Black," *Spin*, October 1990, 70–71; "The Legacy of Malcolm X," *Life*, December 1992, 84–94; *Three Plays*, vii–xiv.

4. August Wilson, "August Wilson Responds," *American Theatre*, October 1996, 108.

5. Toni Morrison, "Memory, Creation, and Writing," *Thought*, December 1984, 385–90; "Unthinkable Things Unspoken: The Afro-American Presence in American Literature," *Michigan Quarterly* 28 (winter 1989): 1–49.

6. Henry Louis Gates, Jr., "The Chitlin' Circuit," in Elam and Krasner, *African American Performance*, 137.

7. See Mike Sell, "The Black Arts Movement: Performance, Neo-orality, and the Destruction of the 'White Thing,'" in Elam and Krasner, *African American Performance*, 56–80.

8. Cherríe Moraga, "Sour Grapes: The Art of Anger in America," in *The Color of Theater: Race, Culture, and Contemporary Performance*, ed. Roberta Uno and Lucy Mae San Pablo Burns (London: Continuum Press, 2002), 115.

9. Brustein's arguments also seem tainted by a personal antagonism: the Yale Drama School came to increased prominence after he was replaced by Lloyd Richards as director and Richards began his collaboration with August Wilson.

10. Harold Cruse, "The Integrationist Ethic as a Basis for Scholarly Endeavors," in *Turbulent Voyage: Readings in African American Studies*, ed. Floyd W. Hayes III, 2d ed. (San Diego: Collegiate Press, 1997), 12.

11. Cruse, "Integrationist Ethic," 12.

12. Wilson, "Black Director," 203.

13. Wilson, "Black Director," 201.

14. Michael Awkward, "'The Crookeds with the Straights': *Fences*, Race, and the Politics of Adaptation," in Nadel, *All Your Fences*, 225.

15. Alan Nadel, "August Wilson and the (Color-Blind) Whiteness of Public Space," *Theater* 27, nos. 2–3 (1997): 39.

16. Cornel West, *Race Matters* (Boston: Beacon Press, 1993).

17. Manning Marrable, "Black Studies, Multiculturalism, and the Future of American Education," in Hayes, *Turbulent Voyage*, 30.

18. Kimberle Williams Crenshaw, "Color-Blind Dreams and Racial Nightmares: Reconfiguring Racism in the Post–Civil Rights Era," in *Birth of a Nation'hood*, ed. Toni Morrison and Claudia Brodsky Lacour (New York: Pantheon, 1997), 111.

19. Nadel, "August Wilson," 40.

20. Nadel, "August Wilson," 40.

21. William Sonnega, "Beyond a Liberal Audience," in Elam and Krasner, *African American Performance*, 90.

22. Sonnega, "Beyond a Liberal Audience," 96.

23. August Wilson, quoted by John Lahr, "Been Here and Gone," *New Yorker*, April 16, 2001, 52.

24. For a discussion of color blindness, history, and cross-racial casting see Brandi Wilkins Catanese, "Casting Away Tradition: The Performance of Blackness in Contemporary American Culture," Ph.D. diss., Stanford University, 2003.

25. Gates, "The Chitlin' Circuit," 133.

26. Moraga, "Sour Grapes: The Art of Anger in America," 115–16.

27. Marion McClinton, quoted by Lahr, "Been Here and Gone," 64.

28. Amiri Baraka, "The Descent of Charlie Fuller into Pulitzerland and the

Need for African-American Institutions," *Black American Literature Forum* 17, no. 2 (1983): 51–54.

29. David Savran, "Ambivalence, Utopia, and a Queer Sort of Materialism: How *Angels in America* Reconstructs the Nation," in *Approaching the Millennium: Essays on "Angels in America,"* ed. Deborah R. Geis and Steven F. Kruger (Ann Arbor: University of Michigan Press, 1997), 34.

30. August Wilson, quoted by Michael Blowen, "Dreaming with Words: Wilson's Plays Are a Matter of Thinking, and Re-thinking What Is on the Page," *Boston Globe,* October 25, 1998, sec. M1.

31. Perhaps in answer to some of the criticism leveled against him, in a desire to practice what he preaches and keep it real on another level, Wilson's revision of his play of the 1970s, *Jitney,* was produced at the Crossroads Theater (a leading black theater) in Newark in 1997 and later was produced at another black theater, the Lorraine Hansberry Theater in San Francisco. Wilson claims that the decision to produce at Crossroads was not a political one but was affected by changes in the production schedule at the Huntington Theatre in Boston, where the play was originally scheduled to be produced in the spring of 1997 (see Joan Herrington, *"I Ain't Sorry for Nothin' I Done": August Wilson's Process of Playwriting* [New York: Limelight Editions, 1998], 142.) Still, the cost of the production at Crossroads equaled the costs of the rest of the theater's season and left it in severe debt. Wilson believed his play was worthy of a standard of production in the smaller black theaters that he had come to expect within the more financially and technically capable majority-white regional theaters.

32. Savran, "Ambivalence, Utopia," 33.

33. Richards, "Yoruba Gods," 101.

34. Victor Leo Walker II, ". . . The Response: The National Black Theatre Summit 'On Golden Pond,'" unpublished summit proceedings, March 1998, 2.

Epilogue

1. Jesse McKinley, "Broadway Theater to Be Renamed for Dying Playwright," *New York Times,* September 2, 2005, sec. A, 20.

2. August Wilson, *Gem of the Ocean* (unpublished manuscript, December 6, 2004), act 2, scene 5, p. 91. Subsequent citations are to act, scene, and page and are given in the text.

3. This section of the poem *Wise, whys, ys* contains this line when published in the online poetry forum "Fooling with Words with Bill Moyer," http://www.pbs.org/wnet/foolingwithwords/mainlst_baraka.html. However, in the published version of the entire poem (Amiri Baraka, "So the King Sold the Farmer #39," *Wise, whys, ys* [Chicago: Third World Press, 1995], 131), this section is omitted.

4. Paul Gilroy, *The Black Atlantic: Modernity and Double Consciousness* (Cambridge: Harvard University Press, 1993).

5. Joseph Roach, *Cities of the Dead* (New York: Columbia University Press, 1996), 4.

6. I thank Margaret Louise O'Leary for this reflection (July 2005).

7. Gunilla Theander Kester, "Approaches to Africa: The Poetics of Memory and the Body in Two August Wilson Plays," in *August Wilson: A Casebook*, ed. Marilyn Elkins (New York: Garland Press, 1994), 108.

8. August Wilson, "Homeward Bound," *American Theatre* 16, no. 9 (November 1999): 16.

Selected Bibliography

Primary Sources

Ma Rainey's Black Bottom. New York: New American Library, 1984.
Fences. New York: New American Library, 1985.
Joe Turner's Come and Gone. New York: New American Library, 1988.
The Piano Lesson. New York: Plume/Dutton, 1990.
Testimonies. In *Antaeus* 66 (spring 1991): 474–79.
August Wilson: Three Plays. Pittsburgh: University of Pittsburgh Press, 1991.
    Includes *Ma Rainey's Black Bottom, Fences,* and *Joe Turner's Come and Gone.*
Two Trains Running. New York: Plume/Dutton, 1993.
Seven Guitars. New York: Plume/Dutton, 1997.
The Janitor. In *Literature and Its Writers: An Introduction,* by Ann Charters
    and Samuel Charters. Boston: Bedford, 1997.
Jitney. Woodstock, N.Y.: Overlook Press, 2001.
King Hedley II. New York: Theatre Communications Group, 2005.

Essays

Foreword to *Romare Bearden: His Life and Art.* Edited by Myron Schwartz-
    man. New York: Harry N. Abrams, 1990.
Preface to *Three Plays.* Pittsburgh: University of Pittsburgh Press, 1991.
"How to Write a Play Like August Wilson." *New York Times,* March 10, 1991,
    sec. 2.5, 17.
"The Legacy of Malcolm X." *Life,* December 1992, 84–94.
"I Want a Black Director." In *May All Your Fences Have Gates,* edited by Alan
    Nadel, 200–204. Iowa City: University of Iowa Press, 1994.
"Living on Mother's Prayer." *New York Times,* May 12, 1996, sec. 4.13.
"The Ground on Which I Stand." Keynote address to the Theatre Communi-
    cations Group, June 26, 1996. *American Theatre* 13, no. 7 (1996): 14–17,
    71–74.
"August Wilson Responds." *American Theatre* 13, no. 8 (1996): 105–7.
"National Black Theater Festival." *Callaloo* 20, no. 3 (1997): 483–92.

Interviews

"August Wilson—a New Voice for Black American Theater." By Hilary
    DeVries. *Christian Science Monitor* 18 (October 1984): 51–54.

"An Interview with August Wilson." By Kim Powers. *Theater* 16 (fall–winter 1984): 50–55.

"A Song in Search of Itself." By Hilary DeVries. *American Theatre* 3, no. 10 (1987): 25.

"August Wilson: Playwright." By Bill Moyers. In *A World of Ideas*, 167–80. New York: Doubleday, 1989.

"Hurdling Fences." By Dennis Watlington. *Vanity Fair*, April 1989, 102–13.

"An Interview with August Wilson." By Yvonne Shafer. *Journal of Dramatic Theory and Criticism* 4 (fall 1989): 161–73.

"August Wilson." By John L. Di Gaetani. In *A Search for a Postmodern Theater: Interviews with Contemporary Playwrights*. Westport, Conn.: Greenwood Press, 1991.

"A Conversation with August Wilson." By Mark William Rocha. *Diversity* 1 (fall 1992): 24–42.

"Blues, History, and Dramaturgy." By Sandra G. Shannon. *African American Review* 27, no. 4 (1993): 539–59.

"The Historical Perspective." By Richard Pettengill. In *August Wilson: A Casebook,* edited by Marilyn Elkins, 235–54. New York: Garland, 1994.

"August Wilson Explains His Dramatic Vision: An Interview." By Sandra G. Shannon. In *Dramatic Vision of August Wilson,* 201–35. Washington D.C.: Howard University Press, 1995.

"Men, Women, and Culture: A Conversation with August Wilson." By Nathan L. Grant. *American Drama* 5, no. 2 (1996): 100–122.

"On Listening: An Interview with August Wilson." By Susan Johann. *American Theatre* 13, no. 4 (1996): 22–23.

"August Wilson." By David Savran. In *Their Own Words: Contemporary American Playwrights,* 288–305. New York: Theatre Communications Group, 1998.

"An Interview with August Wilson." By Bonnie Lyons. *Contemporary Literature* 40, no. 1 (1999): 1–21.

"The Art of Theater XIV: August Wilson." By George Plimpton and Bonnie Lyons. *Paris Review* 41, no. 153 (1999): 66–94.

"Homeward Bound: August Wilson." By Chris Jones. *American Theatre* 16, no. 9 (1999): 14–17.

"August Wilson on Playwriting: An Interview." By Elizabeth J. Heard. *African American Review* 35, no. 1 (2001): 93–102.

Secondary Sources

Books and Articles

Abbotson, Susan C. "From Jug Band to Dixieland: The Musical Development behind August Wilson's *Ma Rainey's Black Bottom*." *Modern Drama* 43, no. 1 (2000): 100–108.

Adell, Sandra. "Speaking of Ma Rainey/Talking about the Blues." In *May All*

Your Fences Have Gates, edited by Alan Nadel, 50–66. Iowa City: University of Iowa Press, 1994.

Ambush, Benny Sato. "Culture Wars." *African American Review* 31, no. 4 (1997): 579–86.

Anderson, Douglas. "Saying Goodbye to the Past: Self-Empowerment and History in *Joe Turner's Come and Gone.*" *College Language Association Journal* 40, no. 4 (1997): 432–57.

Arnold, David L. G. "*Seven Guitars:* August Wilson's Economy of Blues." In *August Wilson: A Casebook,* edited by Marilyn Elkins, 199–225. New York: Garland, 1994.

Arthur, Thomas H. "Looking for My Relatives: The Political Implications of 'Family' in Selected Work of Athol Fugard and August Wilson." *South African Theatre* 6, no. 2 (1992): 5–16.

Awkward, Michael. "The Crooked and the Straights: *Fences,* Race, and the Politics of Adaptation." In *May All Your Fences Have Gates,* edited by Alan Nadel, 204–29. Iowa City: University of Iowa Press, 1994.

Barbour, David. "August Wilson's Here to Stay." *Theater Week,* April 18–25, 1988, 8–14.

Bellamy, Lou. "The Colonization of Black Theatre." *African American Review* 31, no. 4 (1997): 587–94.

Bergesen, Eric, and William W. Demastes. "The Limits of African-American Political Realism: Baraka's *Dutchman* and Wilson's *Ma Rainey's Black Bottom.*" In *Realism and the American Dramatic Tradition,* edited by William W. Demastes, 218–34. Tuscaloosa: University of Alabama Press, 1996.

Bernstein, Richard. "August Wilson's Voices from the Past." *New York Times,* March 27, 1988, sec. 2.1, 34.

Birdwell, Christine. "Death as a Fastball on the Outside Corner: *Fences'* Troy Maxson and the American Dream." *Aethlon* 8, no. 1 (1990): 87–96.

Bissiri, Amadou. "Aspects of Africanness in August Wilson's Drama: Reading *The Piano Lesson* through Wole Soyinka's Drama." *African American Review* 30, no. 1 (1996): 99–113.

Bloom, Harold, ed. *August Wilson.* Broomhall, Pa.: Chelsea House, 2002.

Blumenthal, Anna S. "*Joe Turner's Come and Gone:* Sacrificial Rites and Rebirth of the Self." *Postscript: Publication of the Philological Association of the Carolinas* 15 (1998): 53–65.

———. "'More Stories Than the Devil Got Sinners': Troy's Stories in August Wilson's *Fences.*" *American Drama* 9, no. 2 (2000): 74–96.

Boan, Devon, "Call-and-Response: Parallel 'Slave Narrative' in August Wilson's *The Piano Lesson.*" *African American Review* 32, no. 2 (1998): 263–71.

Bogumil, Mary L. "'Tomorrow Never Comes': Songs of Cultural Identity in August Wilson's *Joe Turner's Come and Gone.*" *Theatre Journal* 46, no. 4 (1994): 463–76.

———. *Understanding August Wilson.* Columbia: University of South Carolina Press, 1999.

Booker, Margaret. *Lillian Hellman and August Wilson: Dramatizing a New American Identity.* New York: Peter Lang, 2003.

Brantely, Ben. "The World That Created August Wilson." *New York Times,* March 27, 1988, sec. 2.1, 5.

Brewer, Gaylord. "Holy and Unholy Ghosts: The Legacy of the Father in the Plays of August Wilson." In *Naming the Father: Legacies, Genealogies, and Explorations of Fatherhood in Modern and Contemporary Literature,* edited by Eva Paulino Bueno, Terry Caesar, and William Hummel, 120–39. Lanham, Md.: Lexington Press, 2000.

Brown, Chip. "The Light in August." *Esquire,* April 1989, 116–25.

Ching, Mei-Lei. "Wrestling with History." *Theater* 20 (summer–fall 1988): 70–71.

Clark, Keith. *Black Manhood in James Baldwin, Ernest J. Gaines, and August Wilson.* Urbana: University of Illinois Press, 2002.

Crawford, Eileen. "The Bb Burden: The Invisibility of *Ma Rainey's Black Bottom.*" In *August Wilson: A Casebook,* edited by Marilyn Elkins, 31–48. New York: Garland, 1994.

Dorsey, John T. "African History in American Plays: August Wilson." In *Methods for the Study of Literature as Cultural Memory,* edited by Raymond Vervliet, 361–67. Amsterdam: Rodopi, 2000.

Dworkin, Norine. "Blood on the Tracks." *American Theater,* May 1990, 8.

Elam, Harry. "August Wilson, Doubling Madness, and Modern African-American Drama." *Modern Drama* 43, no. 4 (2000): 611–32.

———. "August Wilson's Women." In *May All Your Fences Have Gates,* edited by Alan Nadel, 167–82. Iowa City: University of Iowa Press, 1994.

———. "*Ma Rainey's Black Bottom:* Singing Wilson's Blues." *American Drama* 5, no. 2 (1996): 76–99.

———. "The Dialectics of August Wilson's *Piano Lesson.*" *Theatre Journal* 52, no. 3 (2000): 361–79.

———. "Of Angels and Transcendence: A Cross-Cultural Analysis of *Fences* by August Wilson and *Roosters* by Milcha Sanchez-Scott." In *Staging Difference: Cultural Pluralism in American Theatre,* edited by Marc Maufort, 287–300. New York: Peter Lang, 1995.

Fishman (Herrington), Joan. "Romare Bearden and August Wilson." In *May All Your Fences Have Gates,* edited by Alan Nadel, 133–49. Iowa City: University of Iowa Press, 1994.

———. "Developing His Song: August Wilson's *Fences.*" In *August Wilson: A Casebook,* edited by Marilyn Elkins, 161–81. New York: Garland, 1994.

Fleche, Anne. "The History Lesson: Authenticity and Anachronism in August Wilson's Plays." In *May All Your Fences Have Gates,* edited by Alan Nadel, 9–20. Iowa City: University of Iowa Press, 1994.

Freeman, Samuel G. "A Voice from the Streets." *New York Times Magazine,* March 15 1987, 49.

Gantt, Patricia. "Ghosts from 'Down There': The Southernness of August Wilson." In *August Wilson: A Casebook,* edited by Marilyn Elkins, 69–88. New York: Garland, 1994.

Glover, Margaret E. "Two Notes on August Wilson: The Songs of a Marked Man." *Theater* 19, no. 3 (1988): 69–70.

Goldberger, Paul. "From Page to Stage: Race and the Theater." *New York Times,* January 22, 1997, sec. C11, 14.

Gordon, Joanne. "Wilson and Fugard." In *August Wilson: A Casebook,* edited by Marilyn Elkins, 17–29. New York: Garland, 1994.

Harris, Trudier. "August Wilson's Folk Traditions." In *August Wilson: A Casebook,* edited by Marilyn Elkins, 49–67. New York: Garland, 1994.

Harrison, Paul Carter. "August Wilson's Blues Poetics." In *Three Plays by August Wilson.* Pittsburgh: University of Pittsburgh Press, 1991, 291–317.

———. "The Crisis of Black Theatre Identity." *African American Review* 31, no. 4 (1997): 567–78.

Harrison, Paul Carter, and Victor Leo Walker II, eds. "August Wilson's Call." Special issue, *African American Review* 31, no. 4 (1997).

Herrington, Joan. *"I Ain't Sorry for Nothin' I Done": August Wilson's Process of Playwriting.* New York: Limelight Editions, 1998.

———. "On August Wilson's *Jitney." American Drama* 8, no. 1 (1998): 122–44.

———. "'Responsibility in Our Own Hands.'" *Journal of Dramatic Theory and Criticism* 13, no. 1 (1998): 87–99.

Ivison, Douglas. "The Use and Abuse of History: A Naturalist Reading of August Wilson's *The Piano Lesson." Excavatio* 10 (1997): 9–20.

Joseph, May. "Alliances across the Margins." *African American Review* 31, no. 4 (1997): 595–99.

Keller, James R. "The Shaman's Apprentice: Ecstasy and Economy in Wilson's Joe Turner." *African American Review* 35, no. 3 (2001): 471–79.

Kester, Gunilla Theander. "Approaches to Africa: The Poetics of Memory and the Body in Two August Wilson Plays." In *August Wilson: A Casebook,* edited by Marilyn Elkins, 105–21. New York: Garland, 1994.

Kroll, Jack. "August Wilson's Come to Stay." *Newsweek,* April 11, 1988, 82.

Kubitschek, Missy Dean. "August Wilson's Gender Lesson." In *May All Your Fences Have Gates,* edited by Alan Nadel, 183–99. Iowa City: University of Iowa Press, 1994.

Lahr, John. "Been Here and Gone: How August Wilson Brought a Century of Black American Culture to the Stage." *New Yorker,* April 16, 2001, 50–65.

Leverett, James, et al.. "Beyond Black and White: 'Cultural Power': Thirteen Commentaries." *American Theater* 14, no. 5 (1997): 14–15, 53–56.

Marra, Kim. "Ma Rainey and the Boyz: Gender Ideology in August Wilson's Broadway Canon." In *August Wilson: A Casebook,* edited by Marilyn Elkins, 123–60. New York: Garland, 1994.

McDonough, Carla J. *Staging Masculinity: Male Identity in Contemporary American Drama.* Jefferson, N.C.: McFarland, 1997.

Monaco, Pamela Jean. "Father, Son, and Holy Ghost: From the Local to the

Mythical in August Wilson." In *August Wilson: A Casebook*, edited by Marilyn Elkins, 89–104. New York: Garland, 1994.

Morales, Michael. "Ghosts on the Piano: August Wilson and the Representation of Black American History." In *May All Your Fences Have Gates*, edited by Alan Nadel, 105–15. Iowa City: University of Iowa Press, 1994.

Nadel, Alan. "Boundaries, Logistics, and Identity: The Property of Metaphor in *Fences* and *Joe Turner's Come and Gone*." In *May All Your Fences Have Gates*, edited by Alan Nadel, 86–104. Iowa City: University of Iowa Press, 1994.

Pereira, Kim. *August Wilson and the African-American Odyssey*. Urbana: University of Illinois Press, 1995.

Pettengill, Richard. "Alternatives . . . Opposites . . . Convergences: An Interview with Lloyd Richards." In *August Wilson: A Casebook*, edited by Marilyn Elkins, 227–34. New York: Garland, 1994.

Plum, Jay. "Blues, History, and the Dramaturgy of August Wilson." *African American Review* 27, no. 4 (1993): 561–67.

Reed, Ishmael. "In Search of August Wilson." *Connoisseur* 217 (March 1987): 92–97.

Richards, Sandra. "Yoruba Gods on the American Stage: August Wilson's *Joe Turner's Come and Gone*." *Research in African Literatures* 30, no. 4 (1999): 92–105.

Rocha, Mark William. "American History as 'Loud Talking' in *Two Trains Running*." In *May All Your Fences Have Gates*, edited by Alan Nadel, 116–32. Iowa City: University of Iowa Press, 1994.

———. "August Wilson and the Four B's: Influences." In *August Wilson: A Casebook*, edited by Marilyn Elkins, 3–16. New York: Garland, 1994.

———. "Black Madness in August Wilson's 'Down the Line' Cycle." In *Madness in Drama*, edited by James Redmond, 191–201. Cambridge: Cambridge University Press, 1993.

Saunders, James Robert. "Essential Ambiguities in the Plays of August Wilson." *Hollins Critic* 32, no. 5 (1995): 1–12.

Shafer, Yvonne. *August Wilson: A Research and Production Sourcebook*. Westport, Conn.: Greenwood Press, 1998.

———. "August Wilson and the Contemporary Theatre." *Journal of Dramatic Theory and Criticism* 12 (fall 1997): 23–38.

———. "Breaking Barriers: August Wilson." In *Staging Difference: Cultural Pluralism in American Theatre*, edited by Marc Maufort, 267–85. New York: Peter Lang, 1995.

Shannon, Sandra G. *August Wilson's "Fences": A Reference Guide*. Westport, CT: Greenwood Press, 2003.

———. "Audience and Africanisms in August Wilson's Dramaturgy: A Case Study." In *African American Performance and Theater History: A Critical Reader*, edited by Harry J. Elam and David Krasner, 149–67. Oxford: Oxford University Press, 2001.

——. *The Dramatic Vision of August Wilson.* Washington, D.C.: Howard University Press, 1995.

——. "Conversing with the Past: *Joe Turner's Come and Gone* and *The Piano Lesson.*" *CEA Magazine* 4, no. 1 (1991): 33–42.

——. "The Good Christian's Come and Gone: The Shifting Role of Christianity in August Wilson's Plays." *Melus* 16, no. 3 (1989): 127–42.

——. "The Ground on Which I Stand: August Wilson's Perspective on African American Women." In *May All Your Fences Have Gates,* edited by Alan Nadel, 150–66. Iowa City: University of Iowa Press, 1994.

——. "The Long Wait: August Wilson's *Ma Rainey's Black Bottom.*" *Black American Literature Forum* 25 (spring 1991): 151–62.

——. "The Role of Memory in August Wilson's Four-Hundred-Year Autobiography." In *Memory and Cultural Politics,* edited by Amritjit Singh, Joseph T. Skerret, Jr., and Robert E. Hogan, 175–93. Boston: Northeastern University Press, 1996.

——. "Subtle Imposition: The Lloyd Richards–August Wilson Formula." In *August Wilson: A Casebook,* edited by Marilyn Elkins, 183–98. New York: Garland, 1994.

——. "A Transplant That Did Not Take: August Wilson's Views on the Great Migration." *African American Review* 31, no. 4 (1997): 659–66.

Smith, Philip E., II. "*Ma Rainey's Black Bottom:* Playing the Blues as Equipment for Living." In *Within the Dramatic Spectrum,* vol. 6, edited by Karelissa V. Hartigan, 177–86. New York: University Press of America, 1988.

Sterling, Eric. "Protecting Home: Patriarchal Authority in August Wilson's *Fences.*" *Essays in Theatre/Etudes Theatrales* 17, no. 1 (1998): 53–62.

Taylor, Regina. "That's Why They Call It the Blues." *American Theatre* 13, no. 4 (1996): 18–23.

Timpane, John. "Filling the Time: Reading History in the Drama of August Wilson." In *May All Your Fences Have Gates,* edited by Alan Nadel, 67–85. Iowa City: University of Iowa Press, 1994.

Usekes, Cigdem. "'You Always under Attack': Whiteness as Law and Terror in August Wilson's Twentieth-Century Cycle of Plays." *American Drama* 10, no. 2 (2001): 48–68.

Wallach, Allan. "Fenced in by a Lifetime of Resentments." *New York Newsday,* March 27, 1987. *New York Theatre Critics Reviews,* 1987, 319.

Wang, Qun. *An In-Depth Study of the Major Plays of African American Playwright August Wilson: Vernacularizing the Blues on Stage.* Lewiston, N.Y.: Edwin Mellen Press, 1999.

——. "Towards the Poetization of the 'Field of Manners'." *African American Review* 29, no. 4 (1995): 605–13.

Werner, Craig. "August Wilson's Burden: The Function of Neoclassical Jazz." In *May All Your Fences Have Gates,* edited by Alan Nadel, 21–50. Iowa City: University of Iowa Press, 1994.

Wessling, Joseph H. "Wilson's Fences." *Explicator* 57, no. 2 (1999): 123–27.

Wilde, Lisa. "Reclaiming the Past: Narrative and Memory in August Wilson's *Two Trains Running.*" *Theater* 22, no. 1 (1990): 73–74.

Williams, Dana A. "Making the Bones Live Again: A Look at the 'Bones People' in August Wilson's *Joe Turner's Come and Gone* and Henry Dumas's *Ark of Bones.*" *College Language Association Journal* 42, no. 3 (1999): 309–19.

———. "A Review Essay of Scholarly Criticism on the Drama of August Wilson." *Bonner Beitrage* 55, no. 2 (1998): 53–62.

Wolfe, Peter. *August Wilson.* New York: Twayne, 1999.

Dissertations

Cho, Nancy J. "Staging Ethnicity in Contemporary American Drama." Ph.D. diss., University of Michigan, 1995.

Coleman, Wendy R. "The Dramaturgy of Spirit: AfriChristian Spirituality in the Plays of August Wilson." Ph.D. diss., Florida State University, 2001.

Downing, Michael John. "Restoring the Myths: Converting Stereotype to Archetype in Five Plays of August Wilson." Ph.D. diss., Indiana University of Pennsylvania, 1997.

Foster, John Shevin. "The Concept of Black Liberation Theology in the Plays of August Wilson." Ph.D. diss., New York University, 2000.

Gist, Vivan E. "Ritual Use of Death in the Plays of August Wilson." Ph.D. diss., University of Maryland, 2000.

Hayes, Corlis A. "A Critical and Historical Analysis of Five Major Plays by August Wilson." Ph.D. diss., Southern Illinois University, 1993.

Morales, Michael Alexander. "Vivisecting the Nation's Body: Ritual, Blood Sacrifice in the Work of Luis Valdez, August Wilson, and Suzan-Lori Parks." Ph.D. diss., Stanford University, 1999.

Nissen, Jonas K. "Strategies of Coping with Social Oppression in Selected Plays of August Wilson." Ph.D. diss., Bowling Green State University, 2000.

Nobles, Vera Lynn. "EMI: The Concept of Spirit in Selected Plays of August Wilson." Ph.D. diss., Temple University, 1995.

Orr, Leslie Sloan. "Gender Role Strain in Selected Plays by August Wilson." Ph.D. diss., Wayne State University, 1997.

Pinkney, Michael Lynn. "African-American Dramatic Theory as Subject of Cultural Studies: An Historical Overview and Analysis." Ph.D. diss., Ohio State University, 1999.

Staton, Mack Lester. "Power Acquisition Theory and the Tragic Legacy in Selected Works of August Wilson." Ph.D. diss., Indiana University of Pennsylvania, 2000.

Taylor, James Lawrence. "Understanding Wilson's Blueswoman: A Dramaturgical Exploration of August Wilson's Female Characters." Ph.D. diss., Florida State University, 2000.

Usekes, Cigdem. "Racial Encounters in the American Theatre: Whiteness and Eugene O'Neill, Blackness and August Wilson." Ph.D. diss., University of North Dakota, 1999.

Walters, Wendy Susan. "A Dramatic Evolution of the Colonial Subject: Imagining Authorship in the Performance of History." Ph.D. diss., Cornell University, 2000.

Index